The Steel Industry of India

The Steel Industry of India

WILLIAM A. JOHNSON

Harvard University Press
CAMBRIDGE, MASSACHUSETTS · 1966

Distributed in Great Britain by Oxford University Press, London
Library of Congress Catalog Card Number: 66–23471
Printed in the United States of America

To Margie and Eric

Preface

This book is an outgrowth of research in India during the academic year 1962–63 and a brief trip to India in May 1965. Although recent developments in the industry may make the study somewhat dated, this should be of little consequence. I am primarily concerned with developing a better understanding of the process of planned industrial growth and only secondarily with the day-to-day problems confronting the industry.

The attached bibliography contains a number of sources referring to India's steel industry. However, had I relied solely on the published word, this study would have been robbed of much of its meat and probably some of its accuracy. No small part of this book is based upon conversations with over 200 persons associated in one way or another with the industry. In general I have refrained from citing specific individuals by name. Reliance on informants involves some risk of accepting unsubstantiated gossip. However, in all instances I have double and triple checked with other informants to try to separate fact from fancy. Of course, I accept full responsibility for any instances where I have not succeeded.

My initial research in India, in preparation of my doctoral dissertation, was financed by a grant from the Foreign Area Fellowship Program. Subsequent research and rewriting of the manuscript were made possible by The RAND Corporation, which, in addition to its work under contract to various government agencies, supports a broad program of study with its own funds. The dissertation was prepared under the guidance of

Professor Edward S. Mason of Harvard University. Its conversion into a book would have been impossible without his support. I am also indebted to Dr. Morton Grossman of the Ford Foundation in New Delhi for many useful suggestions about issues of importance concerning the Indian steel industry and ways to improve the finished manuscript. Dr. Raymond Ewell of the State University of New York at Buffalo, Eric Jacobsen of Pittsburgh, and G. Ramanathan of New Delhi were especially helpful in enabling me to meet persons associated with the industry and, ultimately, to obtain the materials upon which this book is based. I also wish to thank the managements of India's five major steel mills and Hindustan Steel Ltd. for allowing me to visit their mills and to interview their employees. The manuscript has been read and commented upon by my RAND colleagues Alan Carlin, Jack Hirshleifer, Richard Nelson, Anthony Pascal, and George Rosen, and by Benjamin I. Cohen of Harvard University, J. B. Condliffe of the Stanford Research Institute, T. Gopalakrishnan of Rourkela, and Carl Liedholm of the Economic Development Institute, University of Nigeria. John Young, an independent consulting engineer with a long association with India's steel industry, has made many useful suggestions, particularly about technical matters, and William Hoehn and Michael Intriligator of The RAND Corporation have scrutinized my statistical analysis in Chapters 6 and 7. Kishor Thanawala of Bombay University has also made several observations incorporated in this book. Finally, I wish to thank my wife, Margie, who accompanied me throughout India, typed several initial drafts of the manuscript, and without complaint has endured my interests in India's steel industry since their inception. The views expressed in this book are my own and do not necessarily reflect the views of these people or organizations.

William A. Johnson

Santa Monica, California
June 1966

Contents

MAPS

Tables

Text Tables

Appendix Tables

The Steel Industry of India

1 | Introduction

India's five-year plans have emphasized programs of industrial development. Perhaps the most significant of these programs has been an ambitious expansion in India's steel industry. Heralded as a giant step in the creation of a modern economy, condemned as a gross waste of India's resources, the importance of this expansion to India's achievement of a rapid rate of economic growth is the principal subject of this study.

Much has been written about the process of industrial growth, and, more particularly, the relationship between this process and economic planning. Yet when I began to examine India's steel industry, I was amazed by the dearth of scholarly studies about the industry and, for that matter, most other industries in less developed economies. The need for empirical work was apparent. This book is meant to be a modest beginning toward filling this need.

Why restrict this study to only one industry in one less developed economy? Perhaps a common deficiency of the literature about economic growth has been its generality. A study of a specific industry runs the opposite risk. However, I have tried to minimize this risk by exiling to the appendixes many of the drab details necessary in an industry study. An examination of a specific industry that has grown rapidly during the past decade could help to clarify some of the more general issues mooted by development economists in recent years.

For example, while examining India's steel industry, I shall also consider general factor scarcities in less developed economies and the relationship between these scarcities and economic stagnation. Much of the literature on development published since World War II tends to emphasize domestic savings and occasionally foreign exchange as the critical constraints on a developing economy. More recently economists have turned their attention to other factors such as skills and willingness to work, although an adequate understanding of the role of these factors in development still seems to be a distant goal. Much of the development theory, and policy recommendations derived from it, continues to assume savings and new investment as the primary, if not the sole determinants of increased rates of growth in less developed economies. I hope that this examination of India's steel industry will contribute to a better understanding of critical factor scarcities in less developed economies.

A second basic issue considered in this book is the role of government in the development process. Whether a nation places primary reliance on centralized planning or decentralized decision-making to allocate scarce resources, it is important that its policies contribute meaningfully, or at least do not detract unnecessarily from its assumed objective, economic growth. The Indian government is committed to growth through central planning; probably few governments have had so refined development plans and few nations have been so development conscious as India. Yet growth is only one of many objectives, including some that are motivated by political and social considerations. That noneconomic objectives are important to policy-makers by no means implies a sacrifice in the general welfare of a nation. However, adherence to them can have a cost: All too often government policies appear to be the primary reason for substantial unutilized potential for growth in India's economy. This book, it is hoped, will throw light on why this is so and how policies might be structured to avoid unnecessary sacrifices in India's economic growth.

Three specific questions will also be considered. First, has India been justified in emphasizing iron and steel in her development plans, or is she merely one of many newly independent nations building a steel industry because it is considered a badge of progress? To answer this question I shall examine the costs of producing steel in India, the rate of return on investment in India's steel industry, and the demand for Indian steel both in India and abroad.

Second, is India expanding her steel industry in the most judicious manner possible? For example, are actual and proposed locations for new steel mills fully justified? Are the methods of production adopted by the industry most appropriate to India's economy? Perhaps most important, are difficulties incurred by India's new steel mills a necessary consequence of their newness? Or, with proper planning, could these difficulties be avoided? The answers to this set of questions are of interest not only because they may help to determine whether investment in India's steel industry is justified, but also because they help to clarify matters of more general relevance to industrial growth in nonindustrial economies.

Third, what lessons can be learned about industrial growth from a study of India's steel industry? In particular, what are some of the more important hurdles that will have to be overcome if rapid growth of the steel industry is to be achieved? How might India and other similar nations best overcome these hurdles?

Before turning to these questions, the reader is introduced to the subject of the book. The remainder of this chapter is devoted to a brief description of steel technology; subsequent chapters will concern the history of India's steel industry, factors of production, and the role of government in the growth process.

Steel Technology: A Brief Introduction

An integrated steel mill manufactures steel in all its stages from the initial reduction of iron ore to the final rolling of finished steel.[1] It is a complex of at least five industrial plants related vertically to each other. It also contains a number of ancillary facilities that are not directly involved in the production of steel but are essential to the mill's operations.

A typical steel mill consumes four basic raw materials: coal, iron ore, fluxes,[2] and scrap. It also consumes a number of other essential inputs such as refractories,[3] water, and electric power. At least part of the mill's coal may be washed to improve its chemical and physical properties. Washing usually takes place at or near mines. Washed coal is then shipped to the mill where it may be blended with unwashed coal to obtain a mixture most suitable for the mill's coke ovens, the first major unit of a steel mill. In addition to coke, these ovens produce such important by-products as coal tar and coke oven gas for sale or use as a fuel by the steel mill itself.

The second major unit of a steel mill, the blast furnace, produces molten iron either by smelting lump ore or artificial iron-bearing materials such as sinter or pellets. The reduction of ore or artificial inputs requires a fuel, coke. Coke also serves as a reducing agent, its carbon forming a chemical union with the oxygen in ore. Fluxes are a third essential input of a blast furnace. The desired combination of iron-bearing materials,

[1] The reader who wishes a brief discussion of steel making is directed to: Bethlehem Steel Corporation, *Steel in the Making*, (Bethlehem, Pa.: Bethlehem Steel Corporation, n.d.). For a more comprehensive discussion of steel making I suggest: United States Steel Corporation, *The Making, Shaping and Treating of Steel*, eighth ed. (Pittsburgh: U.S. Steel, 1964).

[2] Fluxes facilitate the separation of metal from impurities in iron ore by rendering these impurities more fusible and furnishing a substance with which they may combine in preference to metal. The most commonly used fluxes are limestone and dolomite.

[3] Refractories are materials used to construct furnaces and to line retaining vessels and conduits exposed to extreme temperatures.

coke, and fluxes is known as the charge. Hot air is blown through the bottom of the blast furnace and, passing upward through the charge, facilitates reduction of iron-bearing materials. The principal product of the blast furnace is hot metal. This may be cast into pig iron and then sold. More often it is transported as hot metal to the next major unit of a steel mill, the steel melt shop. The blast furnace also produces by-product gas, which is usually consumed by the steel mill itself, and slag, a mixture formed by the action of the flux on the fuel and impurities in ore. In the blast furnace, slag serves as a vehicle for separating impurities from metal. When solidified it may have some commercial value.

The steel melt shop adjusts the composition of carbon and other impurities in hot metal to produce steel. By this century Bessemer converters were largely displaced by open hearth furnaces. However, the converter has gained a new prominence since the mid-1950s after the development of oxygen steelmaking processes.[4] A part of the hot metal used to produce steel is melted scrap. In India virtually all the scrap consumed by steel mills is generated by the mills themselves;[5] in more developed economies, large tonnages of scrap are usually purchased from outside sources.

Steel may be cast into ingots. The ingots are then cooled, removed from their molds, reheated, and sent to the fourth major unit of a steel mill, the intermediate rolling mill. Once again, there has been a major technological change since World War II, the development of continuous casting. Increasingly widespread, use of this revolutionary process allows the casting of molten steel directly into intermediate forms. The inter-

[4] The best known and most widely accepted oxygen process is the LD converter. The LD furnace is essentially a top-blown Bessemer converter into which oxygen is injected. It takes its name from Linz and Donawitz, the two Austrian cities where the process was developed.

[5] The principal sources of steel scrap within a mill are the crop ends of intermediate and finished sections and unsalable defective steel.

mediate section produced depends on the finished product of the steel mill. A mill manufacturing rails or heavy structurals will first produce blooms, the mill manufacturing bars and light structurals, billets, and the mill manufacturing flat products, slabs. There is no precise distinction among the three types of intermediate sections. Their size and shape depend primarily on the general size and shape of the finished product. Blooms and billets are relatively long and thin, the billet possessing the smaller cross-sectional area. Both the bloom and billet have round or square cross-sections, whereas the cross-section of a slab is wider and rectangular. Some steel is also cast into ingots or rolled into blooms and billets for forging into such finished products as wheels and axles.

The last major units of an integrated steel mill are its rolling mills. Only a relatively small amount of additional rolling is necessary to produce bars, structurals, rails, and plates. However, to produce sheets, slabs may first be rolled into strips, then finished in a cold rolling mill and, in some plants, galvanized, tinned, or corrugated.

There are also a number of auxiliary facilities at a typical integrated steel mill. A by-product recovery plant processes chemicals captured from the mill's coke ovens. Another plant may produce the oxygen used by several of the mill's units. Water is often cooled in towers and then recirculated through the plant. Ingot molds are turned out by the mill's foundry. These are only a few of the many ancillary facilities usually found at a typical steel mill.

Definition of the Industry

Most industry studies are hampered by the ill-defined boundaries of the industries under examination. This study is no exception. India has six integrated steel mills. There are at least three other types of productive units in India that rightly belong to the steel industry: small pig iron plants; secondary producers and rerolling mills; and alloy, tool, and stainless steel plants. For the most part this study will be concerned only with India's integrated steel mills. When relevant, it will also be extended to other productive units.

Small pig iron plants produce salable pig iron, primarily for Indian foundries. In general they are intended to use methods of production other than the blast furnace. Although many of these plants have been licensed by the government, only two were in operation by the end of 1964. Small pig iron plants are discussed at some length in Chapter 10.

In 1963 nine Indian factories were classified as secondary producers. These are well established companies that purchase most of their semifinished steel from India's integrated mills, converting this steel into such specialized items as wire and tinplate as well as ordinary bars and rods. In addition, there are over 180 registered rerolling mills, generally smaller factories that manufacture bars and rods or draw wire from intermediate forms of steel produced in India's integrated mills or from ingots manufactured from scrap. These mills, in theory at least, produce sections that are demanded in small amounts and are not amenable to rolling by the integrated mills. Presumably, these mills complement rather than compete with the integrated plants. This segment of India's steel industry is not considered at length in this study.

The Government of India has licensed more than a dozen alloy, tool, and stainless steel projects in the private sector. By 1965 there was noticeable progress in only two of these projects. In addition, the government has built a large alloy and tool steel plant adjacent to one of its integrated steel mills. Even though the production of special steels is of no small importance to India's development plans, for the most part I also ignore this segment of the industry.

2 | The Growth of India's Steel Industry

India's Steel Industry prior to World War II

India has possessed a modern steel industry for more than a half century. The existence of the industry prior to Independence has provided Indian planners with an invaluable basis of experience in the manufacture of steel. It also provides the analyst with an opportunity to determine how the industry has grown and what problems have confronted its growth at a time when institutional factors, notably government policies, were less pervasive and market considerations more pervasive influences on India's economy.

Iron ore has been smelted in crude furnaces throughout the Indian subcontinent for at least 3,000 years. Most of these furnaces disappeared during the nineteenth century after the establishment of British rule in India and the incidence of technological advance in Europe. The construction of railways and the more widespread use of money enabled imported iron and steel to penetrate previously inaccessible regions of India. Moreover, after the collapse of Maratha and Sikh power during the first half of the nineteenth century, the market for armaments, in which Indian iron and steel excelled, dwindled. Most of India's demand for iron and steel by the beginning of this century was for forms indigenous artisans could not easily produce—sheets, rails, bars, and structurals—which are shaped in rolling mills, not on the blacksmith's anvil.

India's ores are widespread, easily mined, and, although they contain an undesirable impurity, they also possess a high iron content by world standards. Consequently, prior to the twentieth century there were no less than seventeen attempts to establish Indian iron works using techniques similar to those used in the West.[1] Most of these schemes never materialized. Of the few that did, all but one failed, and that venture barely survived during its fifty years of life.[2]

There were many reasons for the failure of early attempts to introduce European methods of manufacturing iron into India. Charcoal was to be consumed by most plants even though the use of coke allowed lower costs of production and was increasingly widespread. Most plants were to produce pig iron for export at a time when its world price was falling. The use of charcoal impeded reductions in costs and, as a result, Indian iron became progressively less competitive over time. Most schemes were begun with too little capital or with limited access to additional sources of funds. Some plants were to be erected in areas far too inaccessible for the profitable marketing of their products. The central government and the various provincial governments were also inconsistent in their support for many of these ventures. Perhaps most important, those who attempted to establish Indian iron works did not possess the requisite managerial and technical skills. Nor, as a rule, did they employ persons who did.[3]

[1] Mahadev Govind Ranade, "Iron Industry—Pioneer Attempts," *Essays on Indian Economics* (Madras: G. A. Natesan & Co., 1906), Ch. VI, pp. 170–192. Ranade was a well-known Indian jurist, publicist, and nationalist. His essay was written in 1892.

[2] The Bengal Iron Company was founded in 1875. Only after 1899 and several changes in its management did it earn a modest profit. In 1905 the company attempted the manufacture of steel, but soon abandoned this, restricting itself for the next three decades to the manufacture of pig iron for export. During the 1920s the company faltered and in the early 1930s suspended operations. In 1936 it was absorbed by the Indian Iron and Steel Company, which now operates one of India's six integrated steel mills.

[3] Ranade, pp. 189–190. The reader may wish to consult two other sources for discussions of attempts to manufacture iron and steel in India prior to the twentieth century. Lovat Fraser, *Iron and Steel in India* (Bombay: The Times Press, 1919), pp. 3–9; and Daniel H. Buchanan, *The Development of Capitalist Enterprise in India* (New York: Macmillan, 1934), pp. 278–282.

INDIA, 1965

JAMMU & KASHMIR
HIMACHAL PRADESH
Ludhiana
PUNJAB
Hissar
DELHI
Jaipur
UTTAR PRADESH
RAJASTHAN
Kanpur
SIKKIM
BHUTAN
NEFA
Amingaon
ASSAM
NAGALAND
MANIPUR
Patna
Monghyr
Udaipur
Shahabad
BIHAR
Satna
Bokaro
Kulti
W. BENGAL
Ahmedabad
Bhopal
Ranchi
Burnpur
TRIPURA
GUJARAT
Adityapur
Durgapur
MADHYA PRADESH
Purulia
Rourkela
Jamshedpur
Calcutta
Korba
Hirri
Barbil
Bhilai
Hirakud
Haldia
Dhalli-Rajhara
Talcher
MAHARASHTRA
Chanda Dt.
Cuttack
ORISSA
BAY OF BENGAL
Bombay
Khapoli
Bailadilla
Hyderabad
ARABIAN SEA
Kothagudem
Vishakhapatnam
Khammam
Ratnagiri Dt
ANDHRA PRADESH
Hospet
Dhone
GOA
Bellary
MYSORE
Bhadravati
Madras
Bangalore
Salem
PONDICHERRY
Shoranur
Coimbatore
Neyveli
MADRAS
Cochin
KERALA

The first fully successful Indian iron and steel mill was established early in this century by Jamsetji Tata, a Bombay merchant and textile mill owner. In 1899 Tata initiated a scheme for erecting a steel mill in India. Within three years he obtained necessary licenses, contracted with an American firm to design his plant, and began a painstaking search for its location. In 1906, two years after Tata's death, a site was chosen at Sakchi, a village in the southernmost district of the present state of Bihar. This is now Jamshedpur, a city of 300,000 persons built around the Tata Iron and Steel Company (TISCO), its subsidiaries, and other factories erected nearby either to supply the works or to consume its steel.

THE IRON AND STEEL BELT OF INDIA

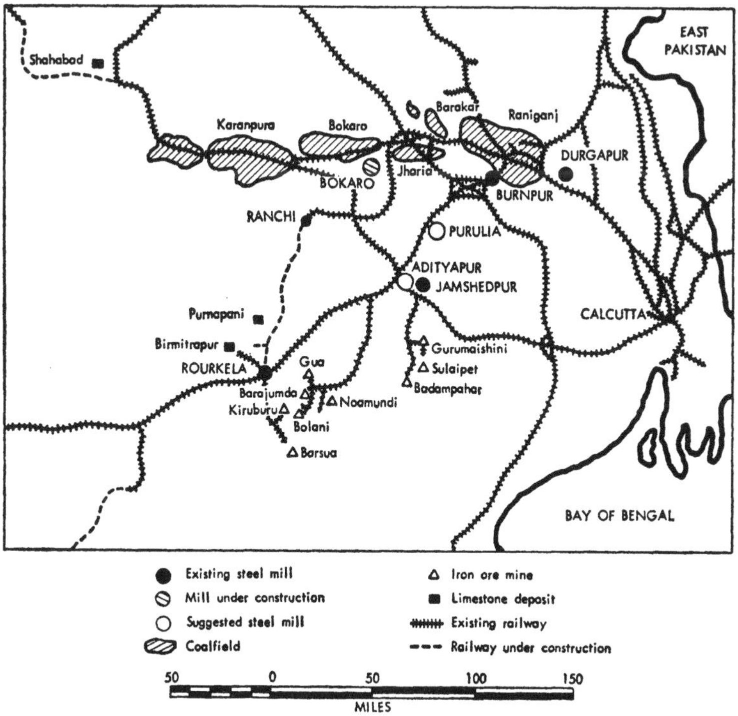

The mistakes of prior attempts to establish a modern iron and steel works in India were consciously avoided by the Tata interests. Coke, not charcoal, was used as a fuel and reducing agent. The mill did not produce pig iron for export, but steel to supply a growing Indian market. Its location was chosen only after thorough investigation guaranteed the proximity of all important raw materials including water. The full cooperation of the government was assured. Perhaps most important, technical skills were imported, not only embodied in the advice of foreign consultants, but also the actual labor of skilled foreign personnel. These directives were largely responsible for the mill's ultimate success.

The Tata Iron and Steel Company grew rapidly. In 1917 TISCO undertook extensions permitting a fourfold increase in its output. By the outset of World War II its capacity had again been doubled. Despite initial difficulties the company underwent almost continual expansion during its first thirty years, achieving an average rate of growth in its capacity of 8 per cent per year.[4] By 1939 TISCO's mill, one of the largest steel mills in the British Empire, was also one of the lowest cost producers in the world. Moreover, data presented in Table 1 indicate that by 1939 TISCO manufactured three-fourths of the steel consumed in India. These achievements resulted in part from the entrepreneurial talents of the Tata family. They also resulted from a favorable environment created by the Indian government, tariff protection and, prior to the 1930s, guaranteed purchases of much of TISCO's output by the government-owned railways.

The Indian Iron and Steel Company (IISCO) was founded in 1918 by British interests in Calcutta, its mill subsequently erected at what is now Burnpur, West Bengal. At first IISCO restricted itself to the manufacture of pig iron primarily for

[4] In 1912 TISCO's capacity was 100,000 tons of finished steel; in 1939, 800,000 tons.

export to the United Kingdom and Japan. In 1936 it acquired the defunct Bengal Iron Company.[5] In the same year the Steel Corporation of Bengal (SCOB) was formed by IISCO's management to undertake the construction of a steel mill adjacent to IISCO's blast furnaces. SCOB first produced steel in December 1939. In January 1953 IISCO and SCOB were formally merged, the new company assuming IISCO's name.

The Mysore Iron and Steel Works (MISW) at Bhadravati, Mysore, is a small plant founded in 1918 by the Maharaja of Mysore. It was originally intended to consume charcoal produced by a wood distillation plant also owned by the Maharaja's government. However, the discovery of methods to produce synthetic wood distillation products during the 1920s made its parent plant obsolete. MISW continued to produce charcoal pig iron. In the mid-1930s it added facilities to manufacture steel and shortly after World War II adopted electric reduction of iron ore. The economics of the Mysore works have always been questionable.[6] In its early years its losses were absorbed by the Mysore Government. More recently it received a subsidy from the Government of India through the price system established over the industry.

This brief discussion of the industry's past serves several purposes, besides providing a necessary background to a study of current planning for the industry's growth. By World War II Indian imports of steel were replaced by output from SCOB's newly built Burnpur plant or consisted of sections demanded in amounts too small for economic rolling in India. India's achievement of virtual self-sufficiency in steel and her production at relatively low costs is very good evidence that India possesses a comparative advantage in the production of steel. Moreover,

[5] This is now IISCO's pipe plant at Kulti. See footnote 2.

[6] For a discussion of the plant, see George B. Baldwin, *Industrial Growth in South India* (Glencoe, Illinois: The Free Press, 1959), pp. 68–84.

Table 1. Indian Production, Imports, Exports, and Consumption of Salable Steel, 1911–1914 and 1920–1939[a]
(thousands of long tons)

	Production			Exports		TISCO's
				and	Approximate	production as a percentage
	TISCO[b]	MISW[d]	Imports[e]	re-exports[e]	consumption[f]	of consumption
1911–12	1	—	779	1	779	g
1912–13	19	—	922	2	939	2
1913–14	49	—	1,215	1	1,263	4
1920–21	122	—	770	1	891	14
1921–22	126	—	703	1	828	15
1922–23	115	—	892	1	1,006	11
1923–24	163	—	872	1	1,034	16
1924–25	248	—	921	2	1,167	21
1925–26	320	—	915	1	1,234	26
1926–27	374	—	877	1	1,250	30
1927–28	429	—	1,258	1	1,686	25
1928–29	288[c]	—	1,165	1	1,452	21
1929–30	425	—	968	1	1,392	31
1930–31	443	—	608	3	1,048	42
1931–32	456	—	369	15	810	56
1932–33	431	—	324	30	725	59
1933–34	535	—	323	47	811	66

Table 1 (*cont.*)

	Production		Imports[e]	Exports and re-exports[e]	Approximate consumption[f]	TISCO's production as a percentage of consumption
	TISCO[b]	MISW[d]				
1934–35	610	—	367	1	976	62
1935–36	661	—	446	2	1,105	60
1936–37	680	3	360	3	1,040	65
1937–38	674	15	365	26	1,028	66
1938–39	715	23	264	24	978	73

[a] Salable steel includes finished steel produced by India's integrated steel mills and also semifinished steel, primarily billets and tin bars produced by these mills and sold to rerollers and secondary producers.

[b] Complete production series are found in any *Annual Report* of TISCO prior to 1959–60. Data for 1911–14 have been recorded from July 1 to June 30; data for 1920–39, from April 1 to March 31.

[c] Year of a prolonged strike.

[d] Production data for MISW are found in M. S. Krishnan, *Iron Ore, Iron and Steel, Bulletins of the Geological Survey of India,* Series A, Number 9, second ed. (Delhi: Government of India Publication, 1961), p. 222. Data are measured in calendar years. MISW did not produce steel prior to 1936.

[e] Government of India, Department of Commercial Intelligence and Statistics, *Annual Statement of the Foreign Trade of India* (New Delhi: Government of India Publication, various years). Data relate to the year April 1 to March 31. Imports and exports of pig iron and scrap have been omitted to make trade statistics comparable with production statistics.

[f] Production plus imports less exports. This is a crude estimate of consumption of steel which disregards changes in inventories.

[g] Insignificant.

the history of India's steel industry indicates a vital private sector in the industry. Finally, the success of India's private sector mills depended in large part on their deliberate avoidance of past mistakes. To some extent the difficulties incurred by India's new public sector steel mills, built since Independence, resulted from their having committed many of these same mistakes.

India's Steel Industry since World War II

Indian production, imports, and exports of steel since 1945 are presented in Table 2. India was able to preserve her relative self-sufficiency in steel until the mid-1950s. After 1954 Indian consumption of steel increased significantly, partly because of a small increase in steel output, but primarily because of substantially greater imports.[7] The inability of the industry to keep pace with Indian demand for steel during the middle and late 1950s can be attributed to its failure to expand during the immediate postwar period.

This inaction did not result from any want of preparation on the part of those responsible for the growth of the industry. In 1945 the government established the Iron and Steel (Major) Panel to investigate India's steel industry and to recommend programs for its future. The Panel's report, completed in 1946, concluded that in addition to the expansion of existing mills, postwar Indian demand for steel would justify the erection of a new mill with an initial capacity of 0.5 million tons of steel, to be doubled immediately, or two new mills, each with an initial capacity of 0.5 million tons. The report was intended merely to serve as a guideline for subsequent studies. Accordingly, several months after Independence, the Government of

[7] Independence in 1947 was accompanied by partition of British India. Continued high levels of production relative to consumption reflect, among other things, some shrinkage of domestic markets as a result of partition.

India commissioned three non-Indian firms to investigate the feasibility of new steel mills in greater detail. All three firms concluded that two new mills should be established, each with an initial capacity of 0.5 million tons of steel. Under the terms of the government's Industrial Policy Resolution, both mills were to be erected by the Government of India, not private interests. Concurrently, India's existing steel companies began preparations for the expansion of their plants.

For several reasons programs for the industry's expansion were postponed until the following decade. The Indian government was preoccupied with Independence and its aftermath. There was also some question about the adequacy of postwar demand for steel. Most important, the primary sources of the industry's financial capital prior to World War II, retained earnings and the sale of shares and debentures, proved inadequate for normal replacement, much less expansion, during the immediate postwar period. The Industrial Policy Resolution of 1948, which declared all new steel mills to be the prerogative of the Government of India and implied nationalization of private sector mills after ten years, the retention of price and distribution controls imposed on the industry during the war, the industry's lopsided capital structure, and the hesitancy of existing and potential shareholders all discouraged the sale of new shares to the Indian public. In addition, the cost of installing new plant and equipment soared during the war and postwar years because of inflation and devaluation of the rupee in 1949. Reserves accumulated prior to and during World War II did not appreciate in value as rapidly and proved inadequate for the postwar expansion programs of the industry. Perhaps most important, until 1951 the government refused to grant producers increments in their controlled prices earmarked for their own rehabilitation and expansion.[8]

[8] The failure of both the public and private sectors to initiate expansion of the industry immediately after World War II has been widely discussed

Table 2. Indian Production, Imports, Exports, and Consumption of Salable Steel, 1945–1964[a] (thousands of tons)

	Production								
	TISCO[b]	IISCO[c] (SCOB)	MISW[e]	HSL[h]	TOTAL	Imports[j]	Exports[j]	Apparent consumption[m]	Production as a percentage of consumption
1945–46	758	200[d]	29[f]	—	987	178	1	1,164	85
1946–47	765	116[d]	25[f]	—	906	64	10	960	94
1947–48	675	202[d]	23[f]	—	900	115	4	1,011	89
1948–49	682	186[d]	22[f]	—	890	166	16	1,040	86
1949–50	739	229[d]	23[g]	—	991	413	18	1,386	72
1950–51	796	205[d]	29	—	1,030	344	9	1,365	75
1951–52	812	268[d]	30	—	1,110	212	10	1,312	85
1952–53	803	317[d]	30	—	1,150	213	18	1,345	86
1953–54	793	297	33	—	1,123	310	10	1,423	79
1954–55	796	469	27	—	1,292	427	7	1,712	75
1955–56	812	460	36	—	1,308	940	4	2,244	59
1956–57	812	451	47[d]	—	1,310	1,705	1	3,014	43
1957–58	799	419	34[d]	—	1,252	1,538	1	2,789	45
1958–59	899	506	37[d]	—	1,442	1,200	(k)	2,642	54
1959–60	1,237	637	34[d]	62	2,006	1,017	3	3,020	66
1960–61	1,263	722	40[d]	566	2,591	1,417	75	3,933	66
1961–62	1,318	737	38[d]	1,093	3,186	1,042	67	4,161	77
1962–63	1,413	795	40[d]	1,704	3,952	933	14	4,871	81
1963–64	1,506	810	41[d]	2,160[i]	4,517	981	33	5,465	83

NOTES TO TABLE 2

[a] Salable steel includes finished steel produced by India's integrated steel mills and also semifinished steel, primarily billets and tin bars, produced by these mills and sold to rerollers and secondary producers. Unless otherwise specified, data refer to the financial year, April 1 through March 31. Prior to 1960 data were measured in British long tons (2,240 lbs.). These have been converted to metric tons (2,204.6 lbs.) to allow comparability with data for later years. Throughout this book the word "ton" refers to the metric ton. Long tons are labeled accordingly.

[b] TISCO, *Annual Report*, 1963–64, p. 6.

[c] Prior to 1953, SCOB, *Annual Report*, various years; after 1952, IISCO, *Annual Report*, various years.

[d] Calendar years.

[e] For 1945–51, Indian Tariff Commission, *Report on the Fair Retention Prices of Steel Produced by the Mysore Iron and Steel Works, 1952* (New Delhi: Government of India Publication, n.d.), p. 6; for 1951–56, Government of India, Planning Commission, *Programmes of Industrial Development, 1956–61* (New Delhi: Government of India Publication, 1956), p. 5; for 1956–57, estimated from Government of India, Directorate of Industrial Statistics, *Census of Manufacturers* (New Delhi: Government of India Publication, 1956 and 1957); for 1958–64, Government of India, Ministries of Steel, Mines and Fuel, Steel and Heavy Industries, and Steel, Mines and Heavy Engineering, Department of Iron and Steel, *Annual Report* (New Delhi: Government of India Publication, various years).

[f] July 1 through June 30.

[g] July 1 through March 31.

[h] Hindustan Steel Limited (HSL), *Annual Report* (various years). HSL did not produce steel prior to 1959–60.

[i] Unpublished information.

[j] Trade in years prior to 1956–57 has been estimated from Government of India, Department of Commercial Intelligence and Statistics, *Annual Statement of the Foreign Trade of India*, (New Delhi: Government of India Publication, various years). Trade in 1955–64 has been estimated from a companion volume, *Monthly Statistics of the Foreign Trade of India*. Trade data for years since 1954–55, particularly import data, are liable to understatement. Some trade on government account has not been recorded by the Department of Commercial Intelligence and Statistics until as much as two or three years after its occurrence. Corrected historical series are available in the *Annual Statement* and are reproduced here. They are not available in *Monthly Statistics*.

[k] Insignificant.

[m] Production plus imports less exports. This is a crude measure of consumption which assumes no changes in inventories of steel from year to year.

Had a new steel mill been established immediately after World War II, rather than during the 1950s, investment in the mill would have been 50 to 60 per cent of investment in each of the three new mills that were eventually erected.[9] In addition, the new mill could have operated at full or nearly full capacity by 1956, barring abnormal delays in its erection and commissioning, thereby negating much of the substantial increase in Indian imports of steel in subsequent years.

Under India's First Five Year Plan, inaugurated in 1951, one new steel mill was to be erected by the Government of India. Even though this project was nebulous at the time the First Plan was published, it was thought that the mill could produce some pig iron by the last year of the plan period. MISW was to triple its output by 1955. The private sector mills were also scheduled to increase their combined capacities by approximately 50 per cent during the plan period.[10]

The only significant increase in steel production during the First Plan period resulted from IISCO's expansion programs.[11] Even so, during the period, TISCO undertook new investments intended to rehabilitate plant and equipment that had deteriorated badly since the outbreak of World War II. In addition, preparations for the construction of three new public sector steel mills were begun by 1956, the last year of the First Plan.

---

in the literature. Although ill-advised government policies were probably the major reason for this failure, the tendency by some to ascribe most if not all the blame to these policies would seem to be somewhat one-sided. The industry's doubts about future steel demand, its unsatisfactory capital structure, and the reluctance of its shareholders to support proposed expansion programs also contributed to its failure to expand during this period.

[9] Lok Sabha, Estimates Committee, *Ministry of Steel, Mines and Fuel, 33rd Report, Second Lok Sabha 1958–59* (New Delhi: Lok Sabha Secretariat, 1959), p. xi.

[10] Government of India, Planning Commission, *First Five Year Plan* (New Delhi: Government of India Publication, 1953), pp. 428, 431, 434, 444, 445, and 447.

[11] See Table 2.

Aside from MISW's expansion program, which was eventually scrapped, substantial progress was made toward fulfillment of all plan objectives.

India's Second Five Year Plan, inaugurated in 1956, established targets for steel that were more than three times India's actual production of steel at the beginning of the plan period. Both public and private sectors were to participate in the growth of the industry, although the share of the public sector was to be predominant. Second Plan targets are indicated in Table 3.

In 1953 the German combine, Krupp-Demag, agreed to establish India's first public sector steel mill. This mill was located at Rourkela, Orissa, in eastern India. In early 1955, the Soviet Union committed itself to the erection of a second public sector mill at Bhilai, Madhya Pradesh. In the same year negotiations were begun with a consortium of British equipment suppliers for still a third public sector mill at Durgapur, West Bengal, culminating in a formal agreement one year later. Most of the foreign exchange costs of the three mills were to be met by loans from the West German, Soviet, and British governments. TISCO and IISCO were also allowed to expand under the Second Plan, in addition to extensions already begun during the First Plan period.

Paradoxically, despite the fact that India's output of steel in 1960–61 fell far short of her production targets, Second Plan programs for the industry's expansion were by and large successful. With the exception of a long-deferred but inconsequential expansion of MISW, all programs for increasing the industry's capacity were fully or largely completed by the end of the plan period. That the industry did not achieve plan targets was primarily a result of relatively minor delays in creating new capacity and initial difficulties in its use.

Under the Third Plan, which began in 1961, the three public sector steel mills were expanded and a fourth mill was to be

Table 3. Second, Third, and Tentative Fourth Plan Steel Targets for India's Major Integrated Steel Mills[a]
(millions of tons of annual capacity)

	Second Plan (1956–1961)			Third Plan (1961–1966)			Fourth Plan (tentative)
Major steel mills	Ingot steel	Salable steel	Finished steel	Ingot steel	Salable steel	Finished steel	Ingot steel
Private sector							
TISCO	2.00	1.50	1.22	2.00	1.50	1.22	2.00[b]
IISCO	1.00	.80	.66	1.00	.80	.66	2.00[c]
Public sector							
Rourkela	1.00	.72	.72	1.80	1.24	1.24	2.50
Bhilai	1.00	.77	.62	2.50	1.95	1.55	3.50
Durgapur	1.00	.81	.66	1.60	1.24	.94	3.40
Bokaro	—	—	—	1.00	.72[d]	.72[d]	1.70
New steel mill	—	—	—	—	—	—	1.50
Total	6.00	4.60	3.88	9.90	7.45[d]	6.33[d]	appr. 16.50

[a] Plan targets for steel, both historical and projected, sometimes vary from source to source. Those indicated in this table are eventual targets established for the Second Plan period, which differ slightly from targets indicated in documents published at the beginning of the period, and initial Third Plan targets. Fourth Plan targets are tentative and subject to change. Data have been drawn from various Planning Commission publications.

[b] TISCO will expand to 4 million tons by the middle of the Fifth Plan period.

[c] Planning Commission's preliminary estimate for IISCO. The company has been reluctant to expand beyond 1.3 million ingot tons capacity by the end of the Fourth Plan period.

[d] Estimate by author.

established at Bokaro, Bihar. The government refused to allow further growth of the private sector plants during the plan period. The expansion of existing public sector mills was delayed for as many as three years and will now be completed only during the first years of the Fourth Plan period. Construction of the Bokaro mill was also delayed. Originally it was thought that the United States would participate in the Bokaro project. However, in the summer of 1963 the U.S. House of Representatives objected to American participation, and within a month India's request for American assistance was withdrawn. Early in 1964 the Soviet Union agreed to finance Bokaro in addition to the proposed expansion of Bhilai. The Bokaro mill will not produce steel until the 1970s. Third Plan targets have failed, not only because of the normal gestation period that must follow the installation of new capacity, but also because of delays in plan implementation.

India's tentative Fourth Plan targets for steel are no less ambitious than those of previous plan periods. A new steel mill is to be completed during the period, in addition to the erection of Bokaro and further expansion of existing mills. The erection of another mill would begin by the end of the period. By mid-1966 the locations of these mills had not yet been determined. Those considered are Goa, the Bellary-Hospet region of northern Mysore, Vishakhapatnam in Andhra Pradesh, and Bailadilla in southern Madhya Pradesh. A third and smaller mill is supposed to be located in Madras, although its erection has been postponed for years and at present seems somewhat problematic.

After an initial period of hesitation following Independence, the growth of India's steel industry has been rapid and will continue to be rapid if future targets are achieved. Direct investment in India's integrated steel mills amounted to 11 per cent of aggregate plan outlay during the Second Plan period. Because the expansion of the industry at that time was intended, in part, to make up for the industry's failure to expand during the previous decade and a half, its claim on Second Plan financial resources was abnormally high. For this reason direct investment in the industry under the Third Plan was to have been 6 per cent of total planned investment, perhaps a more reasonable estimate of the share of India's financial resources allocated to her steel industry in the long run.[12] Nonetheless, this still represents a substantial claim on India's resources.

For the most part, investment in steel has been accorded priority over investment in most other industries. For this reason the steel industry generally has not suffered from retrenchment brought about by unexpectedly scarce resources (or overly ambitious planning, depending upon one's point of view). Nor has it suffered from a want of attention by Indian planners and other officials responsible for administering plan programs. As a result, some unplanned imbalances have been created. Steel scarcities persisting throughout the 1950s have, for many sections, given way to surpluses, which in all probability will continue if plans for steel are implemented successfully in the future.

[12] Estimated from information contained in the annual reports of HSL, TISCO and IISCO, 1960–61, and Government of India, Planning Commission, *Third Five Year Plan* (New Delhi: Government of India Publication, 1961), pp. 59 and 502.

3 | Factor Endowments and Resource Allocation

Much of the theoretical discussion about economic development has stressed a dichotomy of inputs, capital and labor, and has proceeded on the assumption that capital is scarce and labor abundant in underdeveloped economies. Several economists have suggested one or another criterion for the investment of scarce capital or one or another means of more fully employing underemployed labor. At first this discussion led to two basic policy recommendations: that it is best for an underdeveloped economy to invest in labor-intensive as opposed to capital-intensive industries and, in any one industry, to use labor-intensive as opposed to capital-intensive methods of production. More recently economists have begun to consider optimum factor proportions within the context of time and have concluded that savings and investment and, therefore, national income may be maximized in the long run by the choice of more capital-intensive alternatives in the short run.

One drawback with this theorizing is that it is much too simplified for many industries in underdeveloped economies. Undoubtedly, there are instances where a dichotomous approach toward factor availability is relevant. There are also many instances, such as India's iron and steel industry, where it is not.

To the casual observer, no industry would appear less suited to India's factor endowments than steel, the textbook example of capital intensity. However, this initial impression ignores the third factor of the classical triad, land or raw materials. More than of most industries, the economics of steel depends heavily on the presence of all principal raw materials. Despite substantial capital costs, the production of steel in a capital-poor economy may be justified, given the availability of raw materials, because of cost benefits derived from the quality of these raw materials, savings in the shipment of imported steel, and, most important for India, savings in foreign exchange.

It is also a mistake to consider capital and labor homogeneous factors of production. Not all types of equipment are equally difficult to obtain. Rather, in India the problem of securing foreign exchange to pay for the imported component of investment is, for a number of reasons, particularly acute. An optimum investment strategy for India might be capital-intensive if this strategy relies heavily on domestic resources and results in large savings of foreign exchange. Nor is all labor abundant. Skilled and experienced personnel have been among the Indian steel industry's scarcest factors of production, and abundant unskilled labor has been of relatively little use to it. The optimum pattern of investment for India's steel industry could also involve the adoption of capital-intensive, labor-saving methods of production.

Necessary factors of production and optimum factor proportions are subjects that do not lend themselves to simplistic answers. Yet these issues are basic to an examination of investment in India's steel industry. The questions must be asked: What are India's critical factor scarcities? How by effective planning might these scarcities be overcome?

Principal Raw Materials

India possesses all principal raw materials necessary for the manufacture of iron and steel. These raw materials are close to one another and are of sufficiently good quality to allow production of iron in conventional blast furnaces.

India's iron ores account for between 10 and 20 per cent of the world's total and, at present rates of exploitation, could last for nearly a millenium.[1] Not only are India's ores abundant, their iron content, 60 per cent, is high by world standards.[2] Unfortunately, Indian ores also contain a relatively high percentage of alumina, an undesirable impurity. Cost advantages resulting from the high iron content of Indian ores are offset, at least in part, by cost disadvantages resulting from the presence of this impurity.[3]

Most Indian ores occur in three regions, Bihar and Orissa in northeastern India, Madhya Pradesh in central India, and Mysore and Goa in southern India.[4] The first of these regions is less than 150 miles from India's only deposits of coking coal and is adjacent to one of her important deposits of limestone, a proximity of principal raw materials shared by few steel industries elsewhere in the world. All Indian mills are based upon the Bihar-Orissa ores except Bhilai, which draws its ores from deposits in Madhya Pradesh, and MISW, which obtains its ores from deposits in Mysore.

India's reserves of coking coal are more limited. Although coal is found in many areas of eastern and central India, coking

[1] For example, see United Nations, Department of Economic Affairs, *World Iron Ore Resources and Their Utilization* (Lake Success, N.Y.: United Nations Publication, 1950), pp. 10–11.

[2] Some average iron contents of probable ore reserves elsewhere are: Brazil, 65 per cent; Sweden, 64 per cent; Australia, 62 per cent; Venezuela, 60 per cent; Union of South Africa, 47 per cent; United States, 45 per cent; U.S.S.R., 45 per cent; France, 38 per cent; Germany, 32 per cent; United Kingdom, 28 per cent. The average iron content of the world's deposits is thought to be 50 per cent. *Ibid.*, p. 11.

[3] A higher iron content results in greater yields of iron per blast furnace tap. However, a high ratio of alumina to silica, another impurity, results in increased consumption of coke and fluxes. Because the volume of a blast furnace is fixed, greater consumption of coke and fluxes allows less ore smelted per blast and therefore lower yields of iron per tap.

[4] These regions contain 44, 25, and 17 per cent of India's ores respectively. Computed from M. S. Krishnan, *Iron Ore, Iron and Steel, Bulletins of the Geological Survey of India*, Series A, Number 9, second ed. (Delhi: Government of India Publication, 1961), pp. 185–186.

coals occur only in the coal fields of the Damodar Valley of Bihar and West Bengal in northeastern India. Present reserves of coking coal have been placed at between 1.6 billion and 2.1 billion tons,[5] less than 10 per cent of India's ore supplies. Even so, assuming existing reserves of coking coal to be used solely by the steel industry, they would be capable of sustaining at least two new steel mills after Bokaro, each possessing eventual capacities of four million ingot tons. Allowing for improved techniques and increased utilization of scrap, they are capable of supporting as many as six new four million ton plants.[6] India's reserves of coking coal, although limited, need not deter the growth of India's steel industry based on indigenous raw materials for many years to come.

India's coking coals are not of good quality. Although low in sulphur, an advantage, they are high in ash, a substantial disadvantage that results in increased costs of production. The ash content of most Indian coking coals must first be reduced by washing to yield a coke satisfactory for smelting iron ore at reasonable costs.

The scarcest of the Indian steel industry's principal raw materials would appear to be limestone. India's known reserves of flux grade limestone are placed at only 100 million tons,[7]

[5] These tonnages refer to the portion of mined coal that can be beneficiated or washed. The estimate of 1.6 billion tons has been made by a prominent Indian engineer, M. N. Dastur, *Steel in India—Economic and Technological Possibilities,* the fourth Sir M. Visvesvaraya Lecture, delivered at the 41st Annual Convention of the Institution of Engineers (India) (Calcutta: *The Statesman,* Commercial Printing Department, 1961), p. 17. The estimate of 2.1 billion tons has been cited in B. B. Engineer, "Principal Mineral Raw Materials for Iron and Steel Industry," *Symposium on Iron and Steel Industry in India, Jamshedpur, 1959* (Calcutta: Technical Journals of India, Private, Ltd., 1959), p. 101. An intermediate estimate of 1.81 billion tons has been made in Energy Survey of India Committee, *Energy Survey* (Delhi, 1964), p. 109. This estimate assumes a 50 per cent washing yield and the addition of blendable coal. It disregards reserves of coal below 610 meters.

[6] See Appendix A.

[7] Dastur, *Steel in India,* p. 17.

which, at present rates of exploitation, approximately 2.8 million tons per year, would not last for more than 35 years. However, the problem with Indian limestones is not that they do not exist, but that search for new deposits of suitable quality has been limited.

Two types of limestone are essential to an integrated steel mill. Most is consumed in blast furnaces; the remainder, which must satisfy more rigorous quality specifications, is consumed in steel melt shops. Much of the blast furnace grade limestone used by existing plants is obtained from deposits in northern Orissa. These deposits are limited, and, although there are others in Bihar, Uttar Pradesh, and Madhya Pradesh, extensive investigation is still needed to determine whether they are of blast furnace grade and are capable of being quarried at reasonable costs. Steel melt shop limestone is in far more limited supply and further prospecting is necessary to uncover new deposits. Beneficiation of substandard limestone and greater use of dolomite are possible alternatives, although both would result in increased costs of production. It is unlikely that a nation the size of India possesses so little suitable limestone. Were sufficient attention given to finding new deposits or verifying known deposits, India's meager reserves would probably be augmented. For this reason limestone is not generally regarded as a serious limitation upon the expansion of India's steel industry, although relatively long haulage of steel melt shop limestone may become necessary in the future.

Although the quantity of necessary raw materials need not deter expansion of India's steel industry, the quality of these materials and research on them leave much to be desired. High ash in coal, high alumina in iron ore, and high insolubles in limestone all result in high costs of producing pig iron, partly offsetting cost advantages accruing from the high iron content of Indian ores and the proximity of these ores to coking coal and limestone. Moreover, surveys of the industry's raw materials have been wanting. Verification of the quality and quantity of certain deposits, particularly of iron ore and limestone, has too often proved to be inadequate after mills have been erected based upon them. This has been a major fault of planning for the expansion of India's steel industry in recent years, resulting in unnecessarily high costs of production.[8]

The Supply of Capital

Although the rate of savings may be lower in India than in more developed economies, obstacles to India's industrial growth resulting from a scarcity of *domestic* savings can be overstated. Inequalities in the distribution of both personal and corporate incomes are far greater in India than in more developed economies, and, because of the size of India's population, upper income groups, although a small portion of the total population, are not small in absolute numbers. Potential entrepreneurs in upper income groups may not be impeded by shortages of investable funds even for so large a venture as a steel mill. For the most part, economists concerned with economic growth have concluded that an increased rate of savings is essential to development. The contention here is that although this may be desirable, domestic savings available to Indian industry are not as limited as some may believe, and perfection of means of directing existing or potential savings to important investment projects is equally desirable and, perhaps, more easily accomplished.

Capital scarcity was, for the most part, no impediment to TISCO's growth prior to World War II.[9] In 1907 the Tatas sold their first issue of share capital entirely in India and within three weeks after it had been offered to the Indian public. In later years the company was again successful in marketing new

[8] Inadequate attention to raw materials in planning for the expansion of India's steel industry is discussed at length in Chapter 8.

[9] Appendix B contains the following discussion in greater detail.

issues of shares and debentures in India. After 1923 TISCO underwent continuous expansion financed almost entirely from retained earnings. Only once prior to World War II did TISCO obtain funds from abroad—in 1923 when it sold debentures in London; and only once did it have to curtail its expansion programs because of shortage of funds—shortly after World War I when there was widespread concern that the company might be forced to declare bankruptcy. Moreover, rates of interest paid by TISCO were generally modest by Indian standards and very little above rates current in the United Kingdom.

There are several reasons for the ease with which TISCO was able to obtain finances for its mill. Imperfections in India's share markets served to channel funds to the company at relatively low rates of interest. The Tatas are members of the relatively well-to-do Parsee community, which has provided a disproportionate share of the company's capital. To some extent communal loyalties enabled the Tatas to draw upon the savings of the Parsee community more heavily than could non-Parsee business interests. Still more important, by 1907 the Tatas were a well-known business family with an established reputation for competent and honest management and success in its ventures. Little risk was attached to TISCO's issues, an extremely important consideration to the Indian investor. In addition, many of the company's largest investors were highly prosperous businessmen who had had long associations with the Tatas and because of these associations were prepared to invest heavily in their steel mill venture. Disparities in both personal and corporate incomes assisted the mobilization of capital by the Tata Company. Finally, the policies of the Indian government and a peculiarity of India's Independence movement, the Swadeshi or "buy Indian" campaign during the first decade of this century, are said to have enabled the Tatas' accumulation of necessary funds.

Table 4. Capital Costs of India's Public Sector Steel Mills as of March 31, 1963

Plant	Cost per ton of capacity (rupees)		Capacity (thousands of tons)		Percentage of investment in foreign exchange
	Per ton of ingots	Per ton of finished steel	Ingots	Finished steel	
Rourkela					
Million ton plant[a]	2,247	3,121	1,000	720	58
After completion of Third Plan expansion[b]	1,833	2,662	1,800	1,240	52
Bhilai					
Million ton plant[a]	2,009	2,608	1,000	770	49
After completion of Third Plan expansion[b]	1,229	1,562	2,500	1,965	45
Durgapur					
Million ton plant[a]	1,933	2,416	1,000	800	49
After completion of Third Plan expansion[b]	1,433	1,852	1,625	1,259	47

[a] Computed from Hindustan Steel Limited (HSL), *Annual Report, 1962–63,* p. 8.
[b] Computed from U.S. Steel Corporation, "A Techno-Economic Survey of a Proposed Integrated Steel Mill at Bokaro, Bihar State, India" (unpub. report submitted to the U.S. Government, Agency for International Development, March 1963), Vol. III, Exhibit F–1.

Discussion of the steel industry's past not only contributes to a better understanding of the process of industrial growth, but also to a more meaningful appraisal of the financial resources now available to the industry. One argument commonly used in defense of the government's entry into the steel industry is that India's private sector would be unable to raise financial capital sufficient to erect new steel mills.[10] This claim may be correct when one is referring to new steel companies that do not possess the reputations and the means of accumulating retained earnings possessed by TISCO and IISCO. It is also possible that the private sector would be incapable of fulfilling the entire steel target established by India's planners. However, to argue that existing private sector companies would be unable to expand their mills or even to erect new steel mills because they would be unable to raise the necessary financial capital is, in my opinion, unjustified. This claim is not borne out by the experiences of these companies. Nor is it supported by an assessment of price controls over the industry and the strength of India's capital markets, given changes in these controls and other Government of India policies.

Initial investment in each of India's new steel mills, presented in Table 4, was between Rs. 1.9 and 2.3 billion.[11] The present costs of a new one million ingot ton mill would be greater, perhaps as much as three billion rupees, depending on the

[10] This assertion was made in 1963 by Mr. J. R. D. Tata, Chairman of TISCO, in an effort to counter American objections to participation in the Bokaro project because it would be a public sector enterprise. Mr. Tata declared, "The simple fact is that we need more steel and we need it quickly. There is neither time nor sufficient private capital available to develop expanded production soon enough. Starting a new steel company with present costs, especially on a rapid basis, is beyond the financial resources of private enterprise . . ." Quoted in *New York Times*, May 25, 1963, p. 13.

[11] Estimated investment costs for India's public sector steel mills vary from one source to another. Expenditures on Rourkela exceed expenditures on Bhilai and Durgapur partly because Rourkela rolls flat products which demand more expensive rolling mill equipment than other types of steel.

type of product manufactured and assuming an appropriate devaluation of the rupee.[12] Were there an increase in the prices received by India's steel companies equal to Rs. 250 per ton,[13] and were this increase earmarked for the growth of the industry, TISCO could accumulate funds sufficient for a new one million ingot ton plant in less than nine years. Substantial rupee reserves could also be accumulated by IISCO. Because prices received by India's steel mills have been inadequate for most of the postwar period, a matter discussed at length in Chapter 5, it would appear that a major reason why both companies have been unable to accumulate funds sufficient for the erection of at least one new steel mill has been the government's price controls.

Of course, the entire cost of a new mill would not have to be covered by retained earnings. During the 1950s both private sector companies were able to market at a premium new share issues sufficient to obtain one-fourth of the funds necessary for their expansion programs.[14] Neither company encountered exceptional difficulties in the sale of these shares. The consensus in late 1962 among persons associated with Dalal Street and Lyons Range, the Wall Streets of Bombay and Calcutta, was that both companies would again be able to market new issues in substantial numbers *provided* these issues correspond to increased productive capacity and that the government exer-

[12] For certain purposes throughout this book I have revalued the rupee at the shadow rate of exchange, one rupee equal to 14 cents, rather than the official rate prior to June 1966, one rupee equal to 21 cents. My justification for using this shadow rate is given in Chapter 5 and Appendix C. Parenthetically, this estimate of the real value of the rupee has been shared by the Indian government. In June 1966, after this book was completed, the rupee was devalued to 13.33 cents.

[13] The government's price policies are discussed in Chapter 5. In particular, see Table 6. Rs. 250 is, in my opinion, the minimum average increase in prices received by India's steel mills in 1962 justified by the real costs of producing steel in India.

[14] TISCO increased its total share capital from Rs. 105 million in 1953 to Rs. 390 million in 1960. IISCO doubled its share capital from Rs. 79 million to Rs. 150 million during the same period.

cise some restraint in its policies of control over the industry.[15] By mid-1965 this optimism had disappeared.[16] There was little hope that either company could float new issues in large numbers, not because of poor performance—this had actually improved during the two year interim—but because of substantial increases in corporate and dividend taxes in early 1963 that have contributed to the depression of India's share markets.

Prior to 1963 the attitude toward IISCO's shares was optimistic. The company had performed well, raising its after-tax dividend several times since 1960 despite government regulation of steel prices and erratic transportation and raw material supplies. The prevailing attitude toward TISCO's shares was more cautious but still optimistic. During the five years ending March 1963, TISCO maintained its dividend by drawing upon its reserves. TISCO's comparatively poor showing was not only a result of low controlled prices and transportation and raw materials difficulties. The company emerged from its recent expansion program with an unbalanced plant, and, consequently, has had greater problems in adjusting to its additional capacity than IISCO. Many of TISCO's difficulties were corrected by 1965, and, in the opinion of most informants, the company would not encounter much reluctance in marketing new shares were it not for the government's tax policies.[17]

The government made special advances to the companies during the 1950s to enable their expansion programs. It was understood at the time these advances were made that they would be repaid by subsequent increases in steel prices. In

[15] Discussions with persons associated with Dalal Street in August 1962 and Lyons Range in December 1962.

[16] For a more recent assessment of India's share markets, see *Capital*, Feb. 4, 1965, pp. 158–159.

[17] Information on dividends and profits can be obtained from the annual reports of both companies. This same information and the range of the market prices of the two companies' shares over the preceding decade is reproduced in Place, Siddons & Gough, *The Investor's India Year-Book* (Calcutta: Orient Longmans Ltd., various years).

1963 the government decided that they should be repaid by new share issues or a sacrifice in dividends and conferred upon itself the unilateral right to convert these advances into company shares.[18] The possibility that the government might acquire significant voting power in both companies has strained India's relations with the World Bank. Partial nationalization of the companies is thought to be a violation of existing loan agreements which were between the World Bank and the companies and which are also entered into by the government as guarantor. The method of repayment was debated for nearly two years before being settled to the satisfaction of all parties late in 1965. In the meantime, the companies' Fourth Plan expansion programs, to be financed in part by the World Bank, remained in abeyance.

Substantially higher prices for steel could conceivably result in increased savings by the Indian economy. Greater excise taxes and increased profits would divert income to the government or to India's steel mills, which could be compelled, by law if necessary, to reinvest their entire gains. Unduly low steel prices have benefited middlemen who market steel, users of steel, and, in a few instances, ultimate consumers. These parties almost certainly do not invest, or at least save, all or even most of their present gain from lower prices; or, if they do, they probably invest it in inventories or in steel-using industries in which there may be excess capacity.

The profits of government plants are also a potential source of investable funds for their own expansion programs or, eventually, the erection of new steel mills. Each sector has access to

[18] "The Companies (Amendment) Act, 1963," *The Gazette of India* (New Delhi: Government of India Publication, Dec. 30, 1963), p. 561. Another section of the Act declares that voting rights attached to shares held in trust will be assumed by a public trustee appointed by the government (pp. 562–563). If administered, this section could be a severe blow to TISCO. The government's action has been criticized by Mr. J. R. D. Tata in his annual speech to TISCO's shareholders in 1964. See *Economic Weekly*, August 8, 1964, pp. 1366–1367.

sources of domestic savings not available to the other. The purposeful use of prices to accumulate savings could be a powerful tool at the disposal of the Indian Government.

The Supply of Foreign Exchange

Any meaningful discussion of the financial resources available to the industry must distinguish between domestic savings and foreign exchange. During the past decade India's balance of trade has worsened. Her trade deficit has been offset partly by invisibles, but primarily by compensatory transactions, such as the receipt of external assistance and the use of foreign exchange reserves. Rigid exchange control has been instituted to minimize India's trade deficit. For this reason, the ability of a party to raise capital in India is no longer sufficient to assure his purchase of goods and services from abroad.

It is debatable whether India's foreign exchange difficulties are primarily a result of her inability to convert rupee savings into foreign exchange or her unwillingness to institute more effective promotion of exports.[19] Probably both have contributed to India's present difficulties. In any event, it is likely that for many years to come Indian savings will have to be supple-

[19] For a sampling of the literature concerned with India's foreign exchange difficulties and, more particularly, her export problems, see S. J. Patel, "Export Prospects and Economic Growth: India," *The Economic Journal*, LXIX (September 1959), 490–506. See, also, comments by Anne Krueger and P. T. Bauer, *The Economic Journal*, LXXI (June 1961), 436–446, and by Benjamin I. Cohen, "A Comment on S. J. Patel's Analysis of Indian Exports," *The Indian Economic Journal*, XI (July–September 1963), 37–46. The last mentioned article is an outgrowth of Dr. Cohen's doctoral dissertation, "A Study of the Export Policies of the Indian Government, 1951/52–1965/66" (unpub. diss., Harvard University, 1963). The principal conclusions of this dissertation are presented in a subsequent article by Dr. Cohen, "The Stagnation of Indian Exports, 1951–1961," *Quarterly Journal of Economics*, LXXVIII (November 1964), 604–620. Finally, a thorough discussion of Indian exports is made by Manmohan Singh, *India's Export Trends and the Prospects for Self-Sustained Growth* (London: Oxford University Press, 1964). Dr. Singh's conclusions are, in general, identical to those of Dr. Cohen.

mented by foreign investment and economic assistance if desired rates of growth are achieved.

The private sector steel companies might have access to at least three sources of foreign exchange not available to the Government of India: foreign private interests, the United States government, and the World Bank. Several foreign private interests have recently considered erecting new steel mills in India. Their proposals were never very serious, and it is doubtful that the foreign interests were willing to supply, or to arrange to supply, a meaningful proportion of the necessary foreign exchange. Nevertheless, given certain assurances by the government, suitable collaboration between Indian and foreign private interests might be arranged and the foreign exchange needs of a new Indian steel mill either supplied by the foreign collaborator or obtained on the basis of his credit.

Another possible source of foreign exchange for a private Indian steel mill is the United States government. The U.S. House of Representatives balked because the Bokaro project is to be erected in the public sector. It might view assistance to a private venture with considerably less disfavor.

The World Bank has also refused to finance government-owned industrial units as a matter of policy. Yet during the 1950s the Bank did make sizable loans to India's private sector steel mills for their expansion programs. Additional credits covering the foreign exchange costs of a new steel mill would be much greater than past loans to the industry. Even so, it is possible, even likely, that a part of these credits could be shared by the United States government or private banks in the United States, Europe, and Japan. A joint private venture drawing its foreign exchange from several sources is an alternative to government erection of a new steel mill that may be unsatisfactory on ideological grounds. However, this does not mean that it is impossible.

Although the Government of India would not have access to these sources of foreign exchange, it would have access to others not available to the private sector. An example is Soviet assistance for Bhilai and Bokaro. I do not mean to imply that the private sector would necessarily do any better than the public sector in mobilizing the foreign exchange component of a new steel plant, but to point out that there are sources of foreign exchange available to private interests and not to the government, and that these sources would be more assured were the government to modify its controls over the industry.

The belief that India's steel industry will soon be freed from much of its past need for foreign exchange appears widespread in India.[20] This belief centers around the Heavy Engineering Corporation, Limited (HEC), a government factory at Ranchi, Bihar, and several newly established public sector enterprises.[21] These plants will supply Indian steel mills with some of their equipment needs and will allow some lessening of Indian dependence on foreign economic assistance. Yet the notion persists that they will soon be able to build a new steel mill each year, thus enabling India to dispense with most if not all foreign participation in the industry's growth. It could take several decades to develop the skills necessary for the satisfactory production of the complicated and diverse components of a steel mill. To entrust most of the industry's equipment needs to inexperienced and untried companies is to risk inordinate delays in expanding the industry and extraordinary difficulties with its equipment. The role of these companies, until they are able to develop the necessary skills, will be that of manufacturers of relatively simple components for all steel mills, preferably as subcontractors to foreign equipment suppliers.

[20] For an example, see references to statements by a former Minister of Steel and Heavy Industries, Mr. C. Subramaniam, *Overseas Hindustan Times*, New Delhi, Dec. 19, 1963, p. 11, and his successor, Mr. Sanjiva Reddy, *The Times of India*, Bombay, Oct. 30, 1965, p. 6.

[21] Adjoining HEC is a foundry-forge plant, intended to supply HEC with a variety of steel mill components, and a heavy machine tool plant to manufacture tools necessary for maintenance at the steel mills. Heavy electrical plants at Hardwar and Bhopal will also manufacture steel mill components. All plants are government owned and operated.

Some informants think that the government may attempt to finance the foreign exchange costs of new steel mills under short- or medium-term commercial credits because of its inability to obtain long-term loans from foreign sources. If so, the erection of these mills would intensify India's foreign exchange difficulties in the near future. Repayment or renegotiation of these loans would almost certainly precede equivalent savings in foreign exchange made possible by the mills' operations.

The Supply of Labor and Managerial Personnel

Labor needed by the Indian steel industry cannot be considered a homogeneous factor of production. Unskilled labor is abundant and has been drawn to India's steel mills in relatively large numbers. However, this type of labor is of limited use to such industries as iron and steel in which an experienced labor force is needed for the efficient operation of complex, highly automated equipment.

There are some uses for unskilled labor in the manufacture of steel, and for this reason employment in India's steel industry is substantially in excess of employment in steel industries elsewhere. However, these uses are by and large divorced from the immediate operations of India's steel mills. Unskilled labor is employed in great numbers in the mining of ore, the handling of raw materials and finished steel, construction, and other subsidiary activities where speed is unnecessary, dangers to physical well-being small, and the demands upon the energies of workers at a minimum. For most activities within the plants proper there is relatively little scope for employment of unskilled labor.[22]

[22] There are a few exceptions. In one private sector steel mill tribal women with wicker baskets salvage pieces of coal that have fallen to the ground from railway wagons, a tippler that empties these wagons, and conveyor belts that carry coal to the mill's coke ovens. Apparently the slight reduction in fuel costs made possible by these women compensates

It is necessary to specify what I mean by skilled labor. This is, first of all, labor that is capable of performing tasks essential to economic activity, such as the production of steel, and possessing abilities not generally shared by others. Moreover, because many of these abilities can be acquired only on the job, skilled labor is in many instances experienced labor, not simply labor that has undergone formal training. There are many levels of skills. The lowest level may include semi-skilled labor, workers capable of a few of the lesser although still specialized tasks essential for the production of steel and, equally important, willing to submit to the disciplines of factory employment. At the other extreme are managerial skills, talents necessary for supervising and coordinating the operations of entire divisions and, at the highest levels of management, an entire steel mill. By and large, skills concentrated at the lower end of the spectrum seem to have been acquired in a surprisingly short period of time by India's steel industry, given an environment conducive to their acquisition by laborers. On the contrary, it has taken decades or even a lifetime for Indian mills to acquire managerial skills.

What are the sources of the skills needed by a new industrial enterprise? Certainly one source is other units in the same or similar industries. To some extent lower levels of skills are more generalized and therefore more easily drawn from other industries. A mechanic in an assembly plant can, with relative ease, become a mechanic in a steel mill. However, the more specialized the skills, the less the enterprise will be able to borrow from outside the industry without the necessity of re-training. This applies with special force to management. Although competent administrators can be obtained from the

the mill for their employment. In another mill workmen with picks and shovels leisurely remove accumulations of slag that are out of the way of other activities in the mill. At all mills is the ever-present peon, ready to fetch tea or to run some other errand.

government—the favored source of management for the new public sector mills—the top management of an industrial enterprise, such as a steel mill, is a highly specialized function requiring intimacy with the operations of all major units of the plant.

The ability of a new industrial enterprise to borrow skills from other establishments is much more limited in less developed countries. New Indian steel mills have been favored by the prior existence of TISCO and IISCO, drawing heavily upon the reservoir of skills accumulated by these companies during the past half century. Nonetheless, because their reserves are limited, both TISCO and IISCO have been unable to satisfy all the needs of the new mills, particularly their needs for supervisory and managerial talent. For this reason, the principal source of many of the specialized skills needed by new Indian mills may have to be the new mills themselves and, until these skills can be created by them, the import of comparable skills from abroad. The alternative to obtaining needed skills from these sources could well be the improper use and, more particularly, the mismanagement of new steel plants.

Once again, some discussion of the industry's past is both of general interest and relevant to a specific study of current problems in the industry. TISCO's early attempts to create a skilled and stable work force and, especially, a competent managerial staff offer the development economist an invaluable case study of the problems of establishing new industrial enterprise in an essentially non-industrial economy.

In its early years TISCO derived little benefit from an abundance of inexpensive labor in India. Prior to 1923 TISCO's labor costs per ton of output were substantially higher than the labor costs of comparable mills in Europe and the United States. By 1933 there was no appreciable difference between TISCO's direct labor costs and labor costs elsewhere despite the fact that much of the company's foreign personnel had by then been replaced by Indians.[23] Because TISCO provided, in addition to its basic wage, an abnormally large number of amenities to its workers, wages in kind and services, the total cost of its labor probably exceeded the total cost of labor in Europe and the United States for a much longer period of time.

The economist might ascribe the high cost of TISCO's labor to the company's use of labor-intensive methods of production. To some extent this assessment is correct. However, in the steel industry technology is relatively inflexible and the substitutability of labor for other inputs, notably machinery, limited. The labor employed by the company was also costly because of the great expense of the imported technician and the low productivity of the Indian worker.[24] In short, labor employed by the company was not cheap.

At first, skilled labor was said to be one of TISCO's scarcest inputs. In the words of the company:

> [More developed economies] have also the enormous advantage of a reserve of skilled labour on which they can draw. In India there is no such reserve, though one will be built up in time as the industry becomes gradually established . . .[25]
>
> There is no question of the scarcity of [skilled] labour in India. It does not exist at all. It has to be imported.[26]

Foreign personnel was expensive. The salaries of foreign technicians were on average 50 per cent above those earned by comparable technicians in Europe and the United States. Moreover,

[23] Indian Tariff Board, *Report of the Indian Tariff Board Regarding the Grant of Protection to the Steel Industry* (Calcutta: Government of India Publication, 1924), p. 33; and Indian Tariff Board, *Statutory Enquiry—1933—Steel Industry* (Delhi: Government of India Publication, 1934), Vol. II, p. 58.

[24] *Report of the Indian Tariff Board Regarding the Grant of Protection*, p. 33.

[25] Indian Tariff Board, *Evidence Recorded During Enquiry into the Steel Industry* (Calcutta: Government of India Publication, 1924), Vol. I, p. 6.

[26] *Ibid.*, p. 228.

TISCO employed a large number of Indians alongside its foreign staff in order to train them or because India's climate and customs prohibited foreign technicians from performing some of the manual tasks they would ordinarily perform in their home countries.[27] In addition the company incurred a number of other costs associated with its employment of foreign personnel, passage to and from India, payment of wages to foreign workers in transit, and provision of housing and recreational facilities to these workers at little or no cost.[28] For these reasons, during its first thirty years the company suffered a cost disadvantage from its employment of skilled foreign personnel. This disadvantage contributed to its higher labor costs per ton of output.

Much of TISCO's skilled Indian labor force had to be created by the company itself. At first TISCO was primarily concerned with the perfection of its organization and operations and more particularly with the production of good quality steel. Subsequently it was preoccupied with supplying the war needs of the allied armies in Africa and the Middle East. For these reasons, a concerted program of Indianization was delayed until shortly after World War I. In 1919 TISCO established a technical institute to train Indians who would eventually replace

[27] *Ibid.*, p. 223.

[28] In its early years the company experienced an excessive turnover of its foreign staff. In an attempt to reduce this turnover it built, among other things, a race track and stocked this track with horses. John L. Keenan, *A Steel Man in India* (New York: Duell, Sloan and Pearce, 1943), esp. pp. 51–56. Keenan was an American associated with TISCO almost from its beginning. In the early 1930s he was the plant's General Manager. His book, the memoirs of his work in India, is a delightful mine of information about TISCO's difficulties in establishing itself, particularly useful as a source of information about the company's early labor problems. Parenthetically, TISCO's racetrack, aside from reducing turnover, also reduced drinking among TISCO's foreign employees. Hence the title of one of Keenan's chapters: "Racing is Good for the Liver." Ordinarily, such facilities as a racetrack have already been provided by the community or other private interests. At Jamshedpur, a city erected in the midst of the Indian jungle, these facilities had to be provided by the Tata Company itself.

the company's foreign personnel. The curriculum of the institute was later broadened and an in-plant training program created to help fill the company's needs for lower categories of labor. In 1924 TISCO employed over two hundred foreign technicians in the operations of its plant. By April 1933 their number was reduced to seventy.[29] Not until 1936 was the first Indian appointed General Manager of the works, and not until the outbreak of World War II was the works for all practical purposes fully Indianized.[30]

TISCO did not consider the availability of cheap unskilled labor to be particularly advantageous. In the words of a company spokesman:

> We do not think that any person having the least knowledge of the manufacture of iron and steel . . . would consider that it was an advantage . . . to employ Indian labour or that it is notoriously cheap . . .[31]

The low productivity of TISCO's early labor force was not only a result of a lack of skills. India's climate reduced the effectiveness of both Indian and imported workers. Moreover, much of TISCO's unskilled work force came from distant areas and considered its employment to be temporary.[32] At first turnover and absenteeism were high. Skills and disciplines developed by the company were often lost, if not permanently at least periodically, when a worker returned to his village for planting or

[29] Indian Tariff Board, *Report of the Indian Tariff Board on the Iron and Steel Industry*, (Delhi: Government of India Publication, 1934), pp. 83–84.

[30] For a discussion of the company's policy of Indianization, see Keenan, *A Steel Man in India*, pp. 133–141.

[31] *Evidence Recorded*, Vol. I, p. 232.

[32] *Statutory Enquiry—1933*, Vol. I, p. 133. See also United Nations, UNESCO Research Center on Social Implications of Industrialization in Southern Asia, "Report on a Preliminary Enquiry on the Growth of Steel Towns in India, a Study in Problems of Urbanization" (mimeograph, Calcutta, 1959), p. 13.

harvesting or for religious and family celebrations.[33] TISCO provided its workers with a number of amenities intended among other things, to encourage permanent settlement in Jamshedpur. These included subsidized housing and grain sales, free water supply and medical services, a bonus scheme, a provident fund, and other fringe benefits. The costs of these amenities were a part of the costs of creating a permanent work force at the Tata mill.

Initially, TISCO tried to minimize its investment in machinery by using coolie labor, especially in the handling of materials. This is behavior the economist might expect. However, TISCO soon found that in many instances coolie labor did not serve as an acceptable substitute for machinery, and additional investment was required to rectify this error.[34]

Discussion of the industry's past serves several purposes. First, not only was financial capital for the most part easily available to India's steel industry prior to World War II, but skilled labor capable of satisfying many of the industry's essential needs was not very plentiful. Some common notions about factor availabilities in underdeveloped economies would appear to be overly simplistic and, perhaps, fundamentally incorrect when applied to India's steel industry.

Second, despite TISCO's early labor problems, one is impressed by the speed with which the company was able to establish itself and, more particularly, to build a stable, disciplined work force. TISCO's plant was erected in a primitive region of India inhabited by tribes possessing little or no industrial experience. Yet the plant was able to draw its early labor

[33] During the early 1920s TISCO had to carry an extra force of 20 per cent to cover absenteeism. This was subsequently reduced to about 10 per cent, still a large cushion by industry standards. *Evidence Recorded*, Vol. I, pp. 228 and 426; *Statutory Enquiry, 1926, Steel Industry* (Calcutta: Government of India Publication, 1927), Vol. III, p. 90; and *Statutory Enquiry—1933*, Vol. II, p. 199.

[34] *Evidence Recorded*, p. 443. See also *Statutory Enquiry, 1926*, Vol. III, pp. 89–90.

force from these tribes and, more important, from more developed regions of India. Some of these regions are more than a thousand miles from Jamshedpur, a fact that calls into question some common notions about the immobility of Indian labor. By the early 1920s TISCO had developed a permanent Indian work force capable of manning the steel mill satisfactorily. Even though TISCO encountered initial difficulties with its labor, these difficulties were overcome and an acceptable work force was built in a relatively short period of time.[35]

Third, measured by the time needed to build an Indian staff capable of running TISCO's mill properly, a far more difficult problem was the creation of the highest levels of skills, supervisory and managerial personnel. Although TISCO's mill was owned and staffed by Indians from the beginning, its supervision was left to experienced American and English steel men until World War II. Only after a competent Indian staff had been created were TISCO's foreign technicians replaced by Indians—in my opinion a decision that more than any other was responsible for the ultimate success of the company.

On the contrary, many of the difficulties now experienced by India's new public sector steel mills can be traced to a failure by those responsible for the industry's growth to follow TISCO's example. The public sector mills have benefited from the prior existence of the private steel companies by hiring some of their skilled workers. Even so, the public sector mills have employed recent college graduates with little industrial experience in positions normally filled by seasoned technicians.[36] The mills have

[35] A similar conclusion is reached by Morris David Morris in his study of Bombay's cotton textile mills. M. D. Morris, *The Emergence of an Industrial Labor Force in India: A Study of the Bombay Cotton Mills, 1854–1947* (Berkeley, Calif.: University of California Press, 1965). For a brief examination of labor recruitment for India's steel industry, see pp. 208–210.

[36] Fortunately, inexperienced graduate engineers do not appear to be in short supply, at least to the steel industry, and represent the principal future source of the industry's managerial and supervisory personnel. As

also imported skilled technicians from abroad. However, with the exception of Bhilai, in the beginning they employed foreign personnel grudgingly and in too few numbers and refused to allow this personnel full powers.[37] In short, those responsible for the public sector mills did not seem to recognize the central importance of expertise to the industry's growth.

Factor Proportions and Plan Strategies

It is not particularly useful to think of factors of production necessary for the manufacture of steel simply in terms of the traditional dichotomy, capital and labor. One must also consider India's natural endowments. In addition, capital and labor are themselves heterogeneous factors to India's steel industry and, perhaps, to many other industries as well. All types of capital are not equally scarce nor all labor abundant. Therefore, simple policy judgments that Indian planners should discourage investment in capital-intensive industries, such as steel, and encourage investment in labor-intensive industries may be misleading.

Whether or not heavy investment in the steel industry rather than in other industries is justified by India's factor endowments is further complicated by the fact that industries are interrelated in many ways. So large an industrial venture as a new steel mill would require a significant expenditure of foreign exchange and the employment of skilled personnel. However, the alternative to the erection of the mill would be the importation of steel, also at a great cost of foreign exchange, or the curtailment of the growth of industries consuming steel. Many

---

of March 31, 1962, 1,504 graduate engineers and 477 operatives had been sent abroad to receive training in foreign steel mills. The largest single contingent was sent to the Soviet Union; the second largest to the United States under In Step (Indian Steel Training and Educational Program) sponsored by the Ford Foundation with the assistance of various American steel companies, universities and other organizations. Trainees have also been sent to the United Kingdom, West Germany, Australia, and Canada.

[37] This is discussed at length in Chapter 8.

consuming industries, such as construction, port facilities, railways, and the manufacture of bicycles and agricultural implements, could employ relatively large numbers of unskilled or semiskilled workers and indigenous capital and may be more suited to India's relative factor endowments. In addition, most of the industries consuming steel are capital goods industries considered essential to India's economic growth. It is by no means certain that investment in the steel industry, even though it would absorb relatively large amounts of scarce factors of production, would be disadvantageous to the Indian economy considered as a whole.

To what extent can techniques of production in a steel mill be varied to better reflect India's factor endowments? For many years, until new industrial enterprise gains the experience essential for the satisfactory production of the components of a steel mill, opportunities for the use of Indian-made machinery will be limited. Even then, it would be a mistake to regard domestic savings as abundant, and, for this reason, it may be to India's benefit to utilize methods of production that allow minimum use of domestic as well as foreign plant and machinery.

It has already been noted that present techniques of steel manufacture do not allow much direct use of unskilled labor. It might seem that other methods, perhaps older methods of producing steel no longer in general use elsewhere, would allow greater use of manual labor relative to capital and would be preferred. For example, thirty years ago hand hot mills were widely used in the rolling of sheets, but have since been replaced in more developed economies, at least, by semicontinuous and continuous strip mills. The newer mills require more capital relative to manual labor and would appear to be poorly suited to India's factor endowments. However, like many recent innovations in the steel industry, continuous and semicontinuous strip mills, because of their speed, allow greater output per rupee of investment in plant and equipment as well as per rupee spent on virtually every other input. Continuous and semicontinuous mills also enable the rolling of a better quality product. Greater manual movement of semifinished forms of steel from one unit of a steel mill to another, where physically possible, might also appear to be superior to the mechanized methods now used. However, mechanized methods may allow the subsequent processing of intermediate forms with less reheating time, thus reducing fuel costs as well as the investment costs of additional reheating capacity.

In general, those techniques used in the manufacture of steel in more developed economies are not particularly well suited for India's factor endowments but are nevertheless best suited for India because they are, overall, most efficient. Not only do mechanized processes allow lower costs of production, they also enable the manufacture of a better quality product. Opportunities for the advantageous adoption of alternative processes, particularly obsolete processes, are limited.

Perhaps a more controversial issue than the technologies adopted by India's steel industry is whether or not all is being done that must be done to secure the successful use of modern technologies by the industry. With a few exceptions, new Indian mills have been equipped with the latest machinery. Unfortunately, they have not always been supplied with complementary factors of production, particularly managerial and technical skills, to assure that this machinery is used properly.

The importance of skills is not a new concept to economists. During the middle of the nineteenth century Mill recognized superior skill and knowledge to be one reason for the higher productivity of certain types of labor.[38] In 1890 Marshall declared knowledge to be the most important "engine" of production.[39] However, both in the writings of classical economists

[38] John Stuart Mill, *Principles of Political Economy,* ed. W. J. Ashley (New York: Longmans, Green, and Co., 1909), pp. 107–108.

[39] Alfred Marshall, *Principles of Economics,* eighth ed. (New York: Macmillan, 1948), Book IV, p. 138 and pp. 204–219.

and in the literature on economic development that has appeared since World War II, there has been relatively little discussion of skills. Only recently have economists begun to work toward a better theoretical and empirical understanding of the relationship between the creation of skills and the process of economic growth.

Skills are produced means of production. This has at times led to the conclusion that skills, like plant and machinery, are a direct result of investment or, more boldly stated, can be purchased if only planners in less developed economies were to devote more resources to education. However, formal education, although beneficial, may not be sufficient to insure the creation of skills that are most needed by industrial enterprise. It may take decades to create managerial talents necessary for conducting the business of a factory. This expertise cannot always be obtained from within an economy, particularly if the economy has a limited industrial base.

Skills are both an essential input and a by-product of economic growth. Needed skills can be imported until comparable skills have been created by the developing economy. However, this would require some lessening of the desire found in many newly independent nations to minimize the employment of foreign experts or to deny these experts sufficient autonomy to direct the operations of new plants. Development strategies could be designed to allow maximum use of available skills in existing units of an industry. However, this may necessitate some sacrifice of political and ideological considerations if existing units happen to be in the private sector. Similarly, new industrial units may be located near existing units to utilize existing expertise as much as possible. Unfortunately, in India this would run counter to an objective of policy-makers that is also motivated by political and ideological considerations, the dispersal of new units of an industry to as many states as possible. There are ways the developing economy can tailor its investment programs to overcome or minimize skill shortages. However, in India these frequently conflict with objectives other than economic growth.

4 | Government Policies Toward Industry

Chapter 3 contained one principal theme of this book, the need for planners to secure all factors of production necessary for the expansion of India's steel industry and, more generally, the development of her economy. This chapter considers a second theme, government policies toward Indian industry. I attempt to outline the important functions of the government, pointing out how its policies interact and what the consequences of this interaction have been. I do not restrict myself to India's steel industry, nor do I attempt to construct a policy model for the entire economy, seeking instead a middle ground between discussion of the industry and a more general discussion of the role of government in India's economic growth.

A primary justification for Indian planning is the government's desire to accelerate India's rate of economic growth. The government also has other objectives, such as greater equality in the distribution of income and a more balanced regional development of the Indian economy. There is nothing wrong with this. Gross national product can be an inadequate measure of a nation's welfare. However, what strikes the student of India's economy is the extent to which policies justified by these other objectives appear to have resulted in a sacrifice of growth. Some may ascribe India's economic backwardness to such fundamental economic and social factors as lack of savings and motivation. Yet there are many Indians who are capable of surprisingly high levels of savings and can match the entrepreneurship found in more rapidly developing economies. Changes in policies would be simpler than more fundamental changes in Indian behavior and, in my opinion, could also result in substantial economic benefits.[1]

At the outset I must disclaim any desire to become embroiled in ideological controversy. Any criticism of government policies in this book is not meant to be a criticism of an idealized economic system. If anything, my own instincts are those of a plumber. My concern is that the pipes work regardless of whether they were laid for socialist or capitalist purposes. Moreover, the Indian government has demonstrated a remarkable willingness to experiment with its policies. Especially during the past several years, the government has been the impetus for revision of a number of policies thought to have discouraged economic growth. In short, not only will I not discuss policies on an ideological plane, the government has itself tended to lessen the role of ideology in its policy-making. Discussion of ideology would be both inappropriate and futile.

Some Comments about India's Development Planning

Indian planning has been examined elsewhere.[2] Therefore I restrict this section to several observations that are especially relevant to my discussion in succeeding chapters. First, with the

[1] This argument is also made by Charles E. Lindblom, "Has India an Economic Future?," *Foreign Affairs* (January, 1966) esp. pp. 249–252. Lindblom, a distinguished academician, spent several years with the U.S. AID Mission in New Delhi.

[2] Three books were published in 1962 examining various aspects of Indian planning: John P. Lewis, *Quiet Crisis in India: Economic Development and American Policy* (Washington: The Brookings Institution, 1962); Wilfred Malenbaum, *Prospects for Indian Development* (New York: The Free Press of Glencoe, Inc., 1962); and W. B. Reddaway, *The Development of the Indian Economy* (Homewood, Ill.: Richard D. Irwin, Inc.,

exception of her First Five Year Plan, India has consistently opted for ambitious targets. Again with the exception of her First Five Year Plan, many plan targets have not been achieved. Although several arguments can be made in defense of ambitious planning, one of its consequences appears to have been the creation of unplanned imbalances in the Indian economy.

The First Five Year Plan was prepared early in the 1950s largely by drawing together ongoing or already conceived projects. The Plan was successful measured by its own standards. Public sector outlay under the plan fell just short of the plan target and India's official estimates of national income grew, on average, 3.5 per cent per year, enabling a modest increase in India's per capita income by the mid-1950s.[3] Perhaps more important, during the First Plan period many needed institutional changes were set in motion—the beginnings of land reform, consolidation of existing development programs, and the creation of a Planning Commission—that should have enabled more rapid growth in subsequent plan periods. The apparent success of the First Plan was in part a result of favorable monsoons at the end of the plan period and the drawing down of foreign exchange reserves accumulated during World War II. It was also a result of relatively modest targets.

When the Second Plan was being prepared during the mid-1950s there was controversy about its size, advocates of bold targets carrying the field. The Plan was partly based on Professor Mahalanobis' plan frame, an ambitious growth model

1962). Lewis is primarily concerned with existing and proposed strategies for India's economic development, centering his discussion on various sectors of the Indian economy. Malenbaum's book provides a more thorough historical discussion of Indian planning than the other two. Although Reddaway devotes much of his time to a statistical summary of India's Third Plan to determine, among other things, under what circumstances Third Plan targets were feasible, his book is of more enduring interest because of its excellent summary of the Indian planning process.

[3] Government of India, Planning Commission, *Second Five Year Plan* (New Delhi: Government of India Publication, 1956), pp. 2–5.

calling for rapid expansion in all sectors of the Indian economy, but above all in industry.[4] The Second Plan anticipated net investment twice that of the First Plan period and a rate of growth in national income averaging 4.5 per cent per year.[5] In fact, many plan targets were not met. Although official estimates of investment during the period slightly exceeded the plan target, there was also fairly substantial price inflation that helped to hold India's average annual rate of increase in national income to 3.6 per cent, barely greater than that achieved during the First Plan period.[6]

Second Plan targets were not impossible. However, their achievement depended on the fulfillment of a number of assumptions made by Indian planners about the availability of financial resources, particularly foreign exchange, the ability of those charged with implementing plan targets to execute their responsibilities, capital-output ratios in various industries, and the lengths of the necessary gestation periods between the installation of new capacity and its full utilization. Many plan targets were not met because of a worsening balance of payments and a resulting shortage of foreign exchange. Also responsible were shortcomings in plan implementation stemming from procedural delays and in certain instances the nonexistence of necessary administrative machinery. Too little time was assumed for production at reasonably full capacity once capacity had been installed. Although capacity targets were reached in some industries, production fell far below capacity

[4] The plan frame was the subject of numerous papers by Indian scholars in 1955. Both the plan frame and many of these papers are reproduced in Government of India, Planning Commission, *Papers Relating to the Formulation of the Second Five Year Plan* (New Delhi: Government of India Publication, 1955). For a discussion of the plan frame see Malenbaum, *Prospects for Indian Development*, pp. 86–91.

[5] Government of India, Planning Commission, *Second Five Year Plan*, p. 11.

[6] Government of India, Planning Commission, *Third Five Year Plan* (New Delhi: Government of India Publication, 1961), pp. 32 and 35.

because of difficulties in breaking in new plant and equipment, problems in training new workers, and shortages of essential raw materials.[7]

When Third Plan targets were framed there was also controversy about their size, advocates of bold planning once again carrying the field.[8] Although at the time of this writing the Third Plan is still in progress, there are ample indications that many targets will not be achieved. The growth of India's national income was approximately 3 per cent per year during the first four years of the Third Plan period instead of a planned increase of between 5 and 6 per cent per year for the entire period. Much of this unexpectedly poor showing can be attributed to poor crops resulting from bad weather. Even so, the rate of increase in industrial production, which should be less affected by the weather, was slightly lower than 8 per cent per year during the first four years of the period, compared with a planned rate of increase of 11 per cent per year for the entire period.[9] There are reasons other than the weather for the failure of the Third Five Year Plan.

To some extent Indian planners benefited from the experiences of the Second Plan period in framing Third Plan targets. Many of the plan's output targets were set well below corresponding capacity targets in recognition of the need for delays

[7] The reader interested in a more detailed discussion of performance under the Second Plan is directed to Malenbaum, *Prospects for Indian Development*, Chapters 10 and 11.

[8] Lewis, *Quiet Crisis in India*, pp. 71–79.

[9] Indexes of national income are presented in Reserve Bank of India, *Report on Currency and Finance* (Bombay: Government of India Publication, various years); indexes of industrial production in Government of India, Department of Statistics, Central Statistical Organization, *Monthly Statistics of the Production of Selected Industries of India* (Calcutta: Government of India Publication, various months). For an appraisal of the performance of the Indian economy during the first two years of the Third Plan period, including anticipated output at the end of the period, see Government of India, Planning Commission, *The Third Plan Mid-term Appraisal* (New Delhi: Government of India Publication, 1963).

during which new units are brought into full production. Yet it was recognized by the Planning Commission only two years after the beginning of the Third Plan period that many output targets would not be achieved.[10] The reasons for this appear to be, as before, overestimation of real financial resources, particularly foreign exchange, and, perhaps more important, a failure to implement many plan projects on schedule.

It is argued that targets should be ambitious to assure maximum efforts to mobilize resources and to continue the momentum of past growth.[11] Ambitious targets are also supported by such noneconomic objectives as minimization of political difficulties inherent in paring plan targets advocated by a particular state or ministry.[12] No doubt, there are advantages in ambitious planning. However, there are also disadvantages and these should be recognized.

It is of little use to speculate that Second and Third Plan targets could have been achieved if only India's planning apparatus, her government ministries, and public and private sector enterprise could have functioned as smoothly as possible. The fact is that most plan targets have not been achieved and by margins sufficient to justify concern on the part of planners. During the Second Plan period a foreign exchange crisis led to the cutting of plan targets to the "core." Priority was given to expenditures on replacements, completion of partially completed projects, and investment in such industries as iron and steel, mining, and transportation, all considered especially im-

[10] Government of India, Planning Commission, *The Third Plan Mid-term Appraisal*, esp. pp. 24–28.

[11] For example, see Government of India, Planning Commission, *Third Five Year Plan*, pp. 92–93.

[12] For example, in January 1961 the Finance Ministry attempted to cut the states' Third Plan targets to conform with anticipated financial resources. This aroused a storm of protest from the states and resulted in a compromise. Anticipated plan outlay remained unchanged. However, anticipated revenues were reduced to a more realistic level. *Economic Weekly*, Feb. 4, 1961, p. 121.

portant to the growth of India's economy. The mid-term appraisal of the Third Plan, although pessimistic about India's achievement of many plan targets, did not result in a formal redrafting of the plan. However, by mid-1965 recurring foreign exchange difficulties had forced a suspension of imports for many purposes. Under both plans, there was also a *de facto* alteration in plan targets as a result of unforeseen delays in a number of plan programs.

Table 5 reproduces planned and actual production of several Indian industries at the end of the Second and Third Five Year Plans. The industries included in Table 5 were selected both because of their importance and the accessibility of their target and output data. Production fell far short of plan targets in a number of other industries not included in Table 5, such as nonferrous metals and fertilizers. Conversely, plan targets for many machine tools and consumer goods industries were met or, in some instances, more than met by Indian producers.

The Indian government has assumed primary or sole responsibility for development of some industries in which plan targets have been under-achieved. There are several reasons for its inability to meet these targets. Shortfalls in steel at the end of the Second Plan were primarily a result of the necessary gestation period during which new mills were broken in. Shortfalls in electricity stemmed in part from a paring of Second Plan targets in response to a foreign exchange crisis during the plan period. On the contrary, cement, mill made cotton cloth, aluminum, fertilizers, and industrial chemicals are all industries that are or were until recently subject to price and distribution controls by the Indian government and were to be expanded partly or entirely through private sector initiative. The relationship between the government's controls and plan shortages is discussed later in this chapter.

One result of the nonachievement of ambitious targets has been the creation of imbalances in the Indian economy. Both

Table 5. Planned and Actual Production of Selected Indian Industries, 1960–61 and 1965–66[a]

Item	Unit	1960–61 Target[b]	1960–61 Actual output	1960–61 Percentage of target achieved	1965–66 Target	1965–66 Output anticipated by the Planning Commission[c]	1965–66 Percentage of target achieved
Locomotives	Number for the five year period	2,364[d]	1,291	55	1,470	1,470	100
Finished steel	Million long tons	4.3	2.4	56	6.8	5.8	85
Cotton cloth (mill made)	Million yards	8,500	5,048	59	5,800	5,550	96
Cement	Million long tons	13.0	7.8	60	13.0	12.0	92
Soda ash	Thousand long tons	230	145	63	450	350	78
Railway wagons (in terms of four wheelers)	Number in thousands for the five year period	107[d]	69	64	117	157	134
Caustic soda	Thousand long tons	135	97	72	340	340	100
Aluminum	Thousand long tons	25.0	18.2	73	80.0	68.0	85
Sulphuric acid	Thousand long tons	470	354	75	1,500	1,200	80
Electricity (installed capacity)	Million kw	6.9	5.6	81	12.7	12.5	98
Iron ore	Million long tons	12.5	10.7	86	30.0	25.0	83
Coal	Million metric tons	61.0	55.5	91	98.6	89.9	91
Paper and paper board	Thousand long tons	350	343	98	700	580	83

Table 5 (*cont.*)

Item	Unit	1960–61			1965–66		
		Target[b]	Actual output	Percentage of target achieved	Target	Output anticipated by the Planning Commission[c]	Percentage of target achieved
Electric transformers (33 kv and below)	Million kva	1.36	1.39	102	3.50	3.50	100
Electric motors (200 hp and below)	Million hp	0.60	0.73	122	2.50	2.50	100
Sugar	Million long tons	2.3	3.0	131	3.5	3.5	100

[a] Unless otherwise specified, data have been taken from Government of India, Planning Commission, *The Third Plan Mid-term Appraisal* (New Delhi: Government of India Publication, 1963), pp. 24–28.

[b] Unless otherwise specified, Second Plan targets have been taken from Government of India, Planning Commission, *Second Five Year Plan* (New Delhi: Government of India Publication, 1956), pp. 58–61.

[c] Data indicate output anticipated in 1963 and appear to be too optimistic for most industries. The most recent unofficial information available on the achievement of Third Plan targets indicates that finished steel production in the last year of the plan will be about 5.0 million tons; installed electricity capacity, 10.5 million kilowatts; cement production, 10.4 million tons; coal output, 66 million tons; and iron ore production, 16 million tons—all well below the plan target and the Planning Commission's mid-plan expectations. Also well below plan targets are the use of irrigation and improved seeds and the production of food grains, fertilizers, jute, oilseeds, commercial vehicles, diesel engines, newsprint, tractors, and paper and sugar machinery. Among the few industries that have exceeded their targets are aluminum, sugar, and electrical machinery, whereas targets that have been equaled include machine tools, shipping, road building, and port facilities. *The Hindu Weekly Review*, April 11, 1966, p. 16.

[d] Government of India, Planning Commission, *Programmes of Industrial Development, 1956–61* (New Delhi: Government of India Publication, 1956), p. 59. Target represents anticipated purchases by the railways during the period.

the Second and Third Plans were based on rudimentary input-output balances. However, by the plans' end, government controls, shortages of foreign exchange, and inexperience or inefficiency in certain offices charged with implementing plan programs contributed to unplanned imbalances, some of which have had serious consequences for the Indian economy.

Recently economists have debated the merits of balanced and unbalanced growth. Proponents of balanced growth have contended that different sectors of an economy must develop simultaneously if shortages of essential inputs do not hinder the growth of the entire economy. Similarly, an industry may not expand because of limited demand for its products. For economic growth to take place it will be necessary to start a number of industries simultaneously, each industry creating a market for the products of one or several other industries.[13]

By 1958 the balanced growth argument was a commonplace in the development literature. However, in that year Albert Hirschman challenged this theory, contending, among other things, that it is simply an assertion that in economic growth one self-contained economy must be superimposed on another, and not a theory of how growth actually takes place.[14] Balanced growth would involve immense and, perhaps, impossible costs to the developing economy, particularly in its demands on the economy's limited supply of entrepreneurial and managerial

[13] The balanced growth argument has appeared in the writings of a number of economists. Perhaps the earliest modern development economist to present this argument was P. N. Rosenstein-Rodan, "Problems of Industrialization in Eastern and South-Eastern Europe," *Economic Journal*, LIII (June-September 1943), 202–211. Also see Ragnar Nurkse, *Problems of Capital Formation in Underdeveloped Countries*, fifth ed., (Oxford: Basil Blackwell, 1957), Ch. 1; and Tibor Scitovsky, "Two Concepts of External Economies," *Journal of Political Economy*, LXII (April 1954), 143–151.

[14] Albert O. Hirschman, *The Strategy of Economic Development* (New Haven: Yale University Press, 1958), p. 52. Of special interest are Chapters 3 and 4.

ability.[15] Instead, Hirschman argues, imbalances are both a result and a cause of growth. One industry, by creating excess capacity, encourages the growth of other industries consuming its products. It may also encourage the growth of subsidiary industries that supply its inputs. Imbalances can be corrected by market forces. They can also be corrected by the direct intervention of government into the economy. The process of economic development is, therefore, a chain of disequilibria, and the optimum development strategy is the one that orders these disequilibria so that maximum economic growth is induced.

My discussion of Indian imbalances resulting from ambitious targets is not meant to be a criticism of the unbalanced growth argument. Rather, it is to point out, first, that many Indian imbalances are not deliberate. They have occurred, despite the intentions of Indian planners, because of limitations on both financial and human resources. In other words, one consequence of India's ambitious targets seems to have been a partial negation of one of the objectives of Indian planning, balanced growth.

Second, many Indian imbalances are not disequilibria. They need not encourage further growth, but may instead persist for months and even years. The government has instituted price, distribution, and investment controls over a number of industries. These controls have created distortions that have in turn impaired the role of the market mechanism as a vehicle for righting imbalances. Yet in India's mixed economy the private sector has been assigned an important place in development plans, even in many industries that are heavily controlled by the government.

This does not mean that imbalances must persist. More and more the Indian government has been drawn into industries

[15] *Ibid.*, p. 53.

where there is a shortage of capacity to remove imbalances created by the inability or unwillingness of the private sector to expand. However, the ability of the Indian government to right imbalances has been mixed. Some imbalances have persisted for as long as a decade.[16]

Direct Controls over the Indian Economy

The Indian government maintains a number of direct controls over the Indian economy.[17] This section examines only two: regulations on investment by the private sector and controls over the pricing and distribution of industrial commodities. Other direct controls are equally important, examples being regulations affecting foreign exchange and the pricing and distribution of agricultural commodities. However, because these controls are only indirectly relevant to a study of the steel industry, they are not discussed here.

Government controls over private sector investment assume many forms. New investment in an industry may be prohibited in certain states to achieve greater regional dispersal of the industry. The private entrepreneur must secure a number of licenses or permits before investing in new capacity: licenses to insure that his project satisfies the objectives of the plan; licenses for the government's allocation and his receipt of for-

[16] An important example, the production of foundry iron, is discussed in Chapter 10. For more than a decade there has been a persistent shortage of foundry iron in India and idle capacity in India's foundry industry. This shortage has not been redressed because of government policies affecting the pig iron industry and heavy reliance on the private sector to expand pig iron production. Only recently has the government decided to take the initiative by establishing pig iron facilities in the public sector.

[17] Unfortunately I am not at liberty to cite two excellent studies of direct controls over India's economy which form the basis of this section. For a partial discussion, see Government of India, Ministry of Industries, *Final Report of the Industries Development Procedures Committee* (Swaminathan Committee) (New Delhi: Government of India Publication, 1964). Also see Lindblom, "Has India an Economic Future?," pp. 239–252.

eign exchange; quotas for scarce raw materials; and permission to issue share capital. In some industries all new investment by private sector interests may be prohibited. In others, only existing private sector units may be allowed to expand.

There are many reasons for the institution of direct controls. They stem, in part, from the government's sincere belief that controls are essential to planning. They also stem from its wish to stimulate a pattern of growth considered desirable on social and political as well as economic grounds. Controls are not necessarily wrong, given India's objectives. However, they have involved a cost, a constraint upon the role of the private sector in India's development plans and, partly because of this, the creation of long-run imbalances that have probably discouraged a more rapid development of India's economy.

For example, one objective of Indian planning is balanced regional development. Although this objective is primarily motivated by political and ideological considerations, it is also given an economic rationale by Indian planners. By spreading industrial and agricultural development programs to as many regions as possible, it is argued, fewer resources have to be invested in such social overhead capital as urban housing and transportation. Perhaps more important, external economies may be greater if investment is spread over many regions rather than concentrated in a few. The spread effects of development programs will be maximized; a larger proportion of the Indian population will be exposed to improved technologies and standards of living and, for this reason, will be encouraged to better its own lot.

Although claims on its behalf may have been exaggerated, there is something to be said for the balanced regional development of India's economy. Almost certainly at least a vocal adherence to this directive will be necessary, given the political facts of life in India. However, balanced regional development has often been interpreted restrictively to mean the location of each type of development program in as many states as possible.[18] This restrictive interpretation probably would not discourage to any great extent the growth of enterprise for which transportation is a relatively unimportant cost item. Nor need it deter the erection of new units in the private sector even though other locations may be preferred by private entrepreneurs.[19] Yet in some instances it seems to have discouraged private sector development. For example, a number of proposed pig iron plants have not been erected because of their locations and particularly because of doubts about the processes they have been licensed to use to enable their regional dispersal.[20] This is an important reason for the persistence of India's foundry iron shortages for the past decade. Whether or not greater external economies would result from the dispersal of the pig iron industry, rather than industries less affected by their locations, is a moot question. In any event, if the government is to pursue this objective and at the same time rely heavily on private sector development, it is necessary that external economies be internalized; private sector interests must have incentives for dispersal similar to those of the government.

India's industrial licensing procedures are exceedingly complex. They vary depending on the size of a new enterprise, the industry in which it is classified, whether it will require foreign exchange, and even the individuals involved. I make no effort to discuss these procedures here, not because they are a negligible influence on private sector investment, but because they are relatively unimportant for India's steel industry. Of greater

[18] In Chapter 9 I consider at length one example of this restrictive interpretation of balanced regional development, the location of new steel mills in states that do not already possess public sector steel mills.

[19] For example, at the government's insistence a private oil refinery was located at the port of Vishakhapatnam, even though Madras was preferred because of its larger market by the private company setting up the refinery. The erection of this refinery has encouraged some spread of industry. A fertilizer plant is now being built at Vishakhapatnam to utilize the products of the refinery.

[20] See Chapter 10.

interest are restrictions on private sector entry into industry based on the government's industrial policy resolutions.

In 1948 the Government of India issued its First Industrial Policy Resolution specifying those industries that were to become government monopolies, those in which the state would assume sole or primary responsibility for new investment, and those that would be subject only to normal government controls. The iron and steel industry was included in the second category. The 1948 resolution was superseded in 1956, the list of industries to become public sector monopolies and in which the government was to have sole or primary responsibility for new undertakings being enlarged.[21]

Although it increased the number of industries reserved to the public sector, the Second Industrial Policy Resolution was somewhat more conciliatory to private enterprise than its predecessor. Expansion of existing private sector units in reserved industries was not prohibited by the First Resolution, but the position of these units was to be reviewed after ten years. This clause was interpreted as a threat of nationalization and did not reappear in the Second Resolution. Moreover, the expansion of existing private sector units in reserved industries was given explicit approval. The government's decision not to nationalize existing private sector companies, with few exceptions, and to allow existing plants to expand in reserved industries has enabled fuller use of private sector expertise and installed plant and machinery.

Three generalizations about relations between the government and the private sector seem to me to be justified.[22] First,

[21] The 1956 Industrial Policy Resolution is reproduced in Government of India, Planning Commission, *Programmes of Industrial Development, 1961–66* (New Delhi: Government of India Publication, 1962), pp. 700–705. For a discussion of both industrial policy resolutions, see Harry Robinson, *Industrial Development Policy in India* (Menlo Park, Calif.: Stanford Research Institute, 1956).

[22] The first two generalizations have also been made by Lewis, *Quiet Crisis in India*, pp. 206–210.

regardless of the ominous sound of the industrial policy resolutions and the "socialist pattern of society," a declared aim of the Indian Constitution, the government has not been consciously opposed to the private sector. The "socialist pattern" is an amorphous concept that more often than not seems to mean a society in which equality of opportunity and economic security are assured to all citizens. There has been substantial scope for private sector expansion in most Indian industries in recent years, although this expansion has probably been slowed by various regulations instituted by the government.

Second, although they are not opposed to the growth of the private sector, India's political leaders are strongly opposed to the development of concentrations of economic power in this sector. Many industries reserved to the public sector under the industrial policy resolutions are either thought to be strategically placed in the economy or, because of economies of scale, their individual units must be operated on so large a scale that they would become monopolies or large oligopolies. The iron and steel industry satisfies both conditions. Therefore the government has thought it necessary to circumscribe the activities of the private sector in this industry.

Third, even though private sector expansion in India's steel industry has been restricted, there has still been a significant participation by this sector in the industry's growth. Existing mills were permitted to expand during the First and Second Plan periods, providing approximately one-third of increased steel-making capacity created during these periods. The government has also licensed numerous private sector ventures in three sectors of the industry amenable to small-scale production: the rerolling of billets and scrap ingots; the manufacture of special steels; and the production of foundry iron in small pig iron plants.

Although the government's industrial policy resolutions have at times been interpreted loosely, it is my belief that they have still created rigidities in many industries, including steel, and have contributed to periodic imbalances in the Indian economy. For example, shortages of steel during the middle 1950s were partly a result of the government's refusal to permit or at least to encourage the expansion of private sector mills during the late 1940s. Shortages of flat steel during the middle 1960s could have been mitigated had the government not rejected a scheme by TISCO in 1961 to expand its flat product output during the Third Plan period. The government has allowed the private sector a role in developing the steel industry, but usually only after a crisis is imminent and it is too late for the private sector to contribute effectively to forestalling this crisis.

The Indian government and various state governments also set or influence the prices of a number of commodities and services.[23] In many instances controlled prices have been kept relatively low, with the result that prices frequently do not cover all costs of production.[24] Controls have not necessarily

[23] In 1965 commodities subject to statutory price control were: scarce categories of iron and steel (primarily flat steel), certain non-ferrous metals, aluminum, cement, kerosene, sugar, coal, coke, cotton, cotton yarn, some cotton textiles, woolen yarn, woolen articles, worsted weaving and knitting yarn, fertilizers, ethyl alcohol, and molasses. Commodities subject to nonstatutory price control were paper, petroleum and petroleum products, matches, bicycles, and motor vehicles. In addition the government fixes the prices of commodities and services produced by public sector enterprise, an example being railway rates. The central government also influences the prices of agricultural commodities and coastal shipping. Most state and local governments fix electricity rates, hotel rates, and rent ceilings.

[24] This has been the conclusion of studies of at least four basic commodities and services—rail transport, steel, coal, and electricity. It has been alleged for many others. Railway rate policies on coal have been examined in a study prepared for the World Bank. Coverdale and Colpitts, New York City, and Surveys and Research Corporation, Washington, "India Coal Transport Study" (multilith, Washington, 1964), Vol. III. The *ICTS* cost estimates have been criticized by Alan Carlin, *A Possible U.S. Policy Towards Indian Transportation: An Illustration of Improved Sectoral Policies* (Santa Monica, Calif.: The RAND Corporation, RM-4379-AID, June 1965), Appendix B. Both Indian rates on coal and the ICTS cost estimates are thought to be too low. Passenger fares and rates on goods hauled long distances are also thought to be too low and rates on some finished goods too high.

Steel price controls are examined in Chapter 5 of this book. I estimate that, had the average price received by steel mills in 1962 covered all discouraged expansion of those industries in which the government has assumed primary or sole responsibility for new investment. However, in those industries in which private sector expansion is permitted, unduly low prices have acted as disincentives to new investment and are one reason for some of India's frequent commodity shortages.

One example is cement, an industry that has been subject to price and distribution controls and whose expansion has been entrusted almost entirely to the private sector. By the mid-1960s India experienced a severe cement shortage, partly because of price disincentives to the industry.[25] Only after the crisis began did the government consider decontrol and meaningful entry into the industry to rectify these shortages.

Another example is the fertilizer industry. Recent food price increases are said to have encouraged greater demand for fertilizers. At the same time there has been tardy progress in fertil-

---

costs of producing steel, it would have had to be increased by about 50 per cent. Increases in steel prices since 1962 have fallen far short of this percentage.

Coal prices have been examined in a study prepared for the Indian Planning Commission. Planning Unit, Indian Statistical Institute, "Price Policy for Coal Undertakings" (mimeograph, New Delhi, 1963). Suggested coal price changes vary from mine to mine, but on average, would involve a 20 per cent increase over existing prices. *Ibid.*, pp. 32 and 43. The more recent "India Coal Transport Study" has estimated the average cost of coal to the Indian economy to be Rs. 29 per ton, roughly 20 per cent higher than the Planning Unit's weighted average estimate and 40 per cent higher than the weighted average price for standard grade coal charged in 1962. *ICTS*, Appendix C, pp. 58–68.

Electricity prices have been examined in another study for the Planning Commission. Planning Unit, Indian Statistical Institute, "Price Policy for Electricity Undertakings" (mimeograph, New Delhi, 1962). Rate policies vary from state to state. In many states it was found that electricity rates, particularly rates charged to large industrial undertakings and agricultural users, are too low. See also Energy Survey, *Report of the Energy Survey of India Committee* (Delhi: Government of India Publication, 1964), pp. 158–159.

25 For an example of the charge that low cement prices have contributed to shortfalls in cement output, see *Eastern Economist*, May 14, 1965, pp. 1128–1129. See also *Capital*, April 29, 1965, p. 587.

izer projects licensed in the private sector, attributed partly to price and distribution controls enacted by the government.[26]

Not all price controls have succeeded. The government's ability to regulate prices has varied from industry to industry. As a rule the government appears to have been more successful in controlling wholesale prices charged by a few large producers. It has been notably less successful in controlling the prices of goods and services produced by a number of small producers, and especially retail prices charged by middlemen. As might be expected, there are thriving black markets for most scarce controlled commodities.[27]

Evasion of price controls need not be illegal. For example, a person who purchases steel at controlled prices is allowed to resell it at market prices if it has been reprocessed. For this reason, small holes are sometimes punched in the corners of steel sheets before they are sold to final consumers. I have had indirect experience with another price control that is widely disregarded, rent ceilings in Bombay City. Landlords sometimes resort to outright evasion by attaching an additional under-the-table charge to official rent limits. However, such evasion may be unnecessary. Dwellings are also rented under short-term leases because only those rented for relatively long periods of time are subject to rent controls. Or the renter may be required to purchase the right to rent a dwelling in addition to his monthly rental payment. There are a number of other price controls that have also failed because of similar loopholes in control legislation.

[26] For example, see *Capital*, April 15, 1965, p. 518 and Lindblom, "Has India an Economic Future?," pp. 239–240 and 244–245. Some other controlled industries in which the government has placed partial reliance on private sector expansion are aluminum, coal, stainless steel, pig iron, and industrial chemicals. With the exception of coal, the products of these industries were in short supply in 1965. Whether there is a causal relationship between these scarcities and price and distribution controls can only be determined after further research.

[27] The black market for steel is discussed in Chapter 5.

Low prices for basic inputs are defended as stimuli to India's industrial and agricultural growth. In fact, occasional or persistent shortages of such industrial inputs as steel, foundry grade iron, coal, cement, and fertilizers have been major deterrents to India's economic growth at one time or another during the past decade. The government maintains a "banned list" of industries in which further expansion will be denied by licensing authorities because of actual or anticipated excess capacity. Presumably price controls over some Indian industries need not result in distortions in the private sector's investment patterns. In fact, exceptions to the list are frequently made for one reason or another. Moreover, the list is based on the relationship between licensed capacity and plan targets for each industry, not actual utilization of capacity. Because most plan targets are ambitious, it may be quite simple for an entrepreneur to justify new investment in industries in which there is already substantial idle capacity. One result of the interaction of ambitious targets and price controls, despite the banned list, has been an unbalanced economy persisting over a long period of time.

Controls are supposed to stabilize retail prices and benefit small consumers. In fact, it is my impression that the result of wholesale price controls, where effective, has frequently been a flourishing black or gray market or increased profits for industries consuming controlled commodities and able to buy these commodities at controlled prices. As a rule only large consumers capable of buying directly from factories or enforcing government regulations appear to have benefited from the government's price policies. Among the beneficiaries have been the various ministries, agencies, and factories of the government itself.[28]

Unduly low prices for controlled commodities and services are only one consequence of the government's price policies.

[28] As more and more government plants are erected in controlled industries, the government is also becoming a principal loser from its controls.

Small price differentials for various grades of coal may be one reason why India's metallurgical industries are unable to obtain adequate supplies of high-grade coking coal. Small price differentials for various types of steel have also encouraged the production of poor quality steel, relatively heavy sections, and, in general, sections that require comparatively little rolling by India's steel mills.[29] Excessive telescoping[30] of railway rates for bulk goods has encouraged the location of consuming industries in regions relatively distant from their sources of supply.[31] Some of these distortions may be justified by social and political objectives of the government. Even so, they have probably incurred a real cost to the Indian economy, the inefficient use of India's resources.

In December 1963, price and, if in force, distribution controls were removed from sixteen commodities.[32] For most of these commodities, supply already equalled demand at controlled prices. For some, price and distribution controls were known to have failed. Therefore, decontrol was not expected to yield much change in prices unless as a result of collusion in price setting by producers or middlemen. The government has also freed the pricing and distribution of categories of steel in relatively abundant supply, vegetable oils, tinplate, pig iron, and cement and fertilizers sold to the private sector. Decontrol has been partial. The Indian government continues to establish prices for a number of important commodities.

Government Ownership and Operation of Industrial Enterprise

The role of the Indian government as owner and operator of industrial enterprise sometimes conflicts with its role as con-

29 See Chapter 5.

30 The longer the distance a commodity is hauled, the lower its rate per ton-mile.

31 Carlin, *A Possible U.S. Policy Towards Indian Transportation*, p. 20.

32 Rayon yarn, staple fiber, caustic soda, soda ash, hydrochloric acid, chlorine, calcium carbide, bleaching power, Chilean nitrate, muriate of potash, sulphate of potash, washing soap, tires and tubes, sheet glass, paper board, and natural rubber.

troller and planner of industrial activity. For example, the government has erected a number of factories in industries subject to price controls. This is one reason why some public sector enterprises, being unprofitable, have been drains on public revenues rather than contributors to them.[33] Where controls have encouraged shortages of commodities, they have also resulted in the possible abuse of consumers' interests. For example, steel shortages have been one reason for the production of poor quality steel and types of steel that consumers do not always want. An unusually large proportion of the steel produced by the government mills has been scrap or has gone into inventories. Thus the performance of the public sector mills has, to some extent, thwarted the objectives of Indian planners. Some of the steel needed by priority users either has not been produced or, if it has, has not always been of the desired quality or specifications.

Difficulties at India's public sector steel mills appear to have been the rule rather than the exception.[34] Many public sector undertakings have not contributed fully to India's plan objectives because of delays in their establishment and extraordinary difficulties in their operations. There is probably no single reason for these difficulties. To some extent they may be a result of the criteria that have been used to judge the mills' performance. For example, some of the problems at India's public sector steel mills have resulted from their almost singular concentration on achieving output records. Some difficulties

[33] A summary of the financial performance of public sector enterprise is presented in Government of India, Ministry of Finance, *Annual Report on the Working of Industrial and Commercial Undertakings of the Central Government* (New Delhi: Government of India Publication, various years).

[34] In addition to the *Annual Report on the Working of Industrial and Commercial Undertakings of the Central Government*, the interested reader is directed to special studies of public sector enterprise prepared by the Estimates Committee of the Lok Sabha, the lower house of the Indian Parliament, and Om Prakash, *The Theory and Working of State Corporations with Special Reference to India* (London: George Allen & Unwin Ltd., 1962).

have also been created by a lack of coordination among various sectors and industries of the Indian economy. Perhaps most important, some difficulties stem from a lack of experience both at public sector plants and in New Delhi. The inexperience of government officials charged with the growth of an industry, either in planning, building, or operating industrial facilities, has been a frequent cause of delays in erecting these facilities and in obtaining usable output from them. The institution of work practices and other procedures inappropriate to an industry, perhaps as a result of inexperience, have also contributed to these difficulties.

No doubt, the problems faced by public sector enterprises will diminish once they gain the experience possessed by established companies. Although there have been some exceptions, in general, plan projects entrusted to an established Indian organization such as India's railways or let out to a few foreign equipment suppliers on a turnkey basis have been completed on schedule or with relatively minor delays. Plan projects that have been the responsibility of one or more relatively untried ministries or agencies of the government have frequently lagged well behind schedule.

Conclusion

In summary, Indian planners do not seem to have complete or, perhaps, even primary control over the allocation of Indian resources. To some extent ambitious targets have limited the effectiveness of Indian planners. Formal or *de facto* retrenchment was necessary midway during the Second and Third Plan periods. Had this retrenchment been an across the board reduction in plan targets, basic plan balances might have been preserved. In fact, reductions typically have been concentrated in specific industries, partly because of priorities attached to other industries, partly because of commitments already made to certain projects early in the plan periods, and partly because of the nature of the government's controls and the mixed level of skills in its factories, ministries, and agencies.

Nor is the Indian government a uniform advocate of economic growth. This is the primary concern of the Planning Commission. Even then, India's plans have had to be tempered by ideological and political considerations. In addition, various government bodies have differing motives and, contrary to the notion sometimes implicit in much of the literature, these motives may not include economic development or other national economic objectives.

Government bodies are among the most influential interest groups in India. Although there are many high-minded persons within the Indian government, public agencies and officials often appear to act primarily in their own interests. For example, controls over the pricing and distribution of commodities have frequently increased the government's revenues or reduced its costs while assuring that the government's demands for controlled commodities are satisfied. If the government is a major consumer of a price controlled commodity, such as steel or cement, it has tended to keep prices as low as possible. On the other hand, if it is primarily a middleman, as it is for fertilizers, it has bought from producers at low prices and sold to consumers at high prices, keeping the difference as revenues. Steel decontrol was encouraged by the erection of the public sector mills.[35] Cement is now extremely scarce. However, anticipated price increases resulting from the proposed partial decontrol of cement would not affect the Indian budget because the government has not entered the industry and will still be able to purchase cement at controlled prices. In short, controls have helped to direct Indian resources to the government at

[35] One informant closely associated with the decontrol of steel told me that opposition within the government melted only after it was shown that the losses of public sector steel mills resulting from controls exceeded the gains to the Indian exchequer from relatively low steel prices.

relatively favorable prices. Where decontrol has been instituted, oftentimes it has been structured so that the government is not disadvantaged.

Partly because various government policies have conflicted with fulfillment of Planning Commission targets, plans for balanced growth have actually resulted in unplanned imbalances in the Indian economy. Price and distribution controls and restrictions on private sector entry into various industries have impeded the private sector's ability to fulfill plan objectives or to rectify unforeseen imbalances. This does not mean that imbalances will persist. Typically, the Indian economy has progressed from one shortage to another. The Indian government has had to put out the fires of a number of crises, resulting in the steady extension of its activities and the thinning of its talents. Unfortunately, not all scarcities have been eliminated quickly; some imbalances, such as India's electricity, steel, and foundry iron shortages, persisted for more than a decade.

The Indian Planning Commission appears to be only partly responsible for the actual allocation of resources to different sectors of the Indian economy. Resource allocation is also determined by government policies that are rooted in objectives other than economic growth and a number of legal or illegal means of circumventing the government's controls. In the end, the actual pattern of growth of the Indian economy could be quite different from that contemplated by India's planners.

5 | Government Control of India's Steel Industry

Many of the functions of India's steel mills are regulated, or have actually been assumed, by the government. All new investment must be licensed by New Delhi. Minimum wages are set by a Wage Board appointed by the Central Government, and dismissals are circumscribed by the laws of the states. Until recently most steel prices were established by the ministry responsible for the industry. The rolling schedules of each of the integrated mills and the distribution of most types of steel were also determined by an agency of this ministry. Since 1964 there has been some liberalization of these controls. Even so, there continues to be substantial government regulation of the industry.

From this *partial* list of controls it is evident that most activities of both public and private sector mills are influenced directly or indirectly by New Delhi. Yet much that has been written or said about India's steel industry seems to ignore this fact. Indian planners have projected future demand for steel assuming that it would be determined only by rates of growth of the Indian economy and in no way related to steel prices. The belief is widespread that the government must take the initiative in expanding the steel industry because India's private sector cannot or will not do the job. In fact, the government's controls over the industry are pervasive. Before any meaningful discussion of the industry can begin, these controls and their consequences must be examined in depth.

The steel industry has been regulated partly because of the belief, perhaps justified, that steel is especially important to India's economic growth. Unfortunately, many controls have been arbitrary or subject to rules of thumb that often bear little relation to the best interests of the industry or the broader objectives of Indian planning. Some have not been effective. This does not mean that all controls are unnecessary and should be abolished. The government can and perhaps should assume a positive role in economic development. However, controls should contribute meaningfully to this objective, or, at the very least, should not needlessly detract from it. Controls, by their very existence, are not necessarily an attribute of a planned economy.

This chapter is restricted to three types of controls: barriers to private sector entry into the industry, regulation of the prices of both public and private sector mills, and the distribution of steel by official agencies. There are many other types of controls, but for my purposes they are relatively unimportant and are discussed, if at all, in other chapters.

Restrictions upon Entry into the Steel Industry

India's industrial policy resolutions have declared all new investment in the steel industry to be the sole responsibility of the state. Exceptions have been made, when deemed in the national interest, to allow existing private sector units in the industry to expand their plants. Exceptions have also been made for segments of the steel industry amenable to the erection of small units. A number of small pig iron plants, rerolling mills, and special steel plants have been licensed for erection by the private sector since the enactment of India's First Industrial Policy Resolution in 1948.

Thus far, only one concrete proposal for a new private sector steel mill has been rejected by the government because of its industrial policy resolutions. In 1954 the Birlas, one of India's foremost industrial families, concluded an agreement for a new integrated mill with a consortium of British equipment manufacturers. The Birla proposal was turned down partly because private Indian interests were to supply only 10 per cent of the mill's initial capital. The rest was to come from the Government of India or from private British interests under medium-term loans guaranteed by the government. Breach of the Industrial Policy Resolution was thought unwarranted because the Birlas would not have had access to significant amounts of financial capital not available to the government.[1] Several months after the rejection of the Birla proposal the government was able to obtain better credit terms for a larger plant with essentially the same consortium of British interests, its efforts culminating in the Durgapur steel mill. The rejection of the Birla proposal does not seem to have retarded the expansion of India's steel industry.

More recently there was some discussion of participation by foreign companies in new private sector steel mills. These proposals were never very definite, certainly not as definite as the Birla proposal, and informants are divided on whether the opposition of the government or the reluctance of the foreign companies was responsible for the failure of these proposals to come to fruition. In any event, the companies allegedly were unwilling to supply more than a nominal share of the plants' capital and to accept less than a dominant share of their control. If so, there may be some reason to question the value of these ventures to the Indian economy.

The likelihood of foreign investment in India's steel industry is small, certainly under the system of control's governing the industry[2] Yet, foreign private investment would confer at least

[1] Lok Sabha, Estimates Committee, *Ministry of Steel, Mines and Fuel, 33rd Report, Second Lok Sabha, 1958–59* (New Delhi: Lok Sabha Secretariat, 1959), p. 7.

[2] In 1963 a vice president of the United States Steel Corporation, testifying before a subcommittee of the United States House of Representatives, declared that his company would not invest its own money in the

two important advantages that should not be underestimated by India's planners. The foreign exchange component of a new steel mill, if not contributed entirely by foreign companies, might be obtained in whole or in part from the World Bank or foreign private interests on the credit of these companies. Moreover, foreign collaboration is one way technical and managerial expertise can be brought to the industry. India's two fundamental factor scarcities could be lessened by foreign investment in an Indian steel mill.

The importance of expertise, both Indian and foreign, does not seem to have been fully recognized by offices charged with the industry's growth. The Indian government allowed private sector companies to expand their plants under the First and Second Plans. However, in 1961 it rejected a proposal by TISCO to increase its plant's capacity on the expectation that Third Plan targets could be met by expansion of existing public sector mills and the erection of a new mill at Bokaro. Only when it became evident that Third Plan and proposed Fourth Plan targets could not be achieved without private sector participation, did the government give tentative approval to the expansion of both TISCO and IISCO. In effect, those most qualified to take the initiative in developing India's steel industry, by virtue of their long experience in the industry, have been restricted to supplementing the public sector when it is unable to fulfill targets considered necessary by Indian planners.

Moreover, extensions permitted the private sector mills have been suboptimum. By early 1963 TISCO had prepared four proposals for expansion during the Fourth Plan period, one

---

Bokaro mill at the rate of return allowed under the system of price controls that governed the industry. Norman B. Obbard, testimony Aug. 15, 1963, U.S. Congress, House Committee on Appropriations, Foreign Operations Appropriations for 1964, *Hearings Before a Subcommittee of the Committee on Appropriations*, Part 4, 88th Congress, 1st Session (Washington: U.S. Government Printing Office, 1963), pp. 1638–1641.

involving extension to Adityapur, a site across the Kharkai River from Jamshedpur. Although outside the perimeter of TISCO's existing mill, expansion at Adityapur was thought especially advantageous by the company since its Jamshedpur mill is extremely cramped. Because this alternative would involve a new site, it was thought to be in violation of the Industrial Policy Resolution and was at first opposed by the government. Negotiations between the government and the company continued for another two years. Not until late 1965 was a doubling of TISCO's capacity through expansion to Adityapur permitted.

IISCO's Fourth Plan expansion was also circumscribed by the government. The company's original proposal to double its capacity was broken into two phases. The first phase, a balancing program, would carry the plant's capacity to 1.3 million ingot tons. This program was approved by the government, but has been delayed by a disagreement over the repayment of government loans to the company.[3] However, the second phase encountered the opposition of the government, partly because it was thought to be in violation of the Industrial Policy Resolution. IISCO has now accepted the bifurcation of its expansion program. By mid-1965, discouraged by the government's policies, IISCO has allegedly settled upon 1.3 million ingot tons as its ultimate capacity, despite the Planning Commission's two million ton target for the end of the Fourth Plan period.

Officials of both TISCO and IISCO have also expressed some interest in establishing new steel mills provided reasonable rates of return are allowed by the government.[4] TISCO has favored the establishment of a new mill at Adityapur with an eventual capacity of about 4 million ingot tons. This mill would possess a major advantage in its ability to use the managerial

[3] See Chapter 3.

[4] This interest was expressed in early 1963 during conversations with officials of both companies.

and administrative talents now employed at the company's Jamshedpur plant. IISCO's officials have been less specific about a site. One was suggested near the company's ore mines that would enable wagons carrying ore to the Burnpur plant to return loaded with coal.

The government's willingness to permit existing mills to expand within their perimeters reflects its awareness of economies of scale in plant size. In particular, because the expansion of an existing plant generally costs far less than the erection of a new plant, it reflects the government's acceptance of financial capital as a scarce factor of production. However, until recently, interpretation of the industrial policy resolutions to allow only plants, and not companies, to expand as fully as possible reflects a lack of concern for scarcities of expertise. The industrial policy resolutions, adhered to literally, have inhibited the full use of existing Indian skills in the expansion of the industry. For this reason, they have been obstacles to achievement of the most efficient growth of the industry.

The Retention Price System

Prior to March 1964 the prices received by India's integrated steel mills, known as retention prices, were established by the ministry in charge of India's steel industry on the basis of recommendations made by the Indian Tariff Commission. The Commission, in theory an autonomous body, conducts periodic investigations of industries subject to price control or benefiting from tariff protection. Steel price control underwent considerable change since its introduction in 1939. Initially prices of war materiel alone were regulated by informal agreement between the government and the steel companies. Statutory price control was enacted in 1941 and extended to civilian requirements for steel in 1944. In 1948 the Indian Tariff Board, later the Indian Tariff Commission, conducted its first major price inquiry. It subsequently undertook three detailed inquiries to determine new retention prices and many subsidiary inquiries to adjust existing retention prices retroactively.[5]

Until March 1964 the price for steel paid by consumers differed from the price paid to producers. For most of the postwar period the selling price was higher than the retention price, the difference accruing to the government's Equalization Fund. This fund was originally used to equate the import price with the lower domestic price of steel. However, during the 1950s the difference between the two prices diminished, the fund no longer serving its original purpose. By the 1960s the fund was used primarily as a source of government revenues and of subsidies on the haulage of finished steel over long distances.

Before 1950 TISCO and IISCO received identical retention prices based upon the costs of the higher cost producer. In 1950 separate retention prices were established for each producer but were abandoned in 1955 because they did not provide sufficient incentive for cost minimization. The retention price was once again based upon the costs of the higher cost producer, and extra profits accruing to the lower cost producer were earmarked for a special plant development fund. Prior to 1962, the prices of individual categories of steel and the weighted average of prices of all categories were the same for both companies. This was accomplished by adjusting the prices of non-common categories without regard for relative costs of production. After 1962 only the prices of common categories were equated.

Because the Mysore Iron and Steel Works is inherently less efficient than the private sector mills, it was given higher

[5] A brief history of the retention price system and investigations by the Indian Tariff Commission is presented in its last report on the steel industry. Indian Tariff Commission, *Report on the Fair Ex-Works Retention Prices of Steel for the Period 1st April 1960 to 31st March 1962* (New Delhi: Government of India Publication, 1962), Appendix IV, pp. 71–78. Other studies by the Indian Tariff Commission and its predecessor, the Indian Tariff Board, are indicated in the bibliography accompanying this book.

retention prices determined by separate price inquiries. Costs of production at the new public sector plants are necessarily greater than costs at the private sector mills. Even so, the government plants received the same retention prices as the private companies and for this and other reasons have incurred substantial losses.[6]

Retention prices established during the late 1940s were too low to allow accumulation of funds sufficient for replacement, let alone self-financed expansion. The method used to compute depreciation was modified during the 1950s and a special element added to the retention price for rehabilitation and development. This element was discontinued in 1960. In general, price decisions by the government were progressively more conciliatory, enabling the industry to finance no small part of its expansion programs from retained earnings while providing a modest return to its shareholders.

This trend was temporarily reversed with the government's price decision of September 1962. Earlier in the year the Tariff Commission recommended an average retention price of Rs. 550 per ton for the two years ended March 31, 1962. The government rejected the Commission's proposal, partly because the Commission had allowed depreciation and return on capital assuming production at 90 per cent of capacity, a production rate achieved by IISCO and somewhat higher than that achieved by TISCO. In the belief that the companies should be penalized for failing to reach 100 per cent of their capacities, the government reduced the estimate of their capital per ton of output upon which return and depreciation were computed.[7] The reasons given for the government's price decision have

[6] The costs of production and profitability of India's public sector steel mills are discussed in Chapter 8.

[7] Indian Tariff Commission, pp. ii and iii. For an explanation of the Government's action by the then Minister of Steel and Heavy Industries, Mr. C. Subramaniam, see *The Statesman*, New Delhi edition, Sept. 20, 1962, p. 7.

been disputed.[8] Yet during the fourth quarter of 1962, immediately after the decision, output of salable steel by TISCO and IISCO rose from less than 90 per cent to 100 and 106 per cent of capacity respectively.[9] At first sight, the government's decision seems to have had at least one positive benefit.

Unfortunately, because steel is not a homogeneous commodity, increased physical production need not reflect greater value of output. Aside from defectives, there were two general designations for the quality of steel produced in India prior to 1965, tested and untested steel. These terms were not entirely satisfactory. Not only had tested steel been tested, it also satisfied certain physical and chemical specifications and bore a certificate affirming this fact. Untested steel may have been steel that satisfied test specifications but had not been tested, or steel that could not pass test standards and had to be sold as untested or commercial grade steel. For technical reasons production of an additional ton of tested steel necessitates a more than proportionate sacrifice of untested steel.[10]

Increased production by India's private sector mills during the last quarter of 1962 was partly the result of improvements in their operations and some easing of their raw material and

[8] For arguments against the government's decision, the reader may wish to consult newspaper commentaries at the time of the decision and the annual statements to shareholders by the chairmen of TISCO and IISCO for the year 1961–62. The statement by Mr. J. R. D. Tata, Chairman of TISCO, is reproduced by TISCO's *Annual Report* for 1961–62. That by Sir Biren Mookerjee, Chairman of IISCO, has been published separately by his company.

[9] Estimated from data presented in *Iron and Steel Review* (various months). This change has persisted. See Table 14, Chapter 8.

[10] The production of tested steel may necessitate longer processing of hot metal in steel melt shops. This results in lower tonnages per unit of time and greater costs per ton of steel. Also, the rough ends, known as crop ends, of intermediate sections must be removed to insure that in subsequent rolling defects are not rolled into finished steel. The greater the cropping of these ends, the lower the probability of producing untested steel, but also the lower the tonnage of finished steel. Conversely, the less the cropping, the greater the tonnage, but the greater the likelihood of untested steel.

transportation difficulties. It was also the result of a change in their product mixes by sacrificing the quality of their steel, a fact freely admitted by IISCO's Chairman in 1963.

> For two years ended 31st March, 1962, in our fight to maintain quality, we produced to approximately 90% of our rated capacity, about 80% of our outturn of saleable steel being of tested quality . . . A basis of 90% capacity production constitutes . . . practically a world standard for the steel industry . . . Faced with such a position where we have been penalized for our performance in place of the commendation we might justifiably have expected, we have had no option but with the greatest reluctance to lower our standards . . . and attainment of a production of 100% of rated capacity has been achieved only at the expense of a drop in the proportion of tested quality steel to about 60% of the total outturn, the rest being of commercial quality, with further reduction possibly still to come.[11]

It is generally acknowledged, although not openly, that TISCO and the public sector plants also sacrificed quality to achieve output.

It may well be that standards for tested steel were unduly stringent and that the distinction between tested and untested steel was an anachronism long in need of revision. This is a technical matter upon which opinions vary. However, some standards are necessary, particularly where failure to use steel of known high quality could result in the loss of life and property. Tested steel is essential for such investment goods industries as railways, heavy construction, and machine tools. Except for the railways, these industries have frequently failed to obtain amounts of tested steel adequate for their needs. On the other hand, many of the uses for which tested steel is of little matter are concentrated in consumer goods industries. To some extent, the effect of the government's price policies during times of scarcity was a forced diversion of steel from investment

[11] Sir Biren Mookerjee, quoted in *Capital,* Aug. 8, 1963, p. 205. Commercial is the same as untested steel.

to consumption or a sacrifice of standards by investment goods industries. These alternatives are not very desirable in view of the government's attempt to increase the rate of investment of the Indian economy. In addition, the sacrifice of quality may have hindered the sale of Indian steel on the international market. A reputation for bad or variable quality could become a stigma persisting long after it is deserved and impairing the future export of Indian steel for many years to come.

The government's unwillingness to allow the increase in the retention price contemplated by the Tariff Commission, by itself, would not have encouraged greater production of untested steel by India's steel mills. The mills receive additions to their prices, known as price extras, that are supposed to compensate them for the greater costs of producing tested steel. In fact, these extras were not remunerative during the early 1960s. A major reason for this was that those who established prices, with few exceptions, tended to adhere to traditional absolute price differentials within any one category of steel. Many price extras were constant or nearly constant throughout the 1950s despite an increase in the average retention price from around Rs. 300 per ton in 1952 to Rs. 550 per ton in early 1964. The overall effect of adherence to constant extras at a time of rising costs is to make the production of less costly alternatives, such as untested steel, more remunerative to the steel mills. For this reason, the government's price policies encouraged the substitution of untested for tested steel.[12] Paren-

[12] The economist might better understand the relationship between tested and untested steel in terms of the familiar production possibilities curve representing the maximum output of one type of steel possible for any given output of the other. The slope of the production possibilities curve in absolute terms, $|dX_u/dX_t|$, is often referred to as the marginal rate of transformation. For the two types of steel $|dX_u/dX_t|$ is at all times greater than one because, at the very least, untested steel can be produced simply by not testing tested steel. The effect of the government's price policies has been a change in the relative prices of the two types of steel. Because equilibrium is established when the marginal rate of transformation is

thetically, the penalty for production of nonstandard and defective steel was for a long time Rs. 10 per ton, again despite continued increases in retention prices. This may explain the comment of one Indian steelman that defective steel had become the most profitable item his company is able to produce.

Similiar distortions crept into the price differentials for lighter, special, and small-order sections within broad categories of finished steel. Lighter sections generally require more passes through rolls and longer rolling time per ton than heavier sections. Special and small-order sections allow shorter rolling periods than standard sections and, consequently, greater unproductive downtime for roll changes. In both instances output per unit of time is less than for heavier and standard sections and therefore production costs are greater. The extra costs of producing lighter, special, and small-order sections, like the extra costs of producing tested steel, were not covered adequately by price extras, either because of the maintenance of constant or nearly constant price differentials over time or, in some instances, no price differentials at all.[13]

Although there is not much the government can do by direct controls to compel the steel mills to produce high quality steel, the Iron and Steel Controller, who prior to 1964 assigned orders to the various plants, in theory should have prevented distortions in the retention price system from limiting output of

---

equal to the inverse ratio of steel prices, the new equilibrium resulting from price increases by the government would involve greater production of untested relative to tested steel. Only if there has been a technological change over time, so that less untested steel must be sacrificed to produce one ton of tested steel, would the price policies of the government not result in a sacrifice of tested steel.

[13] This criticism has also been made by the Raj Committee, a group headed by a prominent Indian economist which recently examined India's steel price and distribution controls. Ministry of Steel and Heavy Industries, Department of Iron and Steel, *Report of Steel Control* (New Delhi: Government of India Publication, 1963), pp. 13–15. Also see Indian Tariff Commission, pp. 24–25.

lighter and special sections. However, this assumes that controls once enacted were effective. In fact all mills, in various ways, were able to adjust their rolling schedules to fit their own interests.

One example was the unwillingness of the Bhilai and Durgapur plants to install new rolls necessary to produce a greater number of sections. By 1964 these mills still produced only a small fraction of the sections they were supposed to produce because of their limited selection of rolls. Those sections they were able to produce were generally standard items capable of being rolled in large tonnages. It is true that new plants need time to develop experience in steel manufacture before undertaking a wider selection of items, and that new rolls would have to be imported, involving the expenditure of foreign exchange. Even so, a primary objective of the public sector mills was to produce as large a tonnage of steel as possible, and their reluctance to turn new rolls helped them to fulfill this objective. The Iron and Steel Controller had to assign to TISCO and IISCO by default a disproportionate number of sections that do not allow large tonnages per unit of time. Because of the inadequacy of price extras these sections were least profitable and therefore least desirable to the private sector mills.[14]

The private sector mills were also able to adjust their rolling schedules to their own benefit. Until the mid-1960s there was a large backlog of orders on these mills, a consequence of the persistent scarcity of most forms of steel in India. Complicating matters was the liberal issuance of priorities to many customers and overriding priorities to some. With few exceptions the Iron and Steel Controller did not follow up orders once they were assigned to the steel mills, with the result that the mills were

[14] As might be expected, complaints of discrimination were leveled against the Iron and Steel Controller by the private sector mills. Indian Tariff Commission, pp. 25–26. Concentration on output records by the public sector mills is discussed in Chapter 8.

able to pick and choose from the backlog of demands and from the many priorities assigned to them more or less as they wished. In some instances customers received only those parts of their orders consisting of "desirable" sections, although these sections alone may have been useless to them. In other instances "undesirable" sections were shipped to customers long after they were ordered and at a time when they were no longer needed. Both practices were important sources of steel traded in the black market. Regardless of the government's controls over steel production, the result of distortions in the price system was production of various types of steel in proportions preferred by India's steel mills, not India's consumers.[15]

There have been other distortions in the relative prices of various types of iron and steel. In the early 1960s prices of foundry iron and intermediate forms of steel were generally thought less remunerative than the prices of finished steel. The most obvious distortion prior to 1962 resulted from the establishment of the prices of noncommon categories—types of steel rolled by one mill but not another—not with reference to the costs of producing these categories, but merely to equalize the weighted average retention prices received by both companies. This practice was discontinued at the time of the Tariff Commission's last price inquiry.

Perhaps the most serious defect of steel price control was the distortion of both retention and selling prices relative to the prices of other commodities and the real costs of producing steel in India. Although operating or out-of-pocket costs were as a rule fully covered by retention prices, overheads were not. In the past the government attempted to forestall increases in steel prices by paring the return and depreciation granted India's steel mills.

In its 1962 price decision the government allowed return, net of depreciation, at 8 per cent before taxes, a rate that is modest

[15] Raj Committee, *Report of Steel Control*, pp. 8–18.

by Indian standards. Rates of return earned on many relatively risk-free Indian securities are as high or higher than 8 per cent. So, also, are average rates of return earned by most Indian industries.[16] The discounted rate of return allowed India's steel industry should be no lower than the marginal rate of return on Indian capital.[17] If it were, there would be good reason to question the wisdom of expanding India's steel industry. Unfortunately, it is no easy matter to estimate a marginal rate of return on capital even though, in theory, it should equal the market rate of interest. Interest rates are affected by risk, government policies, and a number of non-market considerations. Added to these difficulties, measures of India's marginal rate of return on capital vary widely.[18] In estimating a higher steel price I assume 10 per cent to be the minimum and 15 per cent the maximum marginal rate of return and, therefore, a range indicating the minimum rate of return that should be allowed India's steel industry.

Not only were the rates used in computing overheads inadequate, so were estimates of total investment, or capital block, to which they were applied. In its last inquiry the Tariff Commission used a standard block of Rs. 1,300 per annual ton, assuming production at 90 per cent of capacity. This was reduced to Rs. 1,176 per ton by the government. Both estimates

[16] For rates of return earned by many Indian companies during the past decade as well as rates of interest paid by these companies on debentures and preference shares, the interested reader is directed to Place, Siddons & Gough (Private), Ltd., *The Investor's India Year-Book* (Calcutta: Orient Longmans Ltd., various years). Place, Siddons & Gough is a prominent brokerage house in Calcutta. The Reserve Bank of India collects data on investment and profits for more than thirty Indian industries. These data have been reproduced in various editions of its monthly *Bulletin*.

[17] In theory, investors will choose from alternative investment opportunities those bearing the highest rates of return until all investable funds available to the economy have been committed. The rate of return on the most profitable alternative not selected is the marginal rate of return on capital. In a risk-free, competitive economy the marginal rate of return on capital would determine the rate of interest.

[18] Appendix C.

were derived from the actual purchase costs of TISCO's plant and equipment, much of it installed before or shortly after World War II, and were in no way related to replacement costs.

These measures of capital block were particularly untenable as bases for the computation of return to the government mills. At the end of their initial stages of construction, India's public sector mills had an average capital block of about Rs. 2,500 per ton of salable steel, assuming production at rated capacity. Once their Third Plan expansion programs are completed they are not expected to achieve an average block lower than Rs. 1,950 per ton.[19] The government mills had difficulty meeting out-of-pocket costs from their retention prices and had to borrow from the State Bank of India to cover their deficits. Even if their out-of-pocket costs had been reduced, it would have been impossible for them to earn an adequate return on their investment so long as they received prices based on the out-of-date capital costs of the private sector plants.

Low retention prices were paralleled by low selling prices. Estimation of retention prices on the basis of historical capital costs, in effect, permitted maintenance of selling prices lower than the long-run marginal costs of producing steel in India. Some unjustified demand for steel was probably encouraged by the government's price policies for the industry.[20]

Estimates of average steel prices that would have covered all real costs of producing steel in 1962 are presented in Table 6. My assumptions are discussed at length in Appendix C and need only be summarized here. Two prices are computed, one

[19] Indian Tariff Commission, pp. 93–94. Because in any new steel mill there are certain facilities that need not be duplicated in subsequent expansion programs, the capital block of these mills should eventually be lower than immediately after completion of their initial stages. These facilities include intermediate and final rolling mills, within plant track and road systems, and various ancillary installations.

[20] The relation between the demand and price for Indian steel is discussed at length later in this chapter and also in Chapter 7.

Table 6. Actual and Social Average Retention Prices for Steel in 1962 (Rs. per ton of salable steel)

	Estimated social prices assuming a rate of return equal to:[a]		Price proposed by the Commission[b]	Price established by the Government[b]
	10%	15%		
Capital block	2,438	2,438	1,300	1,176
Work costs	357	357	357	357
Adjustment for revaluation of coal	6	6	0	0
Adjustment for revaluation of the cost of foreign personnel	12	12	0	0
Depreciation	122	122	66	59
Return	244	366	106	94
Interest on working capital	9	13	9	6
Element for repayment of special advances from the government	8	8	8	0
Other expenses	6	6	6	6
Less: Miscellaneous recoveries	−2	−2	−2	−2
Total price	762	888	550	520

[a] See Chapter 5 and Appendix C. Rs. 2,438 is the predicted average capital block of India's three public sector steel mills after their current expansion programs are completed. Costs of imported equipment and foreign personnel have been revalued at one rupee equal to 14 cents. Depreciation has been allowed at 5 per cent of capital block, a reasonable estimate of the rate of replacement in a steel mill. The method used by the Indian Tariff Commission to compute return on working capital, 5 per cent of six months' costs of production, was a rather arbitrary rule of thumb. A cost accountant at one of the private sector mills thought that this return was reasonable. I assume, also arbitrarily, that it works out to an actual rate of return on working capital of 10 per cent. Accordingly, when allowing a 15 per cent return on capital, I assume a 50 per cent increase in interest on working capital. Other cost items are assumed identical to those suggested by the Tariff Commission.

[b] Based on information presented in Indian Tariff Commission, *Report on the Fair Ex-Works Retention Prices of Steel for the Period 1st April 1960 to 31st March 1962* (New Delhi: Government of India Publication, 1962), pp. 44 and 94.

based on a rate of return equal to 10 per cent, the other on a rate of return equal to 15 per cent. Two inputs subject to questionable price administration by the government, coal and foreign exchange, have also been revalued for the purposes of this exercise. Expenditures in foreign exchange in particular have been substantially undervalued in steel prices because of India's unrealistic rate of exchange. The industry's foreign exchange costs are incurred, by and large, in the employment of foreign personnel and the purchase of foreign-made plant and machinery. Accordingly, costs of imported labor and capital block have been adjusted for an assumed "shadow" rate of exchange: one rupee equal to 14 cents rather than the official 21 cents in force before devaluation in June 1966.[21]

It is necessary to specify the precise meaning of the social prices presented in Table 6. They do not represent "fair" prices in the same sense that "fair" prices have been determined in the past by the Indian Tariff Commission. Because an upward revision has been made in actual factor costs, it is probable that all mills would be delighted to receive my prices. Rather, my analysis is an attempt, however crude, to measure social or shadow prices for steel, the true costs to the Indian economy of producing steel in new mills.

Shadow pricing is a risky business. Virtually all prices are subject to some distortions resulting from government policies or market imperfections. Should the wages of unskilled labor be given a zero value because of its alleged zero marginal productivity? Should monopolistic prices be adjusted to levels

[21] This shadow rate of exchange assumes a minimum revaluation of the rupee. Wilfred Malenbaum, "Comparative Costs and Economic Development: The Experience of India," *American Economic Review*, LIV (May 1964), 397. Also see Appendix C. Subsequent to the completion of this manuscript India devalued to 13.33 cents, a rate which supports the shadow rate I have used but which is thought by some observers still to be too high. Which shadow rate of exchange would be appropriate is a moot question. Were the rupee valued still lower, my estimates of social prices for Indian steel would increase.

more appropriate to a competitive economy? Although I run the risk of becoming lost in the shadows, I have to assume this risk. Social prices for steel are used for two purposes in subsequent chapters, to determine whether India has been justified in investing so heavily in her steel industry under her five year plans, and to estimate the proportion of Indian demand for steel that is spurious because of unduly low steel prices. In my opinion, these questions cannot be talked about meaningfully unless the effects of India's price policies are also considered.

Selling Price and Steel Distribution Control prior to March 1964

Prior to March 1964 there was a difference between prices paid by consumers, referred to as selling prices, and prices paid to producers, or retention prices. Selling prices for most types of steel were also established by the Government of India. Although the retention price was increased by about 30 per cent between 1956 and 1962 to cover increased costs of production, the selling price, which was higher, was increased by only 10 per cent during the same period, an amount equal to an excise tax imposed on steel. Not only did the retention price not adequately reflect real costs of producing steel in India, increments in the selling price did not match increments in costs during much of the past decade.[22]

There were at least two ostensible reasons for the government's reluctance to allow an increase in selling prices. First, it was thought that maintenance of low steel prices encouraged India's economic growth by subsidizing the purchase of an important industrial input. Low prices were undoubtedly a boon to some steel consumers. However, they did not necessarily encourage the expansion of India's economy in recent years. For much of the 1950s the Indian economy was hindered by a persistent shortage of most types of steel, resulting to some

[22] Raj Committee, "A Preliminary Report on Steel Control," (mimeograph, New Delhi: Ministry of Steel and Heavy Industries, Department of Iron and Steel, 1963), p. 12.

extent from unnecessary uses of steel encouraged by unduly low prices. By the early 1960s shortages of rails, certain bars, and structurals had changed to surpluses, partly because of the commissioning of new steel mill capacity, but also because of a slowdown in the rate of growth of the Indian economy and an apparent slackening in investment.[23] Production of these types of steel has probably been expanded too rapidly and almost certainly at the expense of growth in other industries. Steel shortages during the 1950s, partly a function of unduly low steel prices, encouraged the establishment of excessive targets for the following decade. All things considered, it is not obvious that low steel prices encouraged a more rapid growth of India's economy.

It has also been argued that steel price increases would contribute to already substantial inflationary pressures in India. Yet the regulation of steel prices alone may not offset inflationary pressures in the Indian economy. Rather, the consequences of the government's regulation of wholesale prices may be inordinate profits accruing to middlemen and to those steel-consuming industries producing commodities that are not subject to price controls.

In 1962 the weighted average import price for steel, CIF, indicated in Table 7, was roughly 10 per cent greater than the weighted average selling price for comparable combinations of steel output.[24] This difference was far greater a decade earlier.

[23] A major reason for surplus structural capacity in mid-1965 was said to be India's cement shortage and a resulting curtailment in the activities of the construction industry.

[24] It is impossible to achieve complete comparability of import and domestic selling prices because steel is not a homogeneous commodity. The average import prices indicated in Table 7, wherever possible, refer to ordinary sections. Even so, it is likely that some of these imports were of relatively specialized sections that are costly to roll and not in sufficient demand to justify their production in India. For this reason, were complete comparability of prices achieved, it is possible that the difference between import and domestic selling prices of steel would be still less than that indicated in Table 7.

Table 7. Prices of Imported and Domestic Steel in 1961–62[a]

	Import prices[b] (Rs./ton)	Selling prices[c] (Rs./ton)	Production in 1961–62 (thousands of tons) All integrated mills[d]	TISCO[e]
Semifinished steel for sale	562	469[f]	1,165.7	384
Structurals	691[g]	630	638.6	41[h]
Rails	617[j]	620	268.2	93[k]
Sheets	898[m]	852[n]	287.6	134
Hoops and strips	800[p]	760[q]	114.8	173[r]
Plates	705[s]	727	149.3	77
Bars and rods	700[p]	616[t]	1,119.3	395[u]
Wire	851[v]	811[w]	42.3	0
Weighted average price assuming the product mix of:				
All mills	670	602		
TISCO	687	623		

[a] I have attempted, wherever possible, to estimate prices for ordinary imported sections comparable to sections produced in India. Import prices include freight and insurance. Selling prices are for untested steel sold by integrated mills, except for rails which, for the most part, must be tested steel.

[b] Computed from data for the period April 1, 1961, through December 31, 1962, presented in Government of India, Department of Commercial Intelligence and Statistics, *Monthly Statistics of the Foreign Trade of India* (New Delhi: Government of India Publication, March and December, 1962).

[c] Government of India, Ministry of Steel and Heavy Industries, Iron and Steel Control, "Price Circular No. 1 of 1962" (mimeograph, Calcutta, June 2, 1962).

[d] Government of India, Ministry of Steel and Heavy Industries, Iron and Steel Control, *Monthly Bulletin* (Calcutta: Government of India Publication, various months).

[e] TISCO, *Annual Report*, 1961–62.

[f] Price of billets only.

[g] Average import price of beams, pillars, girders, angles, and tees.

[h] Heavy structurals only.

[j] Import price of heavy rails only.

[k] Includes sleepers and fishplates.

[m] Import prices of black sheets, plain and corrugated, galvanized sheets, plain and corrugated, and sheets up to 1/8" not galvanized or tinned.

(*Notes continued on next page*)

NOTES TO TABLE 7 (*cont.*)

[n] Weighted average price of plain black sheets and galvanized corrugated sheets.
[p] Approximation from trade statistics.
[q] Selling price of hot rolled strips and skelp.
[r] Includes skelp.
[s] Import price of plates over ⅛″.
[t] Arithmetic average of the prices of light and heavy bars and rods.
[u] Includes light structurals.
[v] Import price of "other" wire.
[w] Price of hard bright wire. Government of India, Ministry of Steel and Heavy Industries, Iron and Steel Control, "Price Circular No. 2 of 1962" (mimeograph, Calcutta, 1962).

Concern for the apparent loss of the competitive advantage held by Indian steel would seem to be merited. However, the use of average import prices as norms for domestic prices involves an implicit acceptance of India's rate of exchange. Because the rupee has been overvalued, it is to be expected that the prices of most Indian goods would compare unfavorably with the prices of imported goods. If import prices prior to 1966 are to be used as norms for domestic prices, they should be adjusted by an assumed devaluation of the rupee. It should also be determined whether or not import prices for steel reflect domestic prices in those countries from which steel is imported. The world market for steel has become highly competitive in recent years and some dumping on the world market has been alleged.

A peculiarity of the selling price for steel is its equalization at all depots throughout India. This policy was instituted in June 1956 because of a desire to encourage a "better geographic distribution of industries and also stimulate the dispersal of industries all over the country."[25] There are circumstances under which regional price equalization would not have this effect. Much of the steel used in construction must be shipped to the

[25] Government of India, Ministry of Commerce and Industry, *Annual Report, 1956–57* (New Delhi: Government of India Publication, 1957), p. 34.

construction site regardless of freight costs. Many steel-consuming industries are normally located near markets for their products or the sources of other inputs, either because their finished products may be comparatively bulky or because steel may be one of their less important inputs. Even so, as long as there is some price elasticity of demand for steel, regional price equalization has almost certainly resulted in greater consumption of steel in regions relatively distant from India's mills.[26]

For most of the postwar period the government maintained direct controls over the distribution of steel. Prior to March 1964 the agency primarily responsible for the distribution of steel was the Office of the Iron and Steel Controller in Calcutta, a subdivision of the ministry in charge of the steel industry. A consumer could place an indent directly on the Iron and Steel Controller for all but exceptionally scarce controlled categories of steel. To purchase scarce categories the consumer first had to obtain a quota certificate from an agency or ministry of the central or a state government.[27] Indents for at least one wagon load, approximately twenty-two tons, were placed on the steel mills by the Office of the Iron and Steel Controller after consultation with representatives of the mills. Smaller orders were placed on middlemen known as stockists who in turn indented on the major producers through the Office of the Iron and Steel

[26] Regional price equalization may have been responsible for a marked change in the regional distribution of steel demand in India since Independence. In 1948, eastern India, the region nearest Calcutta and India's integrated steel mills, accounted for nearly 60 per cent of Indian demand for steel. Prices were then established on the basis of cost plus freight from major Indian ports, a system of price discrimination no more related to actual costs of distributing steel than that now in force. In 1960–61 eastern India accounted for 37 per cent of Indian demand for steel, and, as may be expected, the share of northern India, the region most distant from ports and relatively distant from India's steel mills, had grown most rapidly. For regional demand in 1948, see Koppers Company, Inc., Pittsburgh, Pa., *Indian Steel Report* (Pittsburgh: Koppers Company, 1948), p. 45. For regional demand in 1960–61, see Table F-9.

[27] In 1962 scarce or "restricted quota" categories included thin black sheets, galvanized sheets, and ordinary and hard bright wire.

Controller. All imported steel was also purchased through this office.

There were countless lapses in the system of controls governing the distribution of steel. The Office of the Iron and Steel Controller received no less than 50,000 indents each year. It was expected to scrutinize each indent, but in fact its staff was incapable of more than a cursory examination based on information supplied by the indentor himself. As a result, many indents were accepted or rejected arbitrarily. Consumers in turn padded their indents to obtain the amounts of steel they actually wanted. Screening of indents did not eliminate over-indenting, nor did it pare existing demands for controlled categories to match their availability.[28] Because outstanding orders usually exceeded the tonnages India's mills could produce within a reasonable period of time,[29] it was necessary to issue priorities to selected consumers, and a black market persisted to enable other consumers to purchase steel that could not be obtained quickly through official channels.

The Office of the Iron and Steel Controller was also unable to effect a meaningful audit to assure the use of steel by intended consumers rather than its resale on the black market. In mid-1963 galvanized sheets commanded a price on the black market approximately 100 per cent and other flat products between 15 and 30 per cent above the government's controlled selling price.[30] Because there was little risk of detection, the inducement to resell these types of steel was very great indeed. The black market drew its steel from several sources. Some consumers, having received steel long after it was needed or in proportions other than desired, found sales on the black market

[28] Raj Committee, *Report*, pp. 8–12; "Preliminary Report," pp. 3–5.

[29] For the backlog of orders prevailing in the early 1960's, see Indian Planning Commission, "Steel in the Third Five Year Plan: Requirements, Availability and Allocation" (mimeograph, New Delhi, 1962), p. 23.

[30] Raj Committee, *Report*, p. 53. The black market for most types of steel declined in importance during the early 1960s.

a convenient and profitable alternative to the accumulation of inventories. Many stockists sold on the black market and the trafficking of quota certificates was commonplace. The principal customers for black market steel included manufacturers of such consumer goods as steel furniture, utensils, and automobile and bicycle parts; and individuals desiring various forms of steel directly, notably galvanized corrugated sheets for roofing. Many purchasers were also willing to pay black market prices to obtain the steel they wanted when they wanted it.

Another abuse of the old system of distribution control was the generous issuance of different types of priorities with the result that indents possessing various priority ratings accumulated at the steel mills. In theory the issuance of priorities was based on the importance of particular uses to the fulfillment of plan objectives, defense and capital goods projects being accorded highest priorities. In practice the issuance of priorities was also based on political influence and ministerial pressures from the central and state governments. Because there was no systematic check by the Office of the Iron and Steel Controller to determine whether or how priorities were being respected by the producers, unless the office was subjected to considerable pressure from the indentor or sponsoring authorities, priorities came to have relatively little meaning.[31]

Still another failing of distribution control was the use of steel for purposes that might be considered unnecessary. Government ministries, for the most part, had first place in India's queue for steel because they could issue quota certificates or bring pressures on the Office of the Iron and Steel Controller and other agencies of the government associated with the issuance of priorities. Substantial inventories of steel were accumulated by the railways and several public sector plants that consume steel. A number of government buildings were erected

[31] *Ibid.*, pp. 11–12 and 19–20.

with steel sheets, whereas mud, brick, thatch, and tile, the normal building materials of India, would have sufficed for some purposes.

In effect, under the old system of distributing steel the Office of the Iron and Steel Controller had little independent power to allocate scarce sections. Actual distribution of exceptionally scarce categories of steel was determined by the various ministries. Steel consumed by medium and large-scale industries was allocated by the Development Wing of the Ministry of Commerce and Industry, steel consumed by small-scale industries by the directors of industries of various states, and steel consumed by the ministries or organizations under their direction by the ministries themselves. Even though consumers of some categories were allowed to indent directly on the Office of the Iron and Steel Controller, this office still had little say in the distribution of those forms that were in relatively short supply. The liberal issuance of priorities to consumers possessing ministerial backing in effect circumvented the Office of the Iron and Steel Controller. Moreover, the absence of a means to insure the production of the most desired forms of steel by steel mills and an audit to insure the ultimate use of steel by those for whom it was intended limited the ability of the Iron and Steel Controller to regulate the actual distribution of scarce items of steel. In short, the office was able to distribute only those forms that were not scarce; that is to say, those forms for which distribution control was unnecessary.

Steel Price and Distribution Control after March 1964

The failure of steel price and distribution controls became increasingly obvious during the early 1960s. Through the initiative of the then Minister of Steel and Heavy Industries, Mr. C. Subramaniam, a committee headed by a prominent Indian economist was appointed in 1962 to investigate existing controls and to suggest alternatives. The Raj Committee's preliminary report was completed in January 1963, its final report in October. In both, the committee discussed at length the failings of existing controls, but concluded that some government regulation would have to be retained to insure allocation of steel to essential capital projects and small consumers. For this reason the revisions suggested by the Raj Committee contemplated only partial restoration of a free market for steel.[32] On March 1, 1964, after receiving comments from the industry and other interested parties, the Government of India announced the adoption of a new system for the pricing and distribution of steel incorporating many of the recommendations made by the Raj Committee.

Under the new system a Joint Plant Committee has been formed consisting of representatives from each of the steel companies, the Office of the Iron and Steel Controller, and the Railway Ministry acting on behalf of consumers of steel. This committee scrutinizes indents, plans rolling schedules, fixes prices for relatively abundant categories, and establishes price extras for different qualities and specifications of steel. The prices of scarce categories of steel are still established by the government.[33] Retention and selling prices are now identical and the Equalization Fund has been abolished. No attempt is made to regulate the price of steel after it has left the plants and trade in steel is permitted to anyone. Should inordinate profits accrue to producers, they will be absorbed by the government through the enactment of offsetting excise duties. Steel prices will continue to be equalized throughout India by means of a fund operated by the Joint Plant Committee. Finally, the government will establish priorities when shortages of specific sections impair the activities of essential user industries.

[32] For the recommendations by the Raj Committee, see its *Report*, Ch. III, pp. 19–27.

[33] In late 1965 these categories included only billets, sheets, plates, and other scarce flat products.

Initially these changes appeared to be decontrol in name only. Most scarce types of steel were exempted from decontrol.[34] Controls over nonscarce types of steel were also eliminated during the early 1950s, only to be reimposed when these types of steel once again became scarce. There was little reason to believe that this experience would not be repeated were there renewed shortages of decontrolled categories of steel. Even then the pricing and distribution of decontrolled categories was entrusted to a committee upon which representatives of the government and India's railways sit and, presumably, could exercise veto power. Had market conditions allowed increased prices for decontrolled categories, there was some question whether the committee could establish these prices.

During the year following decontrol the public and private sector mills assumed greater dominance in the Joint Plant Committee than was expected in the beginning. The Joint Plant Committee also assumed effective responsibility for the distribution and placing of indents of scarce categories of steel. Not unexpectedly, the committee's assumption of powers has encouraged the charge that it is a producers' monopoly sanctioned by the government.

Yet the Joint Plant Committee has been popular with consumers. It is credited almost universally for distributing steel more efficiently than the Office of the Iron and Steel Controller, reducing the time needed to process an indent to as little as one week. Although the committee has had several factors in its favor, notably an easing of steel supplies and rail bottlenecks that inhibited the distribution of steel by the Iron and Steel Controller, there is little doubt that it is also a far more efficient organization.

By April 1965 the committee had not significantly increased

[34] Only broad categories of steel not in short supply were decontrolled by the Government of India. Within most decontrolled categories there were specific types of steel that were still scarce.

the prices of decontrolled categories of steel.[35] Nor had it improved rolling schedules by adjusting price extras or standardizing steel sections. However, it subsequently enacted increases both in the base price for steel and in the size and number of price extras for different types of steel. This has allegedly contributed to an increase in the profits of India's steel mills, an improvement in quality, and increased production of hitherto "scarce" commodities such as foundry grade iron, thin sheets, and light sections. Informants have faulted the committee most severely for its failure to improve the distribution of indents to the various steel mills. It would appear that the performance of the committee after two years of operations, although commendable, has been mixed, a not very surprising outcome given its short lifetime and the magnitude of the problems it inherited.

There has also been a major change in steel prices set by the government. In February 1965 India's Finance Minister proposed an increase in excise taxes to divert to the government benefits that had accrued to traders and consumers of several controlled commodities.[36] Subsequently, the Indian Parliament enacted modest increases in excise taxes on relatively abundant types of steel, and substantial increases, ranging as high as 20 per cent, on scarce types of steel.[37]

In my opinion, decontrol has been a step in the right direction. However, decontrol, by itself, may not be fully desirable.

[35] Prices of decontrolled categories were increased in April 1964 by no more than 3 per cent. They were increased once again in February 1965, but only by amounts equal to increases in the excise taxes on steel. Joint Plant Committee, "Announcement by the Joint Plant Committee, Schedule of Prices" (mimeograph, Calcutta, March and April 1964 and February 1965).

[36] Government of India, *Budget, 1965–66, Finance Minister's Speech* (New Delhi: Government of India Publication, February, 1965).

[37] For the magnitude of price increases for decontrolled commodities, see Joint Plant Committee, *Announcement* . . . (April 1964 and February 1965). For the magnitude of price increases for controlled commodities, see *The Gazette of India, Extraordinary,* Part II, Section 3, subsection ii (New Delhi: Government of India Publication, March 1, 1966, and March 6, 1965).

There has never been a truly competitive market for steel in India, nor would there be were the government to give free rein to the Joint Plant Committee. The steel industry is potentially oligopolistic, and it is possible that given complete freedom in pricing, the committee, acting as a producers' monopoly, would establish prices masking inefficiencies in both public and private sector mills. Moreover, the producers' ability to allocate indents according to their own and not consumers' interests lessens competition in the industry. India's mills need not produce steel in exact specifications demanded by consumers, nor do they have to worry about quality, because the Joint Plant Committee assures them a fixed share of the Indian market. Indian policy-makers might well ask the question: How can we now increase competition in the industry for both public and private sector mills?

The persistence of steel shortages throughout the 1950s, the arbitrariness of government controls over steel pricing and distribution, the public sector mills' concentration on setting output records,[38] and a number of other circumstances have encouraged the growth of a "let the buyer beware" mentality in the industry. Cost minimization has been a relatively unimportant objective in India's public sector mills. Production of good quality steel and of types of steel in specifications demanded by consumers has been neglected. Now that many types of steel are no longer in short supply, I see no reason why these practices should persist. Yet they may if there does not develop a minimum level of competition among India's steel mills.

How can the government assure greater competition in the industry? One possibility would be to allow consumers to indent directly on steel mills for relatively abundant sections. Indents would pile up at those mills offering the lowest prices, reflecting

[38] The performance of public sector mills is discussed at length in Chapter 8.

the lowest costs of production, and willing to produce desired types of steel. Faced with a loss in orders for abundant sections, other mills would be forced to improve their standards or settle for idle capacity or greater inventories of unsalable products. The government might also consider relatively free importation of steel at prices reflecting the social value of the rupee. Introduction of this element of competition would place a limit on prices charged by Indian producers. It would also encourage domestic mills to emulate standards of quality prevalent in the world market for steel.

Conclusion

I do not intend this chapter to be an exposé. The defects of past controls over the steel industry are known by the government, and recent policy changes have contributed to their removal. My primary purpose is to point out how the policies of the government have been inconsistent and, consequently, how they have diminished the effectiveness of Indian planning. More generally, my purpose is to indicate the need for coordination of government activities in a planned economy.

The government's industrial policy resolutions and price policies did not discourage public sector development of the steel industry. However, these controls have discouraged private sector expansion, even though this expansion has been sanctioned by Indian planners.[39] Selling prices established by the government have prompted excessive demand for steel and exaggerated plan targets.[40] Price and distribution policies have also encouraged the production of types of steel that are not neces-

[39] That the private sector expanded during the 1950s is not a meaningful exception to this statement. It was understood at that time that special advances from the government, to finance part of this expansion, would be repaid by subsequent increases in retention prices. The government later demanded repayment by other means.

[40] For an estimate of the amount of exaggeration resulting from unduly low selling prices, see Chapter 7.

sarily identical to those wanted by consumers or especially needed to fulfill India's plan programs. In short, many of the government's controls over the industry have, in the past at least, reduced the effectiveness of Indian planning.

Recent policy changes should remove many of the defects of the old system. However, they do not fully alter one policy directive: the desire to limit private sector expansion in the industry. Were the private sector to contribute meaningfully to the growth of the industry, some increase in producers' prices and relaxation of India's Industrial Policy Resolution might be necessary. Public sector ownership of the steel industry is an objective justified on social and ideological grounds. Right or wrong, adherence to this objective does have a cost. Thus far private sector mills have demonstrated their ability to produce steel at a greater profit than public sector mills. Expansion of existing plants would also cost far less than the erection of new plants. Above all, the private sector mills form a reservoir of skills that has not been fully tapped by Indian planners. In short, a major cost of India's reluctance to allow existing steel companies to expand fully has been some sacrifice of a principal goal of planners, India's achievement of a maximum rate of economic growth.

6 | An Economic Justification for Expansion of India's Steel Industry

Has India been justified in developing her steel industry? Or would investment elsewhere be a wiser use of her scarce resources? These questions are basic to any appraisal of India's planning for the expansion of the industry. However, before they can be answered, the role of steel in India's economy and, more particularly, in her plans for economic growth should be established.

Why is steel important? Proponents of bold targets for India's steel industry often cite the fact that all modern economies possess steel industries. Therefore, it is claimed, if India is to modernize her economy, she too must develop her steel industry. This argument, so baldly stated, suffers from obvious weaknesses. An efficient agriculture is also characteristic of a developed economy. So, too, is the production of spark plugs and chewing gum. Greater use of steel in developed economies, by itself, is not a sufficient reason for India to give priority to new steel mills in her Five Year Plans. Why, then, should steel be singled out for special attention?

The economist might argue that India must increase the fraction of her national income devoted to investment if her economy is to grow rapidly. Steel is necessary for the production of machine tools, roads, railroads, and bridges, much of the private and social capital essential for building India's economy and, particularly, her economic infrastructure. This argument is also subject to several limitations. In the first place, not all steel is used in the manufacture of investment goods. Well over half of the steel manufactured in the United States enters directly into the production of consumer durables and other consumer goods. In India this proportion is much lower, probably around one-fifth of total steel output. Nonetheless, it is sufficiently large that increased steel output could conceivably permit an increase in the fraction of India's national income devoted to consumption, not investment. Nor are all increments in investment necessarily advantageous. Excessive production of steel relative to demand may result in investment in unwanted inventories of steel. Finally, one might argue that India should emphasize production for export of commodities other than steel, thereby permitting greater steel imports. Given an open economy, an economy engaged in foreign trade, it is not at all obvious that India must produce steel to achieve economic growth.

The sole objective of Indian planning for steel is assumed to be maximization of India's national wealth and the income derived from that wealth, India's net national product. Whether or not investment in the industry is justified will depend on the relationship between the rate of return earned by the industry and the rate of return earned by the most remunerative extramarginal investment, the marginal rate of return on Indian capital. If the former exceeds the latter, investment in the industry would, in theory, contribute to maximization of India's net national product, assuming for the moment that India's rate of savings is not influenced by the particular set of investment alternatives chosen by Indian planners. At first I estimate a crude measure of the rate of return on investment in India's steel industry, disregarding delays necessarily incurred before a mill receives the full return on its investment. Subsequently,

I attempt to determine an internal rate of return for the industry accounting for these delays by discounting the future income and costs of an Indian steel mill.[1]

Maximization of India's net national product is not the only objective of Indian planning, nor, for that matter, the only welfare criterion for public policy in general. Other objectives such as greater employment and increased equality in the distribution of income have not only been adopted by the Indian government but may actually be in conflict with both the maximization of India's net national product and, more particularly, the expansion of her steel industry. In the following pages no consideration is given to these other objectives. The ostensible reason for investment in the steel industry is that increased supplies of steel would enable India to produce substantially more of the goods and services for which steel is an important input. It is almost unquestioned in India that increasing steel supplies by domestic production represents a more advantageous use of Indian resources than the import of steel from abroad. The most appropriate criterion for determining the correctness of this belief is the rate of return earned by the industry.

Moreover, I attempt to measure the social rate of return that would accrue to the Indian economy from investment in steel, not the actual rate of return earned by an Indian mill. The distinction between the two rates arises from the possible existence of external economies or diseconomies in the industry and, particularly, price administration by the government over steel and various of the industry's inputs.

[1] The theory of investment is widely discussed in the economics literature. For concise presentations of relevant parts of this theory, the reader is directed to Gardner Ackley, *Macroeconomic Theory* (New York: Macmillan, 1961), pp. 460–477, and Jack Hirshleifer, James C. DeHaven, and Jerome W. Milliman, *Water Supply: Economics, Technology, and Policy* (Chicago: The University of Chicago Press, 1960), pp. 152–157. See, also, Jack Hirshleifer, "On the Theory of Optimal Investment Decision," *Journal of Political Economy*, LXVI (August 1958), 329–352.

Whether the steel industry is subject to external economies and diseconomies is a moot question. If so, the return to society from investment in steel would differ from the actual return to a steel mill. One can imagine several examples of external economies. A mill might train workers eventually drawn into other industries. It might contribute to the transformation of an agrarian into an industrial work force willing to submit to the discipline of factory employment. It may encourage the location of new industries in regions opened by its railroads or the production of a marketable surplus of agricultural commodities on nearby farm land. On the contrary, a new mill may result in external diseconomies, perhaps the first to come to mind being the textbook examples of smoke created by its furnaces and problems associated with crowding in its townships.[2] Externalities are notoriously difficult to measure. In this study I assume, arbitrarily, that the classical external economies and diseconomies associated with investment in India's steel industry are, in fact, negligible. In any event, they are probably not very different from externalities resulting from investment in other Indian industries. If so, my neglect of these externalities should not have serious consequences.

However, the effects of the government's price policies cannot be ignored. The prices of steel, several of the industry's inputs, and foreign exchange are all administered by the government and differ from prices that would exist in the absence of the government's controls. Because of these controls, the actual rate of return earned by the industry falls far short of the real rate of return accruing to Indian society from investment in steel. In this chapter I use "shadow prices" to value steel and several of the industry's inputs. Therefore, what is meant by "social rate of return on investment in steel" is that rate of

[2] However, because Indian steel mills typically erect, own, and operate their townships, these diseconomies may, in fact, be internal to them.

return accruing to society but not to Indian steel mills because of the government's price policies.

The internal social rate of return, an approximation of the social marginal productivity of investment in steel,[3] has been criticized on the ground that a developing economy should not maximize the present value of future income on its investment, but rather the rate of capital accumulation and therefore, by assumption, the rate of growth of its national income.[4] This, it is argued, may result in a choice of alternatives that would not be suggested by the social marginal productivity criterion, notably capital-intensive alternatives that would redistribute income in favor of segments of the population saving a larger proportion of increments in their income. Regardless of the merits or demerits of this argument,[5] the steel industry, being relatively capital-intensive, should theoretically satisfy the latter criterion.[6] If, then, it also satisfies the social marginal productivity criterion, India would indeed have the best of both worlds. Investment in her steel industry would be consistent with the maximization of both the present value of return on her investment and her long-run rate of capital accumulation.

[3] For a discussion of this criterion the reader is directed to A. E. Kahn, "Investment Criteria in Development Programs," *Quarterly Journal of Economics*, LXV (February 1951), 38–61; and to subsequent discussion engendered by this article, most notably, H. B. Chenery, "The Application of Investment Criteria," *Quarterly Journal of Economics*, LXVII (February 1953), 76–96.

[4] The best known and, perhaps, the most extreme statement of this view is that of W. Galenson and H. Leibenstein, "Investment Criteria, Productivity, and Economic Development," *Quarterly Journal of Economics*, LXIX (August 1955), 343–370.

[5] Discussion of this argument has been widespread. In particular, the reader is directed to Otto Eckstein, "Investment Criteria for Economic Development and the Theory of Intertemporal Welfare Economics," *Quarterly Journal of Economics*, LXXI (February 1957), 56–85; and A. K. Sen, "Some Notes on the Choice of Capital-Intensity in Development Planning," *Quarterly Journal of Economics*, LXXI (November 1957), 561–584.

[6] In practice it may not because of price controls imposed on the industry.

Social Rates of Return on Investment in the Industry

A crude social rate of return is first estimated without discounting the future benefits and costs of production by the industry. The average works costs of the Tata mill and the capital costs of a new mill producing essentially the same combination of products are used to compute this rate of return. Both have been adjusted for higher shadow prices for coal and foreign exchange. The resulting estimate of costs is meant to be a measure of the social cost of producing a ton of steel in a new Indian steel mill, a crude approximation of the long-run marginal cost of producing steel in India.[7]

Since the alternative to the production of steel in India is its import from abroad, the average landed price of imported steel, revalued at one rupee equal to 14 cents, can be used to compute the social rate of return on investment in India's steel industry. This price is, in effect, the "opportunity cost" of not producing steel in India. Unlike the domestic market equilibrium price for steel, the import price should not be affected by changes in Indian demand, India's imports representing only a small fraction of the steel traded on the world market. For this reason the import price is assumed to be constant for all levels of output.

World markets for steel have been depressed in recent years and some dumping has been alleged.[8] India has benefited from dumping, but whether her advantage would continue for the

[7] For a justification, see Appendix C.

[8] For example, see the testimony of Norman B. Obbard, Executive Vice President of the United States Steel Corporation. U.S. Congress, House Committee on Appropriations, Foreign Operations Appropriations for 1964, *Hearings Before a Subcommittee of the Committee on Appropriations*, Part 4, 88th Congress, 1st Session, (Washington: U.S. Government Printing Office, 1963), p. 1630. See also Sir Jehangir Ghandy, *Steel, Some Problems of Development*, pamphlet published by TISCO based on a speech to the Engineering Institute of India, Calcutta, Dec. 24, 1959, pp. 8–9.

life of a new steel mill is highly problematic. The average import price for steel in 1961–62 may understate the long-run import price and, hence, the long-run social rate of return on investment in India's steel industry. However, any bias introduced by the use of the 1961–62 price would be adverse to the principal argument of this chapter, that investment in India's steel industry is justified, and, for this reason, no effort is made to adjust for it.

The use of the average import price in effect assumes demand for Indian steel to be equal to anticipated output at this price. On the contrary, it is conceivable that demand would not sustain the output of India's marginal firm at a price equal to the average import price for steel. It is even conceivable that demand would not sustain the output of this firm were the price of steel sufficient to allow the minimum rate of return considered necessary for Indian industry, 10 per cent.[9] Demand is essential to an appraisal of the economics of India's steel industry and is examined in the next chapter. For the moment, it is assumed to be of no relevance in computing the social rate of return on investment in the industry.

Social rates of return earned by a representative Indian mill are presented in Table 8. After completion of its first stage and overcoming initial difficulties in its operations, a new mill manufacturing the same types of steel as TISCO would earn 13.0 per cent on its initial investment. After completion of its second stage, some five or six years later, the mill would earn 21.3 per cent. Its capacity might be increased still further to approximately 2.5 million tons of salable steel. Although limitations on data prevent as precise an estimate of the mill's ultimate profitability, rough computations indicate that it would be about 28 per cent.[10]

[9] See Appendix C and Table 6.

[10] This is a rough estimate based on cost estimates for the Bokaro steel mill prepared for the United States Agency for International Development. U.S. Steel Corporation, "A Techno-Economic Survey of a Proposed In-

Table 8. Social Rates of Return on Investment in a New Indian Steel Mill

	Initial capacity	Capacity after expansion
Assumed output (millions of tons of salable steel)	0.77	1.50
Capital cost[a] (Rs. per ton of salable steel)	3,161	2,438
Average import price[b] (Rs. per ton)	1,030	1,030
Less:		
Average costs of production excluding depreciation and return[a, c] (Rs. per ton)	460	388
Depreciation[a] (Rs. per ton)	158	122
Net profits		
Rs. per ton	412	520
As a percentage of capital cost	13.0	21.3

[a] Table 6 and Appendix C.
[b] Table 7. The average import price, assuming TISCO's product mix, has been revalued at one rupee equal to 14 cents, rather than the official 21 cents prior to June 1966.
[c] The element for repayment of special advances to the government is excluded because this is a cost specific to existing private sector mills.

Estimated social rates of return on investment in a new Indian steel mill are extremely sensitive to changes in the as-

tegrated Steel Mill at Bokaro, Bihar State, India," (unpub. report submitted to the U.S. Government, Agency for International Development, March 1963), Vol. III, p. 4. It is estimated that, with its imported component valued at the assumed shadow rate of exchange, the Bokaro mill would cost 19.7 per cent less per ton at the end of its third and last stage than it would at the end of its second stage. Capital costs at the end of the mill's second stage, indicated in Table 8, have been adjusted accordingly. As before, the average import price is taken to be Rs. 1030 per ton. Costs of production excluding depreciation and return are taken to be Rs. 376 per ton, assuming no employment of imported personnel after completion of the mill's third stage. A crude rate of return earned by the mill at the end of its third stage would then be 28.4 per cent.

sumed shadow rate of exchange. The rate used, one rupee equal to 14 cents, in my opinion represents a minimum justified devaluation of the rupee.[11] Were a still greater devaluation assumed, so that one rupee is equal to, let us say, 10.5 cents, the crude social rate of return earned by a new Indian mill would increase to approximately 18 and 29 per cent at the end of its first and second stages respectively. Conversely, were the rupee valued at a price somewhat greater than 14 cents, estimates of the crude social rate of return earned by a new steel mill would fall substantially. For this reason, the important assumption must be made that during the lifetime of a new steel mill there will be no increase in the real value of the rupee that is not accompanied by lower costs of producing steel in India. This assumption seems reasonable. The circumstances that would result in the appreciation of the rupee, such as a lower rate of inflation in India than in hard currency countries, could also result in a smaller increase in the costs of steel production in India than in these countries.

On at least one occasion the divergence between the industry's actual and social rates of return has proved disadvantageous to India. The United States Steel Corporation was contracted by the United States Government's Agency for International Development to conduct a survey of India's proposed Bokaro steel mill. As would any private company reacting to the prices received for its products, it assumed that the expected profitability of the Bokaro mill would be a suitable measure of its economic worth. Not surprisingly, it found that Bokaro would incur losses in its first stage and would earn a crude rate of return of only 9 per cent net of depreciation during its third

[11] This is also the opinion of Wilfred Malenbaum "Comparative Costs and Economic Development: The Experience of India," *American Economic Review*, LIV (May 1964) 397. Subsequent to the completion of this chapter, India devalued to 13.33 cents, a rate that tends to support the assumed shadow rate of exchange.

and last stage.[12] These rates are hardly commendable by economists' standards and were considered wholly inadequate by U.S. Steel were it to invest its own capital in the Bokaro mill.[13] To some extent, the negative impression created by the anticipated actual rate of return to be earned by the Bokaro mill contributed to Congressional opposition to the project.

In fact, were crude social rates of return estimated for the Bokaro project by assuming shadow prices for steel and foreign exchange, the mill would return approximately 12 per cent in its first stage and 24 per cent in its third and last stage. These rates of return are far more favorable to the project than those indicated by U.S. Steel's report. Whether U.S. Steel would still be reluctant to invest its capital in the Bokaro mill were it to receive these rates of return is a matter for speculation. Nevertheless, the project would at least have had a fighting chance.

It is clear that the social rate of return earned by the industry would be substantially greater than that actually allowed by the Indian government. It would also be substantially greater than that rate taken to be a minimum estimate of the marginal rate of return on Indian investment. However, this by itself is not a proper comparison. Before any judgment can be made about the economics of India's steel industry, one must first consider delays incurred before receipt of return on investment in the industry. It is necessary to discount both the future returns and costs of the industry by an appropriate rate of interest. If, then, the present value of future benefits exceeds

[12] This is an approximation based upon data presented in U.S. Steel, Vol. III. It assumes receipt of existing retention prices by the Bokaro mill and excludes excise duties on finished steel.

[13] After repeated questioning by members of the Congressional subcommittee that considered the Bokaro project, Norman B. Obbard, Executive Vice President of U.S. Steel, declared that his company would not invest its own money in Bokaro because the anticipated rate of return did not compare favorably with rates of return earned elsewhere. Testimony, Aug. 15, 1963, in *Hearings*, p. 1641.

the present value of future costs, investment in the industry would be justified.

The internal rate of return is the rate of discount that would equate the present value of revenues resulting from a particular investment with the present value of both operating and capital costs associated with this investment. If b_i represents the revenues and c_i the costs in year i, the internal rate of return, r, for discrete time intervals would be such that:

$$\sum_{i=0}^{n} \frac{b_i}{(1+r)^i} = \sum_{i=0}^{n} \frac{c_i}{(1+r)^i}$$

The longer it takes for an industry to recoup its investment, all other things being equal, the lower will be its internal rate of return. For an industry such as steel, in which the ultimate return on investment is so long delayed, the internal rate of return may actually be quite low despite the apparent profitability of the industry in the long run.

In theory, were alternative investment opportunities independent of each other, they could be ranked by their internal rates of return, those with the highest rates being chosen in preference to all others until the financial resources available to the economy are fully committed. The highest internal rate of return of those alternatives not selected will equal the marginal rate of return on investment. Thus, if investment in India's steel industry is justified, the industry's internal rate of return should at least equal India's marginal rate of return.

I estimate that the *minimum* internal social rate of return on investment in a representative new Indian steel mill is 13.2 per cent. The computations upon which this estimate is based are fully explained in Appendix D. I need only note here that in making these computations I make a number of assumptions that bias this estimate downward. First, I assume that the mill will not be expanded beyond a capacity of 1.5 million tons of finished steel. In fact, the mill would probably be expanded to at least 2.5 million tons. Second, I assume that the mill will have to replace 5 per cent of its plant and equipment each year starting the first year of its operations. Actually, 5 per cent is more properly a long-run rate of replacement for the industry. In its first years, a new mill would incur needed replacements at a much lower rate. Third, I assume a minimum devaluation of the rupee. The greater the devaluation, the greater the rate of return earned by the industry. Fourth, I assume that Indian steel will command a price equal to the average landed price of imported steel, a price allegedly influenced by dumping. Were this price more properly determined by costs of production abroad, the social rate of return earned by the industry would presumably be higher than the rate I have computed. Finally, I assume that all investment takes place at the beginning of a year and that all profits are earned at the end of the year. In fact, there would be both profits and investment throughout the year, and, for this reason, the mill's true internal rate of return would be somewhat higher than that estimated.

The first two assumptions can be relaxed, although somewhat arbitrarily, in an attempt to compute a second, more representative, rate of return for the industry. All other assumptions remaining unchanged, the mill's internal social rate of return would then be 14.9 per cent.

Both estimates are above that rate I believe to be the minimum marginal rate of return on Indian capital, 10 per cent. However, they are not overwhelmingly above this rate and, for this reason, investment in India's steel industry is justified so long as the assumptions upon which this analysis is based are not seriously violated. The industry is sufficiently close to the margin that its economics cannot be taken for granted. A great deal depends on India's demand for steel, a matter considered in Chapter 7. A great deal also depends on whether or not new mills are being located, designed to use the most efficient methods of production, and operated so that the actual rates of return on investment in them approximate the internal social rates of return estimated in this study.

The internal rate of return criterion has been criticized because, under certain circumstances, it may be misleading or fundamentally incorrect.[14] It is not logically identical to the theoretically more acceptable present value criterion and, for this reason, if it is used, the analyst should determine that the two criteria do, in fact, yield the same results. The present value of return on an investment is equal to the total of differences between discounted benefits and costs of that investment. In terms of the notation used to represent the internal rate of return:

$$\text{P.V.} = \sum_{i=0}^{n} \frac{b_i - c_i}{(1 + \rho)^i},$$

where ρ represents an appropriate rate of discount.[15] If this discount rate is identical to the internal rate of return, present value (P.V.) will equal zero. In theory, an investment alternative would be chosen if its present value is positive or, when there is a choice between two or more alternatives with positive

[14] The limitations of the internal rate of return criterion are discussed in Hirshleifer, pp. 344–351, and Hirshleifer, *et al.*, pp. 156–157.

[15] There may in fact be as many discount rates as there are time periods. One advantage of the present value rule is that it enables the analyst to take account of anticipated changes in future discount rates. Once again, the form of this equation assumes discrete time intervals. If instead the future benefits and costs of an investment alternative are discounted continuously at all moments in time:

$$\text{P.V.} = \int_0^n e^{-\rho i}[b(i) - c(i)]\, di$$

where i represents the time period and ρ the rate at which anticipated benefits and costs are discounted. Which form of the present value equation is adopted will depend upon the needs of the analyst. Both are acceptable.

present values, if it possesses the highest present value. For the internal rate of return criterion to be consistent with the present value criterion it is sufficient that, for all discount rates greater than zero and lower than the internal rate of return, present value is positive and, conversely, for all discount rates greater than the internal rate of return, present value is negative. This condition is met by India's steel industry. The present values of return on investment in steel at various discount rates are presented in Appendix D.

Savings in Foreign Exchange

In Chapter 3 it was argued that capital cannot be considered a homogeneous factor of production in India. Although domestic capital may be scarce, foreign exchange and, therefore, the portion of capital that must be purchased from outside India is in far more limited supply. Indian planners have had to give special weight to the foreign exchange costs and returns of each investment alternative.

Annual imports of salable steel accounted for over 10 per cent of total Indian imports between 1956 and 1963. They absorbed nearly 17 per cent of India's export earnings during the same period.[16] It would be wrong to conclude that simply because India appears to have a comparative advantage in the production of steel she should produce all the forms of steel she now imports. Some types of steel are purchased from abroad in quantities too small for their economic rolling in India. Nevertheless, much of the steel imported during the late 1950s and early 1960s could have been produced in India. Although investment in India's steel industry has claimed a substantial proportion of total Indian investment, it is equally true that the import of steel has absorbed a large proportion of the foreign

[16] Estimated from trade data presented in Government of India, Department of Commercial Intelligence and Statistics, *Monthly Statistics of the Foreign Trade of India* (New Delhi: Government of India Publication, various months).

exchange that would have been available for the purchase of imports other than steel.

That investment in India's steel industry would repay its foreign exchange costs in a relatively short period of time is evident when one considers the proposed Bokaro steel mill. Bokaro will allow substantial import substitution. To be sure, the erection of the Bokaro mill will also necessitate large expenditures of foreign exchange, approximately $500 per annual ton at the end of its first stage.[17] However, the average price of the steel produced by the mill would be roughly $172 per ton. The foreign exchange costs of the Bokaro mill would be repaid by import substitution in less than three years, assuming that the mill produces at full or nearly full capacity.

So short a pay-off period for foreign exchange costs is not uncommon for other Indian industries.[18] By itself it does not commend investment in the steel industry rather than, let us say, fertilizers, textiles or agriculture. Mention of the foreign exchange savings resulting from the expansion of India's steel industry is merely intended to point out that if India is to choose between importing steel or steel plant machinery then she would be justified in selecting the latter if her sole concern is minimization of expenditures of foreign exchange in anything but the very short run.

Conclusion

When special attention is given to foreign exchange, one of India's scarcest resources, the argument for investment in India's steel industry is strengthened. Unless India's consump-

[17] U.S. Steel, Vol. III, p. 4. U.S. Steel's cost estimates have been criticized for being too high. However, they are supported by the anticipated costs of Russian plant and equipment to be installed at Bokaro.

[18] This can easily be determined for many Indian industries from data presented in Government of India, Planning Commission, *Programmes of Industrial Development, 1961–66* (New Delhi: Government of India Publication, 1962), various pages.

tion of steel is to be curtailed, the alternative to the production of steel in India could be a substantial and, possibly, intolerable drain on India's foreign exchange earnings. Given that the assumptions made in this chapter are correct, the production of steel would appear to offer India an opportunity for economically defensible import substitution.

In fact, I argue in subsequent chapters that some of these assumptions are incorrect. Future steel targets are based on demand estimates that are exaggerated, in part because of grossly optimistic predictions of future rates of growth of the Indian economy, in part because of the implicit assumption by Indian planners that unduly low steel prices and current steel shortages for certain categories will continue. There is good reason to doubt that the Indian market for steel could sustain an average price equal to the revalued price of imported steel if future targets are achieved. There is also good reason to doubt the validity of the assumption that costs at new public sector mills will be comparable to those at TISCO. In fact, for a number of reasons, India's existing public sector mills have incurred excessive operating and replacement costs which have, in turn, resulted in their earning a *negative* rate of return on investment thus far. Finally, there is reason to question the proposed locations of new steel mills. These locations have been influenced by political and ideological considerations and could result in still higher costs of production at new public sector mills.

Therefore, I do not argue that the rate of return earned by new steel mills will justify the expansion of India's steel industry as now planned. Rather, this rate could justify expansion given improved planning and practices at new steel mills. The difference is important, for in it, in my opinion, lie many of the differences between developed and less developed economies. The exercise performed in this chapter, although necessary, is by itself sterile. If the experience of India's steel industry is to throw light upon the problem of less developed economies, it is also necessary and far more interesting to consider why the actual social rate of return earned by the industry differs from the potential rate estimated here.

7 | The Demand for Indian Steel

For many years after Independence India suffered from shortages of steel. These shortages were particularly severe during the late 1950s, after India's foreign exchange crisis forced a curtailment of imports but before any significant output could be realized from Second Plan programs for the industry's growth. At that time many Indian metal-working industries were operating at considerably less than their full capacities primarily because of their inability to obtain needed iron and steel.[1]

India still suffers from excess demand for certain forms of steel, notably flat products, alloy steels, and billets for rerollers. However, by 1964 she was producing a surplus of many heavy structurals, rails, bars, and rods. Because further growth of India's economy is anticipated, present surpluses may not continue for more than a few years. Even so, persistent shortages of steel in the past are no guarantee that future demand for all types of steel is assured. Plan targets for steel must be established with regard for the likely performance of consuming industries and of export markets.

[1] This was the conclusion of a delegation sent to India early in 1960 by the American Iron and Steel Institute. AISI, "Engineering Data on the Indian Steel Industry" (unpub., New York, 1960), Section III, p. 13. Complaints by various consumer interests about their inability to acquire needed iron and steel are commonplace in Indian business and trade journals. They were particularly numerous during the late 1950s.

Demand for Indian Steel during the Second Plan Period

Estimates of Indian demand for steel, reproduced in Table 9, are based on the total number of indents received by the Office of the Iron and Steel Controller and various sponsoring authorities, the agencies charged with steel distribution prior to March 1, 1964. It would appear that 4.3 million tons of finished steel, the production target for the last year of the Second Plan period, 1960–61, was conservative. Demand in that year exceeded this target by about 18 per cent. It would also appear that demand for steel has been increasing rapidly, by over 6 per cent per year since 1956. Were it to continue to grow at this rate it would reach 6.8 million tons by the end of the Third Plan period, an amount equal to the Third Plan production target for finished steel. Inadequacy of demand would seem to be no problem in both the recent past and the near future.

Table 9. Recorded Indian Demand for Steel, 1956–1962
(millions of tons)

Year	Demand	Year	Demand
1956–57	3.99	1959–60	4.79
1957–58	4.14	1960–61	5.07
1958–59	4.27	1961–62	5.40

Sources are indicated in the notes to Table E–1, Appendix E.

These data are misleading. In the first place there are almost certainly errors in demand data, estimates of demand in some instances varying substantially from one official source to another.[2] Moreover, it is generally accepted that in times of scarcity consumers have inflated their orders to obtain the amounts of steel they actually want, anticipating that their requests will be cut or the delivery of their steel delayed. During the past decade total consumption of steel in no year equalled demand

[2] For a fuller discussion of these errors, see Appendix E.

measured by indents on controlling authorities. Indents were cut by these authorities, often arbitrarily, encouraging multiple indenting and resulting in some overestimation of demand for steel.

Demand for steel is also influenced by the government's price policies, a subject considered at length in Chapter 5. The average selling price for steel was allowed to increase during the first half of the ten year period ending March 31, 1962. However, during the second half of this period it was held virtually constant even though other prices rose each year. To some extent the rapid increase in Indian demand for steel during the latter part of this ten-year period resulted from a cheapening of steel relative to other commodities, not growth of the Indian economy. In addition, because retention prices as a rule did not cover all costs of producing steel in India, and low selling prices reflected low retention prices, some demand was encouraged throughout the ten-year period in excess of what would have existed had Indian steel mills been allowed full cost prices for their products.

Indian demand for steel, given higher prices and the guaranteed supply of all indents, might not have justified the substantial investment in the steel industry during the Second Plan period. Some excess demand for steel could have been eliminated by an appropriate price increase and more effective screening of indents. To determine how much, I have subjected data on demand for steel for the decade ending March 1962 to the familiar statistical tool, multiple regression analysis.

Demand for steel, the dependent variable, is assumed to be a function of three independent variables: industrial production, the ratio of steel prices to India's wholesale price index, and the relationship between steel available for consumption and demand itself. A full description of this analysis, the data used, the variables included, and its limitations, is presented in Appendix E. It need be noted here only that there is a significant relationship between steel demand and each of these variables. As expected, the number of indents placed on controlling authorities is positively related to industrial production and negatively related to both the relative price of steel and the supply of consumers' indents by controlling authorities. Unfortunately, it is possible to obtain several different but nonetheless significant estimates of regression coefficients depending on which data are used or which variables included. The particular regression adopted in this chapter has been chosen for several reasons. First, it is based on observations of demand that, of the several available, would appear to be most reasonable. Second, it provides an excellent explanation of total variance in steel demand. Third, it indicates the lowest price elasticity of steel demand. Therefore, its use to appraise plan targets in effect gives Indian planners the maximum benefit of the doubt.

Indian demand for steel is highly inelastic. Even so, were steel prices in force in 1962 to be increased by the minimum amounts suggested in Chapter 5, data in Table 10 indicate that annual demand during the early 1960s could have been reduced by roughly 0.5 to 0.8 million tons depending on the price increase assumed.[3] Moreover, were indents properly screened by controlling authorities to remove overindenting, annual demand could have been reduced by another .30 million tons. The total reduction in annual demand for steel would have been slightly greater than the annual capacity of each of the new public sector mills built during the Second Plan period.

[3] In Table 6 it was estimated that a more appropriate retention price in 1962 would have been Rs. 762 per ton, allowing a 10 per cent return on investment in the steel industry, or Rs. 888 per ton, allowing a 15 per cent return. These prices are based on the long-run capital costs of new steel mills, capital costs after these mills have been expanded. The average costs of distributing finished steel to markets, Rs. 60 per ton, have been added to these estimates to determine full-cost selling prices and, when used in the regression, reductions in steel demand resulting from price increases.

The relative importance of the estimated reduction in steel demand, given higher steel prices and full supply of indents, is also indicated in Table 10. In all, between 15 and 20 per cent of total Indian demand for steel at the end of the Second Plan period appears to have been spurious. However, the remainder is only slightly less than the Second Plan output target for the industry. Because there were delays in implementing new capacity, the normal gestation period accompanying the erection of new mills, and these delays were to some extent unavoidable, the conclusion would seem justified that the aggregate Second Plan target for steel was supported by real Indian demand.

However, steel is not a homogeneous product. Broadly speaking, it can be divided into four distinct categories—rails and heavy sections, bars and light structurals, flat products, and other types of steel. There is relatively little substitution of these categories for each other either in production or consumption. For this reason demand for a broad category of steel may fall short of a plan target even though, overall, aggregate demand more or less equals the aggregate target for the industry. Recent events indicate that several specific Second Plan targets were, in fact, excessive. Steel sheets and other flat products remain in critically short supply. However, by the 1960s certain bars, rails, and structurals were being produced in excess of demand.

The regression analysis also enables an answer to a question left unanswered in Chapter 6. In estimating the social rate of return on investment in the industry the assumption was made that all steel produced in India could be sold at the Rs. 1030 per ton, the average import price revalued at one rupee equal to 14 cents. Were this, in fact, the price established by controlling authorities, predicted demand for steel during the early 1960s would have been approximately four million tons per year, still well above actual Indian production of steel at that

Table 10. Actual and Estimated Indian Demand for Steel, 1956–1962

Two-year period	Actual demand (millions of tons)[a]	Predicted demand (millions of tons)[b]	Reduction in predicted demand assuming: Full supply of indents (millions of tons)[c]	Reduction in predicted demand assuming: Higher steel prices, return equal to: 10 per cent[d] (millions of tons)	Reduction in predicted demand assuming: Higher steel prices, return equal to: 15 per cent[e] (millions of tons)	Per cent reduction in predicted demand, return equal to: 10 per cent (per cent)	Per cent reduction in predicted demand, return equal to: 15 per cent (per cent)
1956–58	8.13	8.12	.64	.65	1.25	15.9	23.3
1957–59	8.41	8.46	.86	.59	1.19	17.1	24.2
1958–60	9.06	9.04	.96	.68	1.28	18.1	24.8
1959–61	9.86	9.79	.77	.84	1.44	16.4	22.6
1960–62	10.47	10.52	.63	.95	1.56	15.0	20.8

[a] Computed from demand data presented in Table 9.

[b] Computed from the linear regression discussed in Appendix E, assuming official prices and actual consumption in various years.

[c] All indents are assumed filled by controlling authorities; in other words, consumption is assumed equal to demand. See Appendix E.

[d] The estimated long-run selling price in 1961–62, Rs. 822 per ton including Rs. 60 per ton transportation costs, and the wholesale price index for 1961–62 are used to measure an appropriate minimum relationship between the average price of steel and the wholesale price index for all years. See Table 6 and Appendix E.

[e] The estimated long-run selling price in 1961–62, Rs. 948 per ton including Rs. 60 per ton transportation costs, and the wholesale price index for 1961–62 are used to measure an appropriate maximum relationship between the average price of steel and the wholesale price index for all years. See Table 6 and Appendix E.

time. My conclusion that India's steel industry could earn a social rate of return justifying its expansion during the Second Plan period remains unchanged.

It should be stressed that this analysis is of necessity imperfect. Not only will changes in the data and the specification of the model increase the apparent price elasticity of demand, but perhaps worse, the assumption of increased steel prices could affect other independent variables in the model. A part of the increase in steel prices is a consequence of an assumed devaluation of the rupee. Other prices would also be affected by an increase in both the price of steel and foreign exchange. Moreover, devaluation could influence industrial production. Insofar as there is slack in the Indian economy there would presumably be greater domestic production of goods both for export and import substitution. Any discussion of a world that might have been is necessarily "iffy." It is clear that my analysis is no more favored, and its conclusions should be considered approximate at best.

Future Indian Demand for Steel

Demand for much of the additional steel output anticipated under the Second Plan already existed at the outset of the plan period. The number of indents placed on controlling authorities during the first year of the period, 1956–57, was only 0.5 million tons less than demand projected by planners for 1960–61, and imports, incontrovertible evidence of demand in excess of production, equalled the combined capacities of two of the three new steel mills built during the Second Plan period. Indian planners were able to select Second Plan targets with some assurance that most of the contemplated increase in production could be consumed by the Indian economy.

The planned increase in steel output during later plan periods is intended to a far greater extent to satisfy new demand created during these periods. Therefore, whether subsequent targets for steel are justified depends much more on the reliability of projections of future Indian demand for steel. Existing demand cannot be as sure a guide to Indian planners as it has been in the past.

The purpose of this section is to appraise projections of future Indian demand for finished steel by four separate organizations: The National Council of Applied Economic Research (NCAER);[4] M. N. Dastur & Company, Private, Ltd.;[5] The Perspective Planning Division of the Indian Planning Commission;[6] and the United States Steel Corporation which examined the proposed Bokaro steel mill for the United States Agency for International Development.[7] Estimates of demand for the last years of the Third and Fourth Plan periods, prepared by these organizations, are reproduced in Table 11. At first sight these estimates appear to substantiate plan targets for the industry. The Third Plan production target, 6.8 million tons of finished steel, is in most instances, modest in relation to them. The tentative Fourth Plan production target, 12 to 13 million tons of finished steel, is supported by all projections except that

[4] The National Council of Applied Economic Research is a private research institute in New Delhi which has prepared two studies of future Indian demand. The first is NCAER, *Appraisal of Steel Demand* (New Delhi: NCAER, 1960); the second, NCAER, *Reappraisal of Steel Demand* (New Delhi: NCAER, 1963), 2 volumes.

[5] M. N. Dastur & Company, Private, Ltd., Consulting Engineers, Calcutta, "Preliminary Report to Hindustan Steel Limited on the Establishment of an Integrated Steel Works at Bokaro" (unpub., December 1959), pp. 170ff. Dastur's original estimates have been revised since the preparation of its Bokaro report to keep abreast of changing plan targets. These revisions are contained in a subsequent report by the company dated July 1963.

[6] Government of India, Planning Commission, Perspective Planning Division, "Demand for Steel, Special Steel and Pig Iron, India: 1960–70" (mimeograph, New Delhi, 1961). The Perspective Planning Division has also conducted a later demand study dated April 1964.

[7] U.S. Steel Corporation, "A Techno-Economic Survey of a Proposed Integrated Steel Mill at Bokaro, Bihar State, India" (unpub. report submitted to the U.S. Government, Agency for International Development, March 1963), Vol. I.

of U.S. Steel. In fact all seven studies are dependent on one or more assumptions that bias their conclusions upward. There is reason to suspect that these projections overstate India's future needs for steel.

At least three major objections to these studies are warranted. First, use of the relationship between steel demand and investment in a sector may be justified were steel used only in construction, that is to say, in actual investment in the sector. However, its use to project demand for steel by manufacturing

Table 11. Estimates of Indian Demand for Salable Steel in 1965–66 and 1970–71[a] (thousands of tons)

	1965–66	1970–71
National Council of Applied Economic Research		
1960 study[b]	7,283	13,062
1963 study	6,902	13,594
M. N. Dastur & Company		
1959 study[b]	9,100–9,900	13,800–15,000
1963 study	8,740	14,440
Perspective Planning Division		
1961 study[b]	7,659	13,340
1964 study	6,728	13,579
U.S. Steel	6,916	11,236

[a] NCAER, *Appraisal of Steel Demand* (New Delhi: NCAER, 1960); NCAER, *Reappraisal of Steel Demand* (New Delhi: NCAER, 1963); M. N. Dastur & Co., Private, Ltd., *Preliminary Report to Hindustan Steel Limited on the Establishment of an Integrated Steel Works at Bokaro* (unpub., December 1959); Government of India, Planning Commission, Perspective Planning Division, *Demand for Steel, Special Steel and Pig Iron, India: 1960–1970* (mimeograph, New Delhi: 1961); U.S. Steel Corporation," "A Techno-Economic Survey of a Proposed Integrated Steel Mill at Bokaro, Bihar State, India" (unpub. report submitted to the U.S. Government, Agency for International Development, March 1963), Vol. I. Later estimates by M. N. Dastur and the Perspective Planning Division have been obtained from informants.

[b] Data have been converted from long tons to metric tons.

industries, as is done in the earlier NCAER study, is not satisfactory since some of the steel consumed by Indian industries is not related to investment but consumption. Steel is used in the manufacture of bicycles, cooking and eating utensils, automobiles, and other consumer durables produced in India. Steel is also used in the packaging and canning of such consumer goods as food and mineral and vegetable oils and in the production of cotton and jute baling hoops. It is expected by planners that the fraction of India's national income allocated to investment will increase and the fraction allocated to consumption will fall during future plan periods. Therefore, the assumption that all demand for steel is related to investment, rather than some to investment and some to consumption, in effect biases upward the NCAER's earlier demand estimates.

Probably the best method for predicting future demand for steel by manufacturing industries is that used in all other studies, estimation of the future output of these industries and, employing input coefficients, steel needed to achieve this output. However, with the exception of projections by U.S. Steel and the later projection by the Perspective Planning Division for 1965–66, all demand estimates suffer from a second source of upward bias, an uncritical acceptance of Third and proposed Fourth Plan targets for user industries. Plan targets are based upon a rate of growth considered desirable by the Perspective Planning Division, not a realistic assessment of what will happen during the Third and Fourth Plan periods. Under the Third Plan India's national income was to increase by between 5 and 6 per cent per year; her industrial production by 11 per cent. In fact, during the first four years of the plan, India's national income increased by little more than 3 per cent per year and her industrial production by less than 8 per cent.[8] Shortfalls in most plan targets were foreseen early in the plan

[8] Indexes of national income and industrial production appear in many sources. For example, see Government of India, Department of Statistics, Central Statistical Organization, *Monthly Statistics of Production of Se-*

period. It was recognized by the government two years after the beginning of the Third Plan that most targets would not be met, including targets for many industries that consume steel.[9]

Because of anticipated shortfalls in achieving most Third Plan targets the Perspective Planning Division reduced its earlier estimate of demand in 1965–66 by nearly one million tons. Yet it *increased* its earlier projection for 1970–71 to account for exports of steel assumed in its later but not in its earlier study. In short, projections of demand for the Fourth Plan period ignore the fact that Third Plan targets will have failed. They are doubly ambitious. Even assuming that Third Plan targets will be met, achievement of Fourth Plan targets would have required fulfillment of the optimistic assumptions of Indian planners. Given that Third Plan targets will fail, the achievement of Fourth Plan targets will now require, in addition, that the shortcomings of the Third Plan period be righted within five years. Some skepticism about proposed Fourth Plan targets is understandable.

There is little question that some downward adjustment in plan targets is necessary for an accurate estimate of future steel demand. This was in fact the assumption made by the United States Steel Corporation. Benefiting to some extent from hindsight, U.S. Steel considered India's plan targets to be unrealistic. It adjusted targets industry by industry, assuming levels of activity in final plan years approximately 80 per cent of official goals unless knowledge of a specific industry dictated otherwise.

I have also attempted a more realistic assessment of future

---

lected Industries of India (Calcutta: Government of India Publication, various months). See, also, Reserve Bank of India, *Bulletin* (various months), and *The Financial Express,* May 13, 1965.

[9] For an appraisal of the Indian economy's performance during the first two years of the Third Plan period, see Government of India, Planning Commission, *The Third Plan Mid-term Appraisal* (New Delhi: Government of India Publication, 1963). This study anticipated a shortfall in achievement of many plan targets. Even so, its predictions were excessively optimistic.

demand for steel by use of the regression analysis discussed earlier in this chapter. The average annual rate of increase in industrial production anticipated by the Indian Planning Commission for the Third Plan period, 11 per cent, was not achieved. A more likely rate of increase is 8 per cent, more or less the same performance anticipated by the U.S. Steel Corporation. Assuming that the average selling price for steel will continue to bear the same relationship to other prices as it did in 1961–62 and that there will be full supply of all indents, I estimate that demand for steel in 1965–66 will be 6.80 million tons, an amount virtually identical to the projection by U.S. Steel and the later projections by the NCAER and the Perspective Planning Division. On the other hand, were industrial output to increase at the planned rate of 11 per cent per year during the Third Plan period, demand for steel in 1965–66 would be 7.54 million tons, almost identical to the earlier estimate prepared by the Perspective Planning Division. This similarity of estimates, prepared differently, inspires somewhat greater confidence in my regression analysis than I might otherwise have had.

Given no change in relative steel prices, predicted Indian demand for steel in 1970–71 is 11.19 million tons.[10] This projection is based on an assumed rate of industrial growth of 8 per cent per year during the Third Plan period and 11 per cent per year during the Fourth Plan period. Once again the regression analysis yields virtually the same demand estimate as U.S. Steel's study.

There is still a third possible source of upward bias from which all seven projections of steel demand suffer. Many of the input and investment coefficients used in predicting the future needs of steel-consuming industries are not only given by technical relationships but to some extent have also been

[10] This projection is made despite doubts about the feasibility of using the regression model to predict demand beyond the Third Plan period. See Appendix E.

influenced by unduly low prices for steel.[11] The apparent need for steel by consuming industries per unit of product or rupee of investment will vary with the price of steel. Low steel prices have encouraged the holding of unnecessary inventories of steel and some wastage by those users capable of obtaining the steel they want at controlled prices. Low prices have also encouraged the substitution of steel for other materials. For this reason it is to be expected that future demand for steel at a price that will cover all costs of its production and distribution in India might be somewhat lower than estimated by U.S. Steel and by use of the regression model.

How much demand for steel would disappear with steel price increases cannot be easily determined. One may assume that the relationship between an appropriate average price for steel in 1962, estimated in Chapter 5, and other wholesale prices should remain constant in the future. Estimates based on this assumption are presented in Table 12 and, as before, indicate that demand for between 0.5 and 0.8 million tons would be eliminated by an increase in the price of steel.[12] However, this implies, among other things, that the costs of producing other commodities will remain unchanged, an assumption of doubtful validity since an increase in the price of steel and inputs used to produce steel would also raise the costs of producing many of these commodities. There are risks involved in the use of shadow prices. Perhaps all that can be said, or, for that matter, need be said, is that an appropriate increase in steel prices would result in some reduction in Indian demand. A best guess of the amount of this reduction is indicated by estimates presented in Table 12.

[11] However, some of the input coefficients used in the demand studies were taken from outside India and therefore reflect foreign not Indian price relationships.

[12] Once again, these estimates assume a 10 and 15 per cent return on long-run investment in the steel industry. Were return based on short-run investment, the reduction in demand would be still greater.

Table 12. Demand for Salable Steel in 1965–66 and 1970–71 Predicted from the Regression Model[a] (millions of tons)

	The average price of steel in 1961–62 assumed equal to:		
	Rs. 619	Rs. 822	Rs. 948
1965–66			
Annual rate of growth in industrial output during Third Plan period assumed to be:			
11 per cent	7.54	7.06	6.76
8 per cent	6.80	6.32	6.02
1970–71			
Annual rate of growth in industrial output during Fourth Plan period assumed to be:			
11 per cent after an 8 per cent rate of growth during Third Plan period	11.19	10.71	10.41

[a] Estimates of future steel demand have been computed from the linear regression model discussed in Appendix E. In particular, see Table E–6. I assume that all indents are fully satisfied, or, in other words, that consumption equals demand. For an explanation of the assumed selling prices of steel, see notes to Table 10.

The Feasibility of Future Plan Targets for Steel

Thus far demand has been considered in the aggregate, a necessary but undesirable simplification. There are several basic types of finished steel, the production of each type requiring relatively specialized rolling mill equipment. It pays a a steel mill possessing modern plant and machinery and a limited capacity to concentrate on the production of one type only. For this reason, Rourkela produces flat products alone, perhaps the most specialized of all forms of steel. Bhilai now manufactures rails and heavy structurals, and Durgapur light sections, bars, wheels, and axles. There is limited substitution of one type of steel for another in consumption. Railways cannot substitute bars for rails. Nor can rails be used in place of sheets in the manufacture of wagons, automobiles, and trucks.

India's is one of the few underdeveloped economies possessing both a substantial and rapidly expanding market for steel. Yet it may be questioned whether the future growth of Indian markets for specific types of steel will be sufficient to justify planned increases in their production. For the purpose of the following discussion, steel demand has been divided into four basic categories. I have accepted demand projections for each of these categories, prepared by U.S. Steel, as most reasonable *at existing price relationships.* These projections are reproduced in Table 13.

Probable future supply and demand relationships for steel are not encouraging. There will still be a surplus of heavy sections and railway materials, primarily heavy structurals, at the end of the Third Plan period. Excess production of these types of steel throughout the period, which was said to be temporary, may be more permanent than is generally thought. If so, the Bhilai plant, which specializes in these sections, would seem to have been expanded too rapidly, unless, of course, excess production can be exported to India's advantage. On the contrary, there will still be a severe shortage of flat products necessitating continued imports if actual demand is to be met by supply. India's shortage of flat products is a result of her inability to erect the Bokaro mill during the Third Plan period.

If estimates of demand prepared by U.S. Steel are accurate, projected surpluses and deficits at the end of the Fourth Plan period are even more disquieting. In response to current shortages of flat products, the Government of India has decided, tentatively, to expand flat product output at all public sector mills. Not only will increased capacity at Rourkela and Bokaro

Table 13. Estimated Demand, Production and Deficit of Salable Steel in India: 1965–66 and 1970–71
(thousands of tons of salable steel)

	1965–66[a]			1970–71		
	Demand	Production	Deficit	Demand[a]	Production[b]	Deficit
Railway materials and heavy sections[c]	1,691	1,993	(302)	2,591 }	4,103	1,446
Bars and light structurals[d]	1,816	1,705	111	2,958 }		
Flat products[e]	2,737	1,310	1,427	4,523	5,445	(922)
Miscellaneous[f]	672	587	85	1,163	965	198
Total	6,916	5,595	1,321	11,235	10,513	722

[a] Demand and production data have been taken from U.S. Steel Corporation, "A Techno-Economic Survey of a Proposed Integrated Steel Mill at Bokaro, Bihar State, India" (unpub. report submitted to the U.S. Government, Agency for International Development, March 1963), Vol. I, pp. 68–69.

[b] The output of existing units of public sector mills is assumed equal to the anticipated capacities of these mills at the end of the Third Plan period. Government of India, Planning Commission, *Programmes of Industrial Development, 1961–66* (New Delhi: Government of India Publication, 1962), pp. 15–16. The output of existing units of private sector mills and other producers is assumed equal to their anticipated output at the end of the Third Plan period. U.S. Steel, Vol. I, p. 65. The industry's Fourth Plan targets had not been set by mid-1965. It was anticipated that increments in output by the end of the period would be: IISCO, .22 million tons of bars; Rourkela, approximately .5 million tons of flat products; Bhilai, approximately .55 million tons of plates and .225 million tons of forging and tube blooms and other semis; Durgapur, 1.30 million tons of strips; and Bokaro, approximately 1.0 million tons of flat products. Information supplied by the Ministry of Steel and Mines, May 1965.

[c] Rails, sleepers, fishplates, wheels, tires, and axles, structurals, and heavy bars.

[d] Wire rods (bars), bars, and bar shapes.

[e] Hot rolled sheets, strip and skelp, cold rolled sheets and strip, galvanized sheets, electric sheets, tinplate and plates.

[f] Wire rods (wire), special steels, forging blooms and billets, and hot rolled skelp for conversion to tubes.

be devoted exclusively to flat products, as expected, but also Bhilai will install facilities to produce half a million tons of plates and Durgapur to produce more than a million tons of strips. The result of this massive investment in the production of flat products will probably be surplus capacity of nearly one million tons by 1970–71. On the contrary, only small increases in the output of other types of steel are anticipated during the Fourth Plan period, barring the erection of a fifth public sector steel mill or substantial expansion of existing private sector mills. For this reason, in 1970–71 there may be a deficit of more than 1.6 million tons of other types of steels.

Tentative plans for increasing India's output of flat products can be questioned for still another reason. Demand for flat products may be more responsive to price changes than demand for rails, structurals, and bars.[13] Therefore, were steel prices established that reflect all costs of producing steel, demand for flat products would decrease more than in proportion to demand for other types of steel. This possibility is of more than academic interest. U.S. Steel's demand estimates implicitly assumed steel prices in force prior to 1963. Since 1963 flat product prices have been increased more than in proportion to prices of other types of steel and many other commodities.

Predicted Indian demand for steel in the early 1970s exceeds total anticipated production by about 0.7 million tons.[14] This deficit is roughly equivalent to the output of finished steel by the fifth public sector mill now contemplated by the government to come into production by the end of the Fourth Plan period. On the surface, it would seem that India's anticipated deficit in

[13] A disproportionate number of questionable uses of Indian steel, probably encouraged by low steel prices, involve flat products. An example has been the government's use of sheets in village level construction in place of the more traditional mud, thatch, brick, and tile. Another has been the accumulation of excessive inventories of flat products by at least two government factories to hedge against possible scarcities of this type of steel.

[14] See Table 13.

steel would justify this mill, particularly in view of the inevitability of a two or three year delay in reaching production at full or nearly full capacity.

There is reason to question this conclusion. In the first place, were steel prices increased, a best guess of the size of the resulting reduction in steel demand would be 0.5 to 0.8 million tons, more or less the same as the anticipated deficit in 1970–71.[15] A price increase is an alternative to the erection of a new steel mill that should enter into the calculations of India's planners. Moreover, India cannot hope to achieve complete autonomy in steel production at this stage of her development. Some types of steel are demanded in amounts too small for their profitable rolling in India. Others require technical skills that India has not yet developed. Imports of these types of steel will continue to be necessary for many years, even though India may have both the desire and the wherewithal to expand her industry.

An appraisal of plans for increasing India's capacity for producing bars and light sections is further complicated by India's rerolling mills and secondary producers. At present these mills are operating at substantially less than their full capacities. For the most part rerolling mills produce bars and bar sections from billets, an intermediate section supplied to them by the main producers, and scrap obtained from the market. The output of billet and scrap rerollers was only 0.6 million tons in 1961–62. Yet it is claimed by the Steel Rerolling Mills Association of India that, were these mills to operate on two shifts, they could produce 1.4 million tons of finished products.[16] Their inability to operate at a higher percentage of their capacities, it is claimed, is a result of their inability to obtain adequate supplies of billets and scrap.[17]

[15] This was the conclusion of my regression analysis already discussed in this chapter.

[16] Unpublished information supplied by the Steel Rerolling Mills Association of India in Calcutta in January 1963.

[17] Another reason has been a shortage of electricity and fuel.

There is some reason to doubt whether increases in the output of India's rerolling mills would represent worthwhile production. Many Indian rerolling mills, particularly those producing finished steel from scrap, cannot manufacture high quality steel. In addition, they are often equipped to roll or prefer to roll those sections already manufactured by the main producers, not those sections demanded in tonnages too small for economic rolling by the main producers and better suited for rerolling mills.[18] Nevertheless, it is likely that some additional useful output of bars and light sections would result from the fuller utilization of under-utilized rerolling mill capacity. Yet, to my knowledge, no attempt has been made to determine how much or in what way useful additional output of finished steel could be obtained by supplying a greater number of billets and scrap to these mills. Planning for the expansion of India's output of these sections may be condoning some duplication of steel-making facilities.

My analysis supports a far less ambitious program for the expansion of India's steel industry than is anticipated by Indian planners. If tentative plans for the steel industry are implemented, then there is reason for concern that there will be some production of steel in excess of demand, assuming for the moment that surpluses cannot be exported. At the very least, excess production may be disguised by questionable uses of steel encouraged, in part, by low steel prices.

Prospects for Exporting Indian Steel

Thus far one important consideration has been ignored. If Indian steel can be exported in exchange for useful goods or services or a convertible currency, the Indian market for steel need not be a limitation upon plan targets. Then by all means India might consider producing steel for export to earn needed

[18] Raj Committee, "A Preliminary Report on Steel Control" (mimeograph, Ministry of Steel and Heavy Industries, Department of Iron and Steel, 1963), p. 15.

foreign exchange. The possibility of India's developing export markets for her metals industry, particularly her steel industry, has been discussed for many years. Although this subject deserves careful consideration, I attempt no more than a cursory review of circumstances that will affect prospects for the export of Indian steel.

In 1962 I asked several people associated with India's steel industry whether Indian steel could be sold abroad in significant amounts. They tended to answer in two ways. Some declared the question to be entirely academic since Indian demand will be so great that there will be no significant exportable surplus in the foreseeable future. Others declared that Indian steel should in any event have little difficulty competing in foreign markets. This same facile assumption that surplus production could be exported with ease has also crept into some of the official literature.[19]

I am somewhat less sanguine about prospects for the advantageous export of Indian steel, but not because India does not *in theory* possess a comparative advantage in the production of steel. Rather, there are at present certain institutional impediments to the export of Indian steel, perhaps the most obvious being the maintenance of an unrealistic rate of exchange. During the postwar period Indian steel was priced below steel traded on the world market. However, in recent years Indian steel prices have risen relative to world prices, paralleling the progressive overvaluation of the rupee. Although a subsidy is granted on exported steel, as of 1963 it was not sufficient to overcome the price disadvantage suffered by the Indian industry.

This price disadvantage also stems from a developing glut on world markets as a result of surplus capacity in the steel indus-

[19] For example, see Government of India, Planning Commission, *Programmes of Industrial Development, 1956–61* (New Delhi: Government of India Publication, 1956), p. 16. Also in preparing its later demand projection, the Perspective Planning Division assumed that India would export 0.5 million tons of steel in 1970–71.

tries of many nations. World prices have been depressed. It is claimed that export prices have, in some instances, been held below comparable domestic prices or, more to the point, that there has been dumping on the world market.[20]

There should also be concern about the quality of steel produced in both public and private sector mills.[21] Because the Indian market for steel is highly protected by import controls and has for years suffered from excess demand, Indian producers have been able to allow their standards of quality to slip without serious consequence to themselves. World markets are not protected. On the contrary, because they have become so competitive in recent years, they may well demand more rigorous standards of quality than might be considered normal under other circumstances or substantial price concessions as a penalty for acceptance of poor or variable quality.

There have been several instances of the export of poor quality steel that have recently come to light. For example, late in 1962 controversy raged over who was responsible for shipment to the United Kingdom of off-heat ingots produced at one of the government mills. The exporter blamed HSL for having marketed the ingots; HSL blamed the exporter for having misrepresented the quality of the ingots to the foreign buyer. No matter who was at fault, the future export of Indian steel has suffered.

If India is to export significant amounts of steel, she will have to emulate other established exporters not only by reducing the export price of Indian steel and improving quality, but also by

[20] For a discussion of the prospects for exporting Indian steel, world prices for steel, and, in particular, the incidence of dumping, see Sir Jehangir Ghandy, *Steel, Some Problems of Development,* a pamphlet published by TISCO based on a speech to the Engineering Institute of India, Calcutta, Dec. 24, 1959, pp. 8–9. The export of steel has also been considered by Sir Biren Mookerjee, Chairman of IISCO, in several of his annual speeches to shareholders. Of particular interest are those presented in 1959 and 1961.

[21] See Chapters 5 and 8.

matching the attractive credit and deferred payment terms generally granted to foreign buyers. Indian producers would have to establish sales outlets in nations that would become their principal foreign customers and maintain substantial stocks of steel so that foreign orders could be filled without delay. The government would have to remove several of the administrative hurdles that now delay the export of steel. In short, much remains to be done before India will be able to compete actively in foreign markets for steel.

At the beginning of the Second Five Year Plan the government declared that 0.2 to 0.3 million tons of steel could be exported in 1960–61.[22] In fact only 6,000 tons of finished steel and 69,000 tons of intermediate forms—ingots, blooms, and billets—were exported that year. In early 1962 the Office of the Iron and Steel Controller set aside 0.1 million tons of heavy structurals and rounds for export the following year. In fact exports of finished steel rose by only 4,000 tons in 1962–63. Export markets have provided an outlet for surplus production of semifinished steel.[23] However, it should not be presumed that because unwanted surpluses of intermediate forms were disposed of through international trade that the same might also be true of unwanted surpluses of finished steel. In the first place possible future surpluses of finished steel would be far greater than the amounts of both semifinished and finished steel that have thus far been exported. Perhaps more important, semifinished steel does not have to pass as rigorous standards of quality, particularly physical standards, as does finished steel. An ingot, bloom, or billet is reprocessed by its purchaser. Fin-

[22] Government of India, Planning Commission, *Programmes of Industrial Development, 1956–61*, p. 16.

[23] This surplus production was a normal consequence of the phased commissioning of the new units erected under the Second Plan. Exports of semifinished steel were negligible in 1959–60, rose to 69,000 tons in 1960–61, were 57,000 tons in 1961–62, and were once again negligible in 1962–63.

ished steel is generally used in the form in which it is received. It will be far more difficult for India to sell finished steel abroad if the quality of this steel is substandard.

There is reason to question whether the export of steel is necessarily to India's advantage. During the twenty-four months ending March 31, 1963, only 16 per cent of India's exports of finished steel were sold to western Europe, the United States, Australia, and New Zealand. The remainder was sold, for the most part, to countries in Asia, Africa, and eastern Europe, many of which have nonconvertible currencies.[24] How is India being paid for her steel? If she is receiving hard currencies or useful goods and services in return for the steel she exports, then it would be to her advantage to export steel. If, instead, she is accumulating reserves of nonconvertible currencies or purchasing unnecessary goods and services, it is questionable that the export of this steel benefits the Indian economy any more than the currencies or the goods being purchased with it. If she is selling at any price simply to rid herself of unwanted inventories, then the export of steel may not allow adequate remuneration for the plant and equipment used to produce the exported steel. Unnecessary production of certain types of steel may merely be disguised by their disadvantageous export, just as some unnecessary production has already been disguised by artificial demand created by unduly low steel prices.

It is by no means apparent that any excess production of steel can easily be exported to India's advantage. Unless a number of essential steps are taken to promote steel exports, plan targets for the industry should be constrained by probable future Indian demand for steel. This being so, Fourth Plan targets for the industry would appear to be excessive.

[24] Estimated from Government of India, Department of Commercial Intelligence and Statistics, *Monthly Statistics of the Foreign Trade of India* (Calcutta: Government of India Publication, various months).

Summary

In this and the previous chapters I have attempted to determine whether or not India has been justified in investing so heavily in her steel industry under her five year plans. Despite the fact that the steel industry requires a substantial investment in capital and is not well suited to the factor endowments generally ascribed by economists to underdeveloped economies, India is capable of producing steel at a cost to the economy competitive with the real price of imported steel and at a real profit adequate for Indian industry. For this reason, primarily, private interests first developed India's steel industry earlier in this century, when there were few controls over entry, pricing, and distribution, and produced most of the steel consumed in India at the outbreak of World War II. In large part, the cost-competitiveness of Indian steel is a result of India's endowment with adequate supplies of all raw materials necessary for the manufacture of steel and the location of these raw materials in relatively close proximity to one another.

Critics of the emphasis placed on expansion of India's steel industry have suggested that India could more profitably concentrate on such alternatives as social overhead, agriculture, and light industries. I would agree that India's planners have placed too much importance on steel, given a realistic assessment of Indian demand. However, without steel, whether imported or produced domestically, the expansion of India's railways, the development of Indian ports, and the manufacture of locomotives and wagons, would be impossible. The production of agricultural tools and construction of some irrigation projects would be difficult if not impossible. Nor could a number of light industries, well suited for employment of large numbers, expand their activities. Some of these industries, notably the manufacture of bicycles, ceiling fans, and sewing machines, have begun to penetrate markets outside India. Unless steel supplies keep in pace with the demands of her industries, the growth of India's economy will be impeded by a repetition of the steel shortages that hindered its orderly progress during the late 1950s.

Yet simply because India seems to have a comparative advantage in steel and steel has been in short supply in the past does not mean that plan targets for the industry are justified. Projections of steel demand have in various ways been exaggerated. To some extent, by overproducing certain bars, rails, and structurals, India is today paying the price for past adherence to unrealistic demand estimates for these sections. If future plan targets for the industry are to be achieved, the consequences could be much more severe. An unbridled fascination for steel, which would appear to exist among some persons associated with planning for the industry's growth, could result in some misallocation of Indian resources.

The analysis of these chapters is based on certain assumptions. First, TISCO's works costs have been adopted as a measure for the entire industry. In fact the works costs of India's public sector mills are considerably higher, and the real works costs of proposed future mills may be still higher, than those incurred by TISCO. Second, estimated investment costs assume more or less normal usage of plant and equipment. Because of certain malpractices at the government's mills, it is likely that the true investment costs of these mills, if properly measured, would be far higher than has been assumed here. Third, for various reasons the actual useful output of the government's mills has been lower than the production at full or nearly full capacity that I have accepted as a norm for the industry.

The rates of return I have estimated are not an unobtainable ideal for India's steel industry. On the contrary, they are based on the actual costs of India's private sector mills during the early 1960s. Although there is no one reason for the inability of India's public sector mills to match the performance of private sector mills, one important reason has been the policies of the Indian government. The consequences of the government's policies of control were discussed in Chapter 5. In the remaining chapters the consequences of other policies affecting the operations and locations of future public sector mills will also be considered.

8 | The Performance of Indian Steel Mills

India's steel mills, particularly her public sector steel mills, have encountered a number of difficulties during the past several years. Some of these difficulties were necessary "teething troubles" for new enterprise. However, many also resulted from a relative neglect of some of the problems of utilizing new capacity, in addition to creating it, by those responsible for the industry's growth.

By and large this chapter is a description of the performance of India's steel mills through the first quarter of 1963. Some of the conditions at these mills appear to have improved since that time. Although my discussion may be dated, I do not consider this to be a serious problem. This chapter is not meant to be an exercise in muckraking, but rather an academic appraisal of new industrial enterprise in an essentially nonindustrial economy. By using India's steel industry as one example of recent industrial expansion, I hope to throw light on more general and longer range problems of industrial growth in less developed economies.

Production as a Measure of Performance

Production as a percentage of capacity, although not a meaningless measure of a plant's success, may be misleading. Rated capacity is an ambiguous concept that varies from mill to mill. There is also some reason to question the relevance and even the accuracy of production data themselves. Despite misgivings about the usefulness of this measure, the output of each of India's major steel mills, computed as a percentage of rated capacity, is presented in Table 14. This statistic, properly interpreted, gives some indication of the relative performance of each of India's steel mills.

During the early 1960s TISCO produced salable steel at a higher percentage of capacity than ingot steel. The company emerged from its most recent expansion program with some difficulties in its primary iron and steel making units. It was able to compensate for its inability to produce ingot steel at anticipated levels by rolling abnormally large tonnages of salable products. To some extent, this accomplishment was made possible by changes in the composition and quality of its output.

By contrast, IISCO has been a mill in balance. Throughout the early 1960s its plant produced ingot and salable steel at the same levels of capacity. However, late in 1962 there was a substantial increase in its production, immediately after the government's controversial retention price decision. IISCO's output returned to its previous level in mid-1964, primarily because of a mishap in its blast furnaces. The promise by the company's chairman to produce at full capacity, even at the sacrifice of quality, seems to have been no idle threat.[1]

Judged by output as a percentage of its capacity, Bhilai has not only outperformed the other two public sector mills, but since 1962 has outperformed the two private sector mills as well. Bhilai's success has been real. However, for reasons discussed below, Bhilai's production statistics are misleading, giving the impression of substantially better performance than has actually been achieved.

Rourkela has been known as the problem child of the industry, and unfortunately even its most trivial difficulties have

[1] Sir Biren Mookerjee, quoted in *Capital*, Aug. 8, 1963, p. 205.

Table 14. Production of Steel as a Percentage of Capacity at India's Major Steel Mills, 1961–62 through 1964–65[a]

Type of steel	TISCO	IISCO	Rourkela	Bhilai	Durgapur
INGOT STEEL					
Annual capacity (millions of tons)	*2.00*	*1.00*	*1.00*	*1.00*	*1.00*
Production as a percentage of capacity					
1961–62	82	93	35	79	46
1962–63	90	100	70	105	73
1963–64	95	103	80	114	97
1964–65	98	95	98	113	101
SALABLE STEEL					
Annual capacity (millions of tons)	*1.50*	*.80*	*.72*	*.77*	*.81*
Production as a percentage of capacity					
1961–62	88	92	26	65	45
1962–63	94	99	58	102	62
1963–64	100	101	78	114	89
1964–65	105	94	96	118	89

[a] For convenience I have used unpublished production data supplied by John Young, an independent consulting engineer who is familiar with the Indian steel industry. These data are, for the most part, identical to production data published elsewhere. Monthly data up to January 1963 are presented in Government of India, Ministry of Steel and Heavy Industries, *Iron and Steel Control, Monthly Bulletin* (Calcutta: Government of India Publication, various months). Annual production data are found in the annual reports of the various steel companies.

become front page copy for many Indian newspapers.[2] By 1962 Rourkela had reached its nadir. Not only was it producing well below its rated capacity, it also suffered from labor troubles, demoralization of skilled personnel, and some destruction of equipment. Although Rourkela was able to produce both ingot and salable steel at nearly full capacity by 1964, its production data are also misleading. Rourkela's greater output of salable steel measures, among other things, the production of steel of limited usefulness to the Indian economy.

Durgapur's problems have not been as thoroughly publicized. A bottleneck in the mill's steel melt shop was overcome late in 1962 enabling near capacity production of ingot steel. However, continued difficulties in the plant's intermediate rolling mills and certain of its finishing mills prohibited corresponding increases in salable steel output, with the result that Durgapur's mill was unbalanced long after its completion. Durgapur's output statistics are also misleading. Like Bhilai and Rourkela, it has produced abnormally large amounts of steel of limited usefulness to the Indian economy.

At least until 1964 the principal, if not the sole, criterion by which the public sector mills were judged was output. As a result, there was an incentive for the mills to neglect other important objectives if they conflicted with output—the production of good quality steel, the creation of balance between

[2] Occasionally, the industry's difficulties are also publicized with unusual candor by the government. Several years ago a team of experts was sent to India by the West German government to investigate Rourkela's difficulties. Its report, made public by the Indian government, for the most part dismissed claims that Rourkela's difficulties were a result of faulty equipment. It instead placed most blame on mismanagement and improper operation of the Rourkela mill. Solveen Committee, "Report of Experts on the Rourkela Iron and Steel Works" (mimeograph, New Delhi, 1962). Rourkela has also been investigated by several government committees, the most recent being the Committee on Public Undertakings of the Lok Sabha early in 1965. This committee found several "disquieting features" about the performance of the Rourkela mill. For press comment on the committee's report, see *Hindustan Times*, May 12, 1965, p. 5.

their units, minimization of costs of production, and adherence to satisfactory maintenance procedures.

The problems of the Rourkela and Durgapur mills were complicated by the frequent and, in this instance, invidious comparison with Bhilai. Bhilai rolls the simplest of products, heavy sections which require less reprocessing than the lighter sections rolled by Durgapur and the flat products rolled by Rourkela. Partly for this reason, Bhilai was able to achieve full capacity production earlier than the other two plants. Moreover the concept of capacity varies. Although actual capacity is probably greater than rated capacity at most mills, Bhilai's actual capacity is substantially in excess of its rated capacity.[3] Built-in excess capacity has provided Bhilai with an initial advantage. Because the plant has met its output targets with relative ease, its management has been able to tackle other equally important problems. Several of the difficulties incurred by Rourkela and Durgapur have resulted from their attempts to emulate Bhilai's output achievements without this cushion, encouraging the sacrifice of other objectives that conflict with production.

All public sector mills have from time to time manufactured certain types of steel in excess of demand in an attempt to establish output records.[4] Both Bhilai and Durgapur have also been reluctant to turn new rolls to increase the number of sections they produce. Because of their limited selection of rolls, the mills are, as a rule, able to produce only standard items for

[3] Production consistently in excess of 110 per cent of capacity gives one cause to wonder how the term capacity has been defined at the Bhilai plant. The former Minister of Steel and Heavy Industries, Mr. C. Subramaniam, has stated that Bhilai's capacity should be placed at 1.25 rather than 1.00 million ingot tons. *Hindustan Times*, Oct. 25, 1962, p. 7. The capacity of the Bhilai mill has been set at 1.20 million tons of ingot steel and slightly less than 1.00 million tons of salable steel in Hindustan Steel Ltd., *9th Annual Report*, 1962–63, p. 19.

[4] For example, in mid-1963 Durgapur overproduced a certain section and then dumped it on the Calcutta market, depressing its price. The mill's objective was to set an output record. *Capital*, July 18, 1963, p. 73. Other instances of this practice have been cited by informants.

which there is a bulk demand adequate for long rolling periods. The rolling of these sections minimizes unproductive downtime for roll changes. Moreover, these sections are often comparatively heavy, thus permitting greater tonnages per unit of time. Rourkela has also concentrated on the production of heavy finished products, notably plates, in part by decision but also by default. By 1963 its cold rolling mill was still unable to operate at anywhere near its full capacity and large tonnages of plates provided a convenient and, so far as the plant was concerned, rewarding outlet for some of its semifinished steel.

Many Indian consumers have had to accept whatever steel they receive, even if it does not meet their exact specifications.[5] Some indentors have been shipped only a part of their orders, often those sections that can be rolled in large tonnages. If overproduction of certain types of steel relative to demand encourages greater conformity to standards, the attempt by India's steel mills to maximize output with only secondary concern for demand may be beneficial. One problem facing India's steel industry is the multiplicity of the sections it is expected to roll. However, if overproduction of certain sections encourages conformity to heavier standards, such as the use of a plate instead of a sheet, then this practice could result in the wasteful use of steel and the inefficient application of Indian resources.

The government plants have also produced large tonnages for their own inventories. This is to be expected during the first years of the mills' operations. However, data presented in Table 15 indicate that by March 1963 inventories of finished and semifinished steel at each of the mills were as great as or greater than those held by IISCO, a plant with essentially the same

[5] Although many sections are no longer in short supply, the inability of consumers to indent directly on steel plants, rather than through the Joint Plant Committee, in effect insures continuation of a producers' monopoly and the possible neglect of consumers' wants. See Chapter 5.

capacity but a substantially higher volume of sales. Inventory accumulation at Bhilai appears to have been halted by 1963.[6] However, inventory accumulation of Rourkela and Durgapur showed little sign of letting up.

It was obvious to even a casual observer that inventories at the government plants were becoming excessive by early 1963. Durgapur and Bhilai had amassed abnormal stocks of ingots and blooms, intermediate forms of steel that have little marketability. Rourkela had also accumulated large stocks of semifinished steel and coils, a product of its hot strip mill that generally requires further processing before sale. Unusual difficulties have plagued some of the units that roll ingot and semifinished steel, notably Durgapur's blooming and billet mills and Rourkela's slabbing and cold rolling mills. Yet activities in preceding stages of iron and steel production have often not been curtailed to allow a reduction in inventories of semifinished steel. The pressures to maintain ingot and semifinished steel production at the highest levels attainable to fulfill and in some instances to over-fulfill output targets have been far too strong.

Excessive inventories not only mean the unremunerative use of India's resources, they have contributed directly to some of the difficulties of the public sector plants. To some extent the movement of products from one unit of a mill to the next has been impeded by accumulations of semifinished steel.[7] Some storage of steel in open fields has also been necessary. Under such circumstances the consequences of continued high levels

[6] However, according to several informants Bhilai has reduced its inventories by selling its steel at unremunerative prices.

[7] Early in 1963 one of India's public sector mills had encountered a bottleneck in its soaking pits. (Soaking pits are ovens that reheat ingots to a uniform temperature suitable for rolling.) An official of the mill blamed this bottleneck on an initial error in the plant's design. A non-Indian technician blamed it on an excessive accumulation of ingots in front of the soaking pits. These ingots inhibited the movement of hot ingots, increased reheating time, and reduced the effective capacity of the soaking pits.

Table 15. Sales and Inventories of Semifinished and Finished Products by Indian Steel Mills, 1960–63[a]

(Rs. million)

	Rourkela	Bhilai	Durgapur	TISCO	IISCO
1960–61					
Sales less rebates payable to government	91	216	102	791	539
Changes in inventories of finished and semifinished products	36	19	15	12	15
Inventories of finished and semifinished products	62	37	19	115	44
1961–62					
Sales less rebates payable to government	146	338	225	863	584

	Rourkela	Bhilai	Durgapur	TISCO	IISCO
Changes in inventories of finished and semi-finished products	14	41	17	−9	14
Inventories of finished and semifinished products	76	78	36	106	58
1962–63					
Sales less rebates payable to government	343	527	362	995	638
Changes in inventories of finished and semi-finished products	30	−10	22	6	0
Inventories of finished and semifinished products	106	68	58	102[b]	58

[a] Data have been computed from information presented in the annual reports of TISCO, IISCO, and HSL, various years.
[b] Rs. 10 million discrepancy not explained.

of production in preceding stages of steel manufacture may be still greater difficulties in subsequent stages and some production of semifinished steel that will eventually have little more than scrap value.

The quality of steel produced by the public sector mills has also been criticized by informants. In any new enterprise it will take a while before the skills and procedures necessary for the manufacture of a consistently good quality product can be developed. Even so, emphasis on production at the public sector mills has resulted in some neglect of quality. Several times I was told that for many consumers the testing of steel had become a mere form, and that test certificates, affidavits of good quality, were being attached to inferior steel. The output of steel can also be maximized by the deliberate production of steel that, if not of poor quality, has a higher probability of being of poor quality than steel produced under more rigorous standards.[8]

Mills have been able to dispose of poor quality products because of persistent shortages of some forms of steel, and the system of distributing steel, which forces most consumers to purchase from plants not necessarily of their own choosing. However, some consumers are sufficiently influential to impose standards of quality on India's steel mills, perhaps the most prominent being the railways. India's railways station inspectors at mills that produce railway materials, and these inspectors are empowered to reject steel if it does not meet test specifications. Government oil companies are major consumers of tubes produced at Rourkela and are also able to reject steel that does not meet their standards. Since there is little market

[8] See footnote 10, Chapter 5. For example, in one public sector mill, early in 1963, the shears that crop the ends of blooms were not functioning. Nevertheless, blooms were still being rolled and passed on to the next unit uncropped in order not to stint on output, substantially increasing the outturn of defective steel and also the likelihood of roll damage.

for rejected railway materials and tubes, the principal alternative to the production of suitable quality steel in these categories is the production of scrap.[9]

At some risk of oversimplification, good quality steel is needed for many purposes by investment goods industries, while poor or middling quality steel can be used more extensively in the manufacture of consumer goods. The production of poor quality steel has, to some extent, diverted steel from investment to consumption, that is to say, from uses that have been accorded highest priorities by Indian planners to uses that have not. The production of poor quality steel has also jeopardized the future export of Indian steel in significant quantities.[10] In some instances, it has resulted in the mills' unnecessary processing of steel that will have only scrap value.[11] When passed on to consumers, poor quality steel can lead to needless haulage by India's railways and unnecessary reprocessing by users.[12] It is not obvious that the marginal increments in output made possible by sacrificing quality are worth these costs, particularly now that India produces many sections in excess of demand.

The managements of the public sector mills have had an incentive to maximize output because this is the principal criterion by which they have been judged. Labor has also had

[9] Second class rails can be used in sidings. By early 1963, output of second class rails outstripped India's demand for sidings with the result that the mill accumulated substantial inventories of unsalable rails.

[10] See Chapters 5 and 7.

[11] For example, in early 1963 one public sector mill produced ingots with excessive refractory inclusions, small particles that enter crude steel in open hearth furnaces. This steel was not rejected, allegedly to maximize the melt shop's output of ingot steel. For the most part defective steel was passed on to consumers. Some was also forged into railway wheels at the mill. When machined, excessive refractory inclusions are said to have caused abnormal breakage of the wheels and, at times, damage to machinery.

[12] One informant described a consumer who was shipped plates of uneven thickness, including one that had a piece of furnace brick imbedded in it. Most of these plates probably had little more than scrap value.

a similar incentive. Bonuses have been related to physical output, not to profits, nor even to the value of steel produced. At one mill it was explained that any attempt to produce thinner gauge products could result in labor unrest because it would reduce the physical output of the mill.

Production statistics are misleading. This is particularly true of the most often quoted statistic, output of ingot steel. As a rule ingots cannot be sold, and a significant number have gone into excessive inventories. Output statistics for salable steel are also misleading. Production of salable steel includes blooms, coils, and second class rails that, despite their generic classification, are largely unsalable. Even sales data do not necessarily measure useful or at least needful production. Some finished steel is being sold without regard for consumer wants and at prices that do not cover costs of production.

One economist, after hearing the conclusions expressed in this section, exclaimed, "This is the Soviet Union during the 1930s." Interestingly, the Soviet Union has now come a long way from its own original emphasis on output, and its experience could serve as a guideline for India. Perhaps a more appropriate measure of the performance of India's public sector mills would be the value of their output or, better, the value of their sales. However, consideration must also be given to the value of the resources consumed to produce this output, the mills' costs of production. The yardstick that encompasses all these measures is profitability, the criterion used in capitalist countries and used increasingly even in the Soviet bloc.

Costs of Production at Indian Mills

In Chapter 6, I used TISCO's works costs to determine the rate of return to the Indian economy resulting from investment in steel. At least until 1964 all public sector mills incurred substantially higher operating costs than India's private sector mills, despite the fact that their equipment is newer and, presumably, more efficient.[13] Until a new mill has normalized its operations, it will almost certainly incur greater production costs than an established plant. Even so, costs of production at the public sector mills have been unnecessarily high, primarily because of circumstances that were avoidable and not because of an intrinsic disadvantage suffered by these mills. My use of TISCO's works costs was necessary to determine whether, in theory at least, expansion of India's steel industry has been justified.

During the early 1960s HSL's operating costs per rupee of sales were roughly 20 to 30 per cent higher than at the private sector plants.[14] The public sector mills have suffered a cost disadvantage in raw materials, including freight, and, to a lesser extent, maintenance and the consumption of power, fuel, spares, and stores. On the contrary, all three mills seem to have had lower labor costs than both TISCO and IISCO.

There is no need to undertake a detailed cost comparison for India's steel mills. Not only are the cost data highly imperfect, a detailed cost analysis is not particularly relevant for my purposes. Instead I restrict myself to a brief discussion of three major components of the mills' operating costs, raw materials, freight, and labor. A discussion of these components highlights some of the difficulties and shortcomings of Indian planning for the growth of her steel industry.

Raw Materials Difficulties

Since the late 1950s all Indian steel mills have encountered a number of extraordinary difficulties with their raw materials

[13] This is, perhaps, the primary reason why the HSL plants have incurred losses, even though they receive the same prices as India's private sector mills. HSL's total book loss, after providing for depreciation and interest, was Rs. 48 million in 1963–64. *Indian Financial Express*, Bombay, Dec. 4, 1964. This compares favorably with a total book loss of Rs. 237 million in 1962–63 and Rs. 166 million in 1961–62.

[14] Computed from profit and loss statements contained in the annual reports of HSL, TISCO, and IISCO.

and rail services.[15] With the possible exception of Bhilai, the public sector plants have not been as well equipped as TISCO and IISCO, particularly by their experience in the industry, to adjust to these difficulties.

The ash content of the coal and the alumina content of the ore consumed by the industry have increased since the mid-1950s. To some extent this deterioration in the quality of the industry's raw materials was an unavoidable consequence of expansion. For years the private sector mills consumed the best grades of coking coal and ore found in north India. However, deterioration in the quality of the industry's raw materials was also a result of poor planning. During the 1950s the government decided to erect five new coal washeries, which beneficiate coal by lowering its ash content. It refused to allow private sector erection of these washeries, even though two were to supply private sector steel mills. By the end of the Second Five Year Plan only two of the five had been established, one by the government's National Coal Development Corporation, the other at Durgapur, built in conjunction with the Durgapur Iron and Steel Works. The other three washeries, to be erected independently by HSL, were not completed until well into the Third Plan period. Delays in their erection necessitated consumption of coke possessing an unusually high ash content and, hence, resulted in unnecessarily high costs of production.

Informants labeled administrative sluggishness on the part of Hindustan Steel Limited, the organization charged with erect-

[15] The reader interested in a published discussion of the industry's raw material and transportation difficulties is directed to Indian Tariff Commission, *Report on the Fair Ex-Works Retention Prices of Steel for the Period 1st April 1960 to 31st March 1962* (New Delhi: Government of India Publication, 1962), pp. 15–20. Also of interest are the annual speeches by the chairmen of TISCO and IISCO to their companies' shareholders and a report on India's recent coal transportation crisis prepared for the World Bank. Coverdale & Colpitts, Consulting Engineers, New York City, and Surveys and Research Corporation, Washington, "India Coal Transport Study" (unpub., 1964), Vol. I.

ing four of the five washeries, as the principal cause of delays. Significantly, the Durgapur washery, although nominally under HSL's control, was included in the contract with the British consortium and erected at the same time as the Durgapur mill. However, responsibility for the other three HSL washeries was divorced from responsibility for the erection of new steel mills or expansion of existing mills. Planning for growth in India's washed coal capacity was not coordinated with planning for growth in India's steel capacity, with the result that a serious and costly imbalance was built into the industry. It is now recognized that delays in building coal washeries were a mistake. Accordingly, the government has sanctioned the establishment of new washeries by India's private sector steel mills and is planning to associate increased washed coal capacity more closely with the expansion of its own plants.

The industry's problems with coking coal have also resulted from a need for rationalization of India's coal industry. For example, during the mid-1950s IISCO obtained its coal from less than a dozen collieries. By 1963, as a result of the reassignment of collieries to the various steel mills, IISCO obtained its coal from as many as thirty, making the uniform blend of coals for which its plant was designed far more difficult. The consistency of the coals received by other steel mills has also suffered. Some consolidation of colliery operations would be desirable. So, also, would be a change in coal price policies to encourage the production of coking coal possessing a uniform high quality.

To some extent the increased content of alumina and other impurities in Indian ores was an unavoidable consequence of the industry's expansion. The mechanization of several ore mines, made necessary by the industry's expansion, has resulted in a deterioration in the quality of its ores. The industry's ore difficulties are also a result of inadequate planning. Partly because of incomplete and misleading tests on their proposed ore deposits, both Rourkela and Durgapur have had to consume ores with higher alumina and fines contents and lower iron contents than had originally been anticipated. This has necessitated blending with ores from other mines and some increase in the cost of ores consumed by these plants. Adding to the production costs of the Durgapur mill has been its purchase of ore through the government's State Trading Corporation at relatively high prices. The State Trading Corporation, acting as a middleman, obtains its ores from a number of small private mines. For this reason, Durgapur's procurement of a uniform blend of ores has proven to be especially difficult.

Transportation Difficulties

The most important cause of India's transport crisis during the early 1960s is thought to have been the failure of the railways to provide sufficient transport capacity, particularly rolling stock, to meet increased demands for railway services.[16] In only a few instances, persons associated with India's steel industry with whom I spoke early in 1963 complained about an overall shortage of wagons. India's steel mills have, for the most part, been given priority over other customers by the railways. Rather, primary blame for the mills' transportation difficulties was attributed to the "bunching" of wagons, the receipt of the wrong types of wagons, and mixing of different types of wagons in the same train and of different types of coal in the same wagon. These practices were probably encouraged by India's wagon shortage.

India's steel mills have been designed to handle a specific number of wagons at any one time. Unfortunately, the movement of wagons to and from the mills has been erratic, especially during the early 1960s. Several trainloads of a particular raw material may arrive within a short time of one another and

[16] Coverdale & Colpitts, Vol. I, p. 31.

then may not be followed by other trainloads for a long period of time. The bunching of wagons has resulted in the levy of demurrage, a charge placed on the mills by the railways for unusual detention of wagons. Bunching has also made it difficult for Indian mills to consume desired blends of coal. Frequently, excessive amounts of one type of coal have been shipped to a mill and, because of limited storage space, have necessitated coking in proportions different from those desired.[17] The result is the production of coke not always ideally suited to the blast furnaces of India's mills. Bunching has also resulted in occasional crises or near crises accompanying the dimunition of the plants' stocks of raw materials. In a few extreme instances stocks of certain raw materials have fallen to as low as one day's supply.

Complaints by the steel mills about their receipt of raw materials in the wrong types of wagons have been directed at two wagons in particular, the BOX wagon, a new 55 ton carrier introduced in the late 1950s to expedite the haulage of coal, and the closed 22 ton wagon which is normally used to haul finished products. No mill is ideally equipped to receive iron ore and limestone in BOX wagons. Therefore, their occasional use to haul these materials to the mills has necessitated hand unloading and demurrage. By and large, Bhilai and TISCO have had little difficulty with coal shipments, although small amounts of coal received in closed 22 ton wagons have been a nuisance. Both mills are equipped with tipplers capable of handling BOX wagons, the type in which most of their coal is received. However, at Rourkela BOX wagons are side-discharged into bunkers or a coal storage yard. Although not intolerable, this method of emptying these wagons is time con-

[17] When bunching at Durgapur entails excessive deliveries of Jharia coal, which should be washed, Durgapur's washery may be over-taxed. On the other hand, the washery may remain idle if no Jharia coal is available. Bhilai, however, has a well-designed and spacious blending yard which better enables it to tolerate bunching.

suming and when accompanied by bunching has resulted in inordinate delays and demurrage charges. Durgapur and IISCO have had the greatest difficulties with BOX wagons because at first neither plant was equipped to handle them. Durgapur has now installed the proper tipplers. IISCO is erecting a 42 mile ropeway to free itself entirely from dependence on India's railways for hauling coal to its plant.

The inability of Rourkela, Durgapur, and IISCO to accommodate BOX wagons was avoidable. The decision to adopt these wagons was made by the railways at the time the public sector mills were being erected and IISCO expanded. Yet no modifications or additions were made in the mills' plans to install apparatus capable of handling BOX wagons. There was, in short, a lack of coordination between planning for expansion of the railways and the steel industry.

Labor Costs

It is not too surprising that labor costs have been a larger proportion of the value of the private sector mills' output. The average wages of these mills are higher, their bonus systems more extensive, and their employment per ton of capacity greater than at the public sector plants.[18] As is to be expected, manpower in Indian mills is substantially in excess of manpower in comparable mills in more developed economies.

Greater employment at India's private sector mills is partly a result of circumstances beyond their control. These mills are older and less mechanized. Moreover, because of the relative cheapness of Indian labor, the private sector mills have in the

[18] In early 1963 TISCO's two million ingot ton plant employed slightly more than 30,000 persons within the plant itself. IISCO, with half the capacity, employed approximately 17,000 persons; the three HSL mills between 13,000 and 15,000 persons. In addition, all mills employ large numbers in such non-works activities as construction, townships, mines, and administrative offices. Since early 1963 employment at the public sector mills, particularly Bhilai, has increased. Employment data have been supplied by each Indian steel mill.

past hired large numbers of unskilled and semiskilled labor, much of it in subsidiary activities such as construction and materials handling. During World War II emphasis on production displaced emphasis on profit maximization, substantial additional help being hired to enable marginal increments in output. Since World War II laws have been enacted restricting the dismissal of employees for retrenchment and making dismissal for infractions of work rules difficult, if not impossible.[19]

Even in the absence of these laws, it is doubtful that either company would engage in a general layoff. Indian labor is not that expensive; nor are the companies insensitive to the social complications and labor unrest created by mass retrenchment. Yet the private sector mills have not been powerless or unwilling to reduce their labor costs. Through natural attrition and, more important, expansion of their plants, both TISCO and IISCO have been able to reduce their work forces and their labor costs per ton of output since the mid-1950s.

Although employment per ton of capacity at the public sector mills is slightly lower than at the private mills, it is far greater than had originally been anticipated. Initially, the public sector mills were to hire between 6,000 and 8,000 persons within their plants.[20] The work forces of these mills are now double original estimates, and the sanctioned strength of each plant is substantially in excess of actual employment.[21]

[19] For a discussion of Indian laws governing the employment of labor, the reader is directed to U.S. Steel Corporation, "A Techno-Economic Survey of a Proposed Integrated Steel Mill at Bokaro, Bihar State, India" (unpub. report submitted to the U.S. Government, Agency for International Development, March 1963), Vol. II, pp. 127ff.

[20] Initial estimates of employment at the public sector mills can be found in the project reports for the Rourkela and Bhilai mills. See also American Iron and Steel Institute, "Engineering Data on the Indian Steel Industry" (unpub., New York City, 1960), Section VI, pp. 9 and 56.

[21] In late 1963 men in position constituted only 83 per cent of the sanctioned strength of the three HSL mills. HSL, "Manpower Situation in Bhilai, Durgapur and Rourkela" (mimeograph, Ranchi, Bihar, 1964), p. 3.

There are many reasons for the unanticipated manpower employed by the public sector mills.[22] Perhaps most important, initial work-force estimates understated the actual demands of a new steel mill in India. The needs of several plant units were ignored by some of these estimates. Employment needs characteristic of India, but not of more developed economies, were also ignored. These include requirements resulting from an allegedly high rate of absenteeism, the relatively low productivity of Indian labor, and Indian customs that encourage extreme job specialization.[23]

The Bhilai mill also retained much of its original construction staff, even though this staff remained idle for several years after Bhilai's initial plant and equipment were erected. This has enabled the retention of skills and disciplines for use in Bhilai's expansion programs, and has had political and humanitarian benefits. However, it has also involved an expense to the Bhilai mill, unnecessarily high costs of production.

Emphasis on production and a relative disregard for cost minimization have encouraged the hiring of additional workers to obtain marginal increments in output. Given the low real cost of unskilled and semiskilled labor, there may be good reason for the employment of large numbers by an Indian mill. However, it is debatable whether all or most of the abnormally large manpower at each mill can, in fact, be justified by cost considerations alone. Although I lack cost data necessary to make this assertion, I suspect that the marginal cost of employing additional labor at an Indian steel mill would far exceed the marginal revenue derived from it.[24]

22 *Ibid.*, pp. 14–15.

23 A technician in an Indian mill generally has several assistants and servants to perform some of the menial jobs normally done by the technician himself in more developed economies.

24 This impression is bolstered by one common feature at all Indian mills, the amount of manpower that appears to remain idle for long periods of time.

Finally, excessive employment has resulted from a juxtaposition of powers at two of the three public sector mills. At least until early 1963, promotions and dismissals that are normally line functions performed by plant superintendents and foremen were often made by the mills' chief personnel managers and general offices. Conversely, plant superintendents and foremen were, in effect, allowed to establish or to influence the standard labor forces of their units, usually a function of a mill's cost department. Perhaps because of inexperience, the personnel offices of the public sector plants have not always been able to distinguish between legitimate and spurious requests for additional labor. Given the pressures on middle management to produce large tonnages of steel, the result, predictably, has been excessive staffing of many divisions.

For some purposes the maintenance of a large labor force has probably been advantageous. Indian labor is relatively inexpensive. Moreover, the Bhilai mill, by retaining its construction staff intact, has minimized future problems of assembling the labor skills necessary for expanding its plant. Some redundant labor is also learning industrial skills and disciplines that will be needed in the future. However, the maintenance of a large number of employees also contributes to unduly high costs of production, undesirable work practices, and labor difficulties arising from confusion about the duties and functions of individual employees. Whether excessive employment is, overall, beneficial is not altogether obvious.

Other Problems at the Public Sector Mills

Certain practices have prevailed at one or more of the public sector mills that, if they have not appreciably increased the current costs of production of these mills, have increased their future real costs. These practices have, to some extent, been changed since the end of 1962. Perhaps the best publicized has been abnormal deterioration in the equipment of the Rourkela and Durgapur mills. Instances of unusual destruction of Rourkela's equipment have been well documented by the Solveen Committee and the Indian press. Destruction of Durgapur's equipment, although less publicized, has also been excessive. The destruction of equipment has necessitated some premature replacement by the mills. However, many of the costs of this destruction are yet to be paid.[25]

Destruction of equipment at Rourkela at one time necessitated some stripping of parts from one unit of a mill to replace parts in another.[26] This practice was prompted by an inadequacy of spare parts and, to some extent, poor inventory control, some available spares actually being unknown to the plant's management. Inadequate stocks of spare parts were partly a result of an initial niggardliness in the provision of inventories, and partly a result of breakage of equipment for which spares are not normally held.[27]

Complicating the replacement of parts at both Rourkela and Durgapur has been the imposition on these plants of a cumbersome administrative organization in their own offices, at Hindustan Steel Limited at Ranchi, and in New Delhi. At Rourkela:

> It has been found that urgent requirements were seriously delayed by offices incapable of judging either the necessity or the urgency of the procurement. Reminders of the different plant sections were not attended to. At present [1962] the period from the date an item is needed and ordered until delivery is estimated in some instances to be as much as 24 to 36 months.[28]

[25] For example, the frequent banking of blast furnaces and coke ovens has reduced their life expectancies. See Solveen Committee, p. 8.

[26] For several examples of cannibalization at Rourkela, see *ibid.*, p. 27. See also *Hindustan Times*, Aug. 11, 1961, p. 7.

[27] Solveen Committee, p. 20.

[28] *Ibid.*, p. 27.

At Durgapur, also, red tape has hindered the purchase of parts essential for restoring crippled units of the plant to full operating efficiency.[29] Following the investigation of the Solveen Committee and a change in management at both mills, the procurement of needed replacements appears to have been hastened.

Some destruction of equipment at Rourkela and Durgapur was caused by negligence and misuse resulting from the inexperience of the plants' management and labor. Some can also be attributed to inadequate maintenance.[30] At both Rourkela and Durgapur maintenance staffs were at first subordinate to the superintendent of each division. Because production is the principal if not the sole criterion by which the performance of a unit is judged, maintenance was often subordinate to production. Conversely, at Bhilai maintenance has from the beginning been fitted into the rhythm of the plant's day-to-day operations with a specific time devoted to the maintenance of a unit as a matter of course. This is one reason for the overall success of the Bhilai plant. Maintenance personnel at both Rourkela and Durgapur have now been placed under one officer responsible for maintenance in all units. This officer is in turn responsible only to the general superintendent of a plant. Maintenance is said to have improved at both plants since 1962, perhaps in part because of this organizational change.

A second practice that was inimical to the long-run performance of India's public sector mills, at least prior to 1963, was

[29] For example, in January 1963 a manipulator in Durgapur's blooming mill was out of commission. (A manipulator turns blooms for subsequent rolling.) An ingenious but laborious substitute had been devised. However, this tied down one of the mill's overhead cranes and reduced the effective capacity of the blooming mill. This part had been out of commission for a number of months. According to a technician at the plant, the primary reason for the delay in replacing the manipulator was lethargy in administrative offices either at the plant, Ranchi, or New Delhi.

[30] For example, see Solveen Committee, pp. 5–6 and 25.

the neglect of training by one of these mills, Durgapur. At both Bhilai and Rourkela reasonably effective training programs had been established by the spring of 1963, combining in-plant with institutional training of both operative and lower supervisory personnel. However, by early 1963 in-plant training at Durgapur had not been recognized in principle by the plant's management, all training having been relegated to a modest "institute" at great distance from the plant. Training should receive priority at India's steel mills. The staffing of these mills with skilled and semiskilled personnel is a major problem confronting their expansion programs, not to mention the erection of new mills contemplated by Indian planners. Durgapur, of all mills, should be most concerned with training since, being the last of the Indian mills to be erected, it has had the last pick of the experienced personnel released by India's private sector steel companies.

At least two reasons were given for Durgapur's neglect of training. First, there was no provision in the original project report or the contract with the British consortium for the erection of a training institute. Durgapur's present institute was established long after other units of the plant. Second, training at Durgapur has not received the wholehearted support of the plant's management and in-plant training, at least early in 1963, was opposed by it. To some extent this was said to be a matter of tradition, in-plant training not being widely accepted in the United Kingdom. It was also a result of emphasis on maximizing short-run output. In-plant training, if it is to be meaningful, may necessitate some interference with and possibly some marginal sacrifice of production by the plant.

A third practice at the public sector mills that has had adverse consequences has been the demoralization of skilled personnel. This is particularly true of young graduate engineers who, in many instances, have been recruited directly out of colleges, their only prior experience with steel manufacture being a brief residence abroad.

To some extent the disillusion of graduate engineers stems from what were, perhaps, excessive aspirations.[31] Even so, their grievances and those of the plants' more experienced middle management have been legitimate. One source of disillusion has been the undue concentration of powers in the hands of the top managements of the plants, or, in some instances, HSL in Ranchi. Several instances of misplaced authority have already been indicated. The purchase of needed replacements has been delayed by a cumbersome system of requisitions through administrative offices that do not possess the technical background necessary to judge the importance of a purchase. Persons charged with quality control and maintenance have in the past been overruled by those charged with production, at times with the sanction of the top managements of the plants. Promotions and dismissals have been assumed by the personnel directors of the plants and the head office at Ranchi even though the middle managements in the plants are best equipped to select or at least recommend those persons meriting promotions and are responsible for the performance of those receiving them.[32] The complaint has also been commonplace that con-

[31] In 1960 a United States steel industry delegation was sent to India, in part to study the effects of a U.S. program for training Indian steel industry technicians. This delegation found that trainees were at times impatient with the failure of plants to run as smoothly as the plants at which they had worked in the United States and often sought unsuccessfully to introduce new ideas learned in the United States but not accepted by their superiors. American Iron and Steel Industry Delegation, *India Report, February–March 1960* (New York: American Iron and Steel Institute, 1960), Section III, p. 10.

[32] For example, I was told by one plant superintendent that four times during his tenure at one of the public sector mills he had been asked as a matter of form to recommend someone for promotion within his unit and each time his recommendation was ignored, the persons receiving the promotions, in his opinion, being inferior or wholly unqualified for the positions they assumed.

siderations other than the performance of individuals have all too often influenced hiring and promotion. Prominent among these other considerations have been age, extent of formal education, regional origin, and political influence.

Fortunately, the need for some devolution of authority to the plants has been recognized by the Indian government. Early in 1963 the powers of Ranchi and New Delhi governing the hiring and promotion of employees and the approval of expenditures were substantially curtailed. However, it is not certain that at the same time there was a parallel and equally necessary devolution of authority from the plants' top managements to their middle managements.[33] Insofar as this devolution has not occurred, demoralization of the plants' middle management could very well persist.

A second source of disillusion has been the occupancy of top managerial positions both at the plants and in Ranchi by persons with little experience in the steel industry. By 1962 top managerial positions had become the preserve of the Indian Administrative Services, India's civil service. On the other hand, middle and lower management groups consisted for the most part of experienced technicians, drawn from the private sector mills or imported from abroad, and trained but inexperienced graduate engineers. That the administrative offices of the plants were inadequate and, worse, were thereby preventing middle and lower managements from performing their functions properly had become a widespread belief by 1963.

There seem to have been some improvements in the plants' top managements during the past several years. Effective if not formal management has always rested with Soviet technicians stationed at the Bhilai mill. The Russian general superintendent has full responsibility for running the mill, despite an Indian

[33] In some matters there has probably been too much devolution of authority. The example of middle managment's ability to influence standard work forces has already been noted.

general manager who, in theory at least, is its highest official. Rourkela's general managers have been drawn from the Indian Administrative Services. However, by 1964 effective control over the Rourkela mill appeared to have passed to its German staff and in particular to its German general superintendent. In 1963 a Briton was appointed for the first time to be general manager of the Durgapur mill. He was followed in 1965 by an Indian who, having served at Durgapur, has had experience in the steel industry. Voids in the top managements of India's public sector steel mills seem to be at an end.

A third source of disillusion among some of the young graduate engineers at Rourkela and Durgapur has been their placement in positions for which they were not trained.[34] Informants cited many instances in which engineers were given jobs only indirectly related to their abilities, the most extreme examples being graduate engineers charged with servicing office air conditioners and administering the motor pool of the plants to which they were assigned. On occasions the misplacement of graduate engineers has resulted from personal differences and political machinations. For the most part it has resulted from inadequate planning for the staffing of these plants.

Some Reasons for Difficulties at India's Public Sector Plants

There is no one reason for the difficulties encountered by the public sector steel mills. Some must be attributed to the newness of the plants. However, to ascribe most if not all of these difficulties to "teething troubles" would be incorrect. The problems of the public sector mills are also a result of other, more basic, deficiencies in planning for the expansion of India's steel industry.

[34] Lok Sabha (House of the People, Indian Parliament), Estimates Committee, *Ministry of Steel, Mines and Fuel, 33rd Report, Second Lok Sabha, 1958–9* (New Delhi: Lok Sabha Secretariat, 1959), p. 86.

Some difficulties have also been attributed to defects in the equipment and design of new plants. Although it is true that in a few instances there have been defects that may, with justification, be blamed on the equipment suppliers or contractors, to attribute the problems of the public sector plants wholly or even primarily to defective machinery or plant design is also unjustified. In my opinion, any appraisal of the performance of the public sector mills should begin with the assumption that initially these plants were basically sound.[35]

There are several fundamental reasons for the difficulties encountered by India's public sector steel mills which, in my opinion, illustrate some of the more basic problems confronting industrial growth in a planned economy. First, there is a problem of choosing the proper criterion for judging the performance of an industrial unit. Until recently, production has been used almost exclusively as a measure of the public sector steel mills' success. This has encouraged the manufacture of types of steel that allow the greatest tonnages even though they may not be most needed by the Indian economy. Emphasis on production has also resulted in some sacrifice of quality and efforts to minimize costs of production. Preoccupation with achieving high levels of output in the short run has also encouraged the sacrifice of two long range objectives. At the Rourkela and Durgapur mills it has, in the past, contributed to a neglect of maintenance and, as a result, the life of equipment. At Durgapur it has also encouraged a sacrifice of in-plant training programs and, hence, the creation of the scarce skills needed by the industry.

The public sector mills' sole emphasis on production may be over. It is recognized by many persons associated with these mills that a more suitable measure of performance should encompass both the value and the cost of output. The obvious measure is the profitability of these mills, or more appropriately,

[35] This was the opinion of the Solveen Committee and several steelmen familiar with the public sector plants.

since investment in the public sector mills and the ability of these mills to earn profits varies, the rate of return criterion used in Chapter 6. Criteria for the performance of India's steel mills should also have a time dimension. If the present production costs of a mill are excessive, but it can be established that this is necessary because of practices that will in the long run benefit the Indian economy, then higher costs might be condoned. On the other hand, if a mill is earning high profits by destroying its capital, then its management should be penalized.

Finally, given higher prices, the public sector mills might be judged by their ability to plan, finance, and implement their own expansion programs or, eventually, the erection of new mills in coordination with planning authorities. They might also be encouraged to seek out export markets to satisfy their own foreign exchange needs. The ability of India's public sector mills to fulfill these two functions, in addition to their ability to earn a satisfactory rate of return, would be most appropriate criteria by which their success or failure could be judged.

A second basic reason for the difficulties of the Rourkela and Durgapur mills, at least until 1963, was their failure to secure managements capable of directing their operations satisfactorily. Indian planners have, as a rule, concerned themselves primarily with the installation of new capacity, the setting of targets, and the purchase and finance of new plant and machinery. They have not concerned themselves to any great extent with obtaining the managerial expertise needed for the public sector steel mills. A mill's middle management has usually been drawn from the private sector plants or from abroad. However, prior to 1963 a mill's top management was in most instances drawn from the Indian Administrative Services and all too often consisted of persons with little industrial experience.

As might be expected, the initial organizations at the mills and at Ranchi were patterned after the Indian civil service. Authority was concentrated in the general managers and their administrative offices. Many decisions that should normally be made by the plants' middle managements were referred to the general managers or their immediate subordinates, notably chief personnel and finance officers. For this reason, decisions about promotions and dismissals, the purchase of spare parts and replacements, and a number of other matters, some extraordinarily trivial,[36] were often delayed. The plant's financial advisors have been especially difficult obstacles to day-to-day decision-making and, in some instances, have even vetoed decisions by their nominal supervisors, the general managers.

Adding to the difficulties created by this system was the seeming inability of the plants' administrative offices to make many of the decisions referred to them. The general manager and his subordinates frequently had a distinguished record with a state or central ministry. Often the general manager was nearing retirement or was brought out of retirement to manage the plant. Thus, Rourkela has had seven general managers in about as many years; Bhilai and Durgapur have each had four. Some plant officials have regarded their tenures at the plants as way stations in their careers not to be tarnished by a wrong decision. For this reason many issues have been referred to HSL's head office in Ranchi. Ranchi has also been unable to make decisions rapidly and many matters that should have been settled by it or even by the plants have frequently been referred to New Delhi.[37] The result, according to one wag, has been the public sector mills' production of greater tonnages of paper than of steel.

[36] For example, a foreign employee at one of the mills spent months trying to get the general manager of the mill, to whom his request had been referred, to approve his moving from one bungalow to another unoccupied bungalow on an adjacent street.

[37] Perhaps the most celebrated example of delays in Ranchi is the now famous case of the stopwatches. In June 1960 a requisition was submitted for four stopwatches. By July 1961, although the requisition had gone through eighty-nine steps toward its approval, including references to HSL's chairman, secretary, and finance officer, the stopwatches had not yet been purchased.

Not all powers have been passed upward. Some which might best be held by the top managements of the plants have fallen to their middle managements. Examples have been the determination of the number of persons employed in a unit and control over quality and maintenance by a division. The staffing of top management positions with inexperienced personnel has resulted in the misplacement of powers in both directions.

In some instances administrative officers who are willing to make decisions have done so with unfortunate consequences. For example, a former general manager at Rourkela determined that his mill could from the start dispense with most of the German personnel scheduled to fill positions of responsibility. Instead Rourkela was staffed primarily with well-meaning but poorly qualified Indian personnel. Perhaps more than any other single act, this decision resulted in the sorry condition of the plant during the early 1960s.

A partial exception has been the Bhilai mill. On the insistence of the Soviet government, Bhilai's Russian staff has from the beginning had complete control over the mill's operations, although working with Indian administrators and technicians drawn from the Indian Administrative Services and the private sector mills. Bhilai's Russian staff is said to have worked closely with its Indian counterparts and, as a result, has developed an Indian organization that will some day be capable of running the mill effectively. More recently, control at Durgapur and Rourkela appears to have passed to reasonably competent Indian and foreign steelmen. Voids in the top managements of both plants may be at an end.

India's experience would indicate that there is more to industrialization in a less developed economy than simply the installation of new plant and equipment. The establishment of an organization and the procurement of managerial and technical expertise necessary to operate new plant and equipment satisfactorily are also essential, and neglect of these complementary factors of production can result in unfortunate consequences for both the plant and the economy.

A third basic reason for the steel industry's difficulties has been a repeated lack of coordination between the parties responsible for its operations and growth. Planning for the industry's raw materials and transportation services did not keep in step with planning for the industry's expansion during the Second Plan period. Controls over pricing have inadvertently conflicted with some of the objectives of India's planners. There has been some lack of coordination among those charged with the operations of India's steel mills and those charged with their expansion. Finally, there has been lack of coordination between the various units of the plants themselves, one division of a mill often conducting itself as if other divisions did not exist.

To some extent greater coordination might be achieved by greater centralization of authority at the mills. Some imbalances between the various units of the Durgapur and Rourkela mills, at least, could be eliminated by more effective direction from the mills' administrative offices. There might also be greater coordination between the development of raw materials and the erection of washeries on the one hand and the expansion of the steel industry on the other were the individual steel mills made responsible for the development and operation of their own mines and washeries. Greater coordination between the expansion and operation of India's steel mills might also be achieved if the mills were allowed a greater say in the timing of their own expansion programs.

However, the redrawing of organization charts may not, by itself, be sufficient to insure balance within a mill and between the mill and the rest of the Indian economy. Other measures may have to be devised to assure that the actions of one segment of the industry do not thwart the operations of another. Some may prefer to rely upon a more perfected system of direct controls. Another means of coordination that might be considered is a workable price mechanism possibly influenced by judicious intervention by the Indian government.

An effective price mechanism might enable coordination of the mills' production with consumer demands. It could also help to coordinate the growth of the steel industry with the need for this growth through the accumulation of retained earnings. In addition other price incentives might be instituted affecting the industry's inputs. For example, the government might consider a system similar to demurrage whereby the railways would pay a penalty to the mills for extraordinary bunching, undue delivery of raw materials in the wrong types of wagons and, if it should become a serious problem, shortfalls in the number of wagons delivered to the mills. The government might also allow greater price incentives to coal mines not only for the production of low ash coal but also for the production of coal possessing a consistent ash content. A similar arrangement could be made for ore and limestone purchased from non-company mines. A workable price mechanism could become an important source of coordination for the industry. To some extent, absence of a workable price mechanism has been an important source of its difficulties.

9 | The Location of Indian Steel Mills

Introduction[1]

One objective of Indian planning is balanced regional development.[2] Accordingly, an attempt has been made to situate new steel mills in as many states as possible. The locations of India's public sector steel mills have not been determined by economic and technical considerations alone.

Although the Rourkela site was recommended by a German delegation that visited India in December 1953, its formal designation by the government required three cabinet meetings, consultations with the chief ministers of several states, and a month's delay because of noneconomic considerations that are necessarily a part of planning.[3] The choice of a second site, Bhilai in Madhya Pradesh, was also influenced by these considerations. Bhilai was one of several potential locations visited by Russian technicians late in 1954. None was in Orissa. Bhilai not only fulfilled the prerequisites of a mill site, it also satisfied the government's ideological and political objectives. Of all

[1] It is impossible to talk meaningfully about the location of India's steel mills without becoming involved in a number of relatively specific issues. Many of the details essential to this chapter have been relegated to Appendixes F and G. Even so, the casual reader may prefer to stop at the end of the introduction, where the more important conclusions of this chapter are summarized.

[2] Government of India, Planning Commission, *Third Five Year Plan* (New Delhi: Government of India Publication, 1961), Ch. IX.

[3] For example, see *Hindustan Times*, Feb. 12, 1954, p. 6; Feb. 15, 1964, p. 1; and Feb. 18, 1954, p. 7.

major Indian states, Madhya Pradesh is one of the least developed and, of all states within reasonable distances from India's coking coals, by 1955 only Madhya Pradesh had not had or been promised a steel mill.[4] A British mission that visited India in 1955 was shown locations in only two states, West Bengal and Bihar. When Durgapur in West Bengal was selected for the British mill it was announced that a fourth public sector plant, erected during the subsequent plan period, would be situated at Bokaro in Bihar.[5] Once a state was allocated a public sector mill it was removed from all further consideration.

Iron ore is found throughout the Indian peninsula. Nature's generosity, although seemingly advantageous, has actually encouraged pressures on the center for the location of steel mills and pig iron plants within various state borders. State interests have frequently sent memoranda to the center in support of particular locations. Officials of state governments and local Congress Party organizations and members of state legislative assemblies have often conferred with officials of the central government and the national Congress Party on the location of new mills. Some states have actually initiated work on steel mills before the selection of locations in attempts, not always very subtle, to influence the center's choice.[6]

[4] Four states possessing significant ore deposits are relatively near the Bengal-Bihar coalfields: West Bengal, Bihar, Orissa, and Madhya Pradesh. IISCO is in West Bengal, TISCO in Bihar, and Rourkela in Orissa.

[5] *Hindustan Times*, Sept. 25, 1955, p. 1.

[6] Perhaps the most celebrated instance of a state's effort to obtain a steel mill occurred during the mid-1950s. The Government of West Bengal first supported the unsuccessful Birla scheme. When this was rejected by the center, it proclaimed its own plans to build a mill and then a coke oven battery at Durgapur, buying up properties and drawing up plans for the Durgapur site. By the time a location for the British mill was chosen, sufficient popular support had been created in West Bengal for a Durgapur mill that selection of any other site would have been politically inexpedient. Other state governments have attempted to build small pig iron plants. Some have taken it upon themselves to sponsor experiments with ob-

Unfortunately, India's only coking coals are situated in West Bengal and Bihar in northeastern India, reasonably close to the ore deposits of only four Indian states, Bihar, West Bengal, Orissa, and Madhya Pradesh. The proximity of four state boundaries to India's only deposits of coking coal has been fortuitous. Thus far, it has allowed the dispersal of new mills without serious mislocation of the industry.

The location of a fifth public sector mill is a matter of current interest in India. Locations under consideration are in south India, in Goa, Mysore, Madras, Andhra Pradesh, and, possibly, southern Madhya Pradesh. Adherence to the "one mill one state" rule will continue, barring location of another mill in Madhya Pradesh, to further the regional dispersal of India's steel industry. No alternative sites in northeastern India are under serious consideration.[7]

That regional interests should try to influence government policy is certainly not unique to India. However, regional loyalties are particularly strong because state boundaries are not only administrative demarcations but also borders between

---

viously inferior raw materials, to purchase ore properties and lands surrounding potential mill sites, and to publish studies purporting to show the advantages of one site over another. For examples, see A. K. Guha, *Location of the New Steel Plant and Its Economic Aspects* (Alipore: West Bengal Government Press, 1954); H. B. Mohanty, *Location of a Steel Plant in Orissa* (Industries Department, Orissa Government Press, n.d.); Government of Madhya Pradesh, *New Iron and Steel Plant, Supplementary Memorandum* (Nagpur: Government Printing Madhya Pradesh, 1953); and Government of Madras, *Consulting Engineers' Report on Neyveli-Salem Steel Project—A Summary* (Madras: Government of Madras Publication, 1964). The last mentioned study is a reproduction of a summary report by M. N. Dastur & Company, and is discussed at some length in Appendix H.

[7] In late 1965, the Planning Commission urged that central and state governments be guided wholly by economic and technical considerations when choosing the locations of major development projects, and suggested in particular that new steel mills be located within the coal-steel belt of northeastern India. To my knowledge this is the first and only time that a responsible government body has questioned south Indian locations. *The Statesman Weekly*, Calcutta, Nov. 27, 1965, p. 10.

distinct cultural and linguistic areas. To some extent, Indian planning has to take into consideration regional pressures. Yet an attempt to satisfy these pressures by spreading industries to as many states as possible could result in the mislocation of industry, excessive costs of production, and needless use of scarce capital either in the erection of producing units themselves or the expansion of associated industries such as railways, power generation, and mining.

The purpose of this chapter is twofold: first, to consider to what extent mislocation of the industry could result from the Indian government's desire to produce steel in as many states as possible; second, if there will be some mislocation of the industry, to assess its costs to the Indian economy. I come to the conclusion that only under favorable circumstances would south Indian locations enable lower costs of producing and distributing steel than alternative north Indian sites. In particular several assumptions must be fulfilled, perhaps the most important being that south Indian steel mills be able to distribute their steel to relatively nearby markets. There are reasons to doubt the validity of these assumptions, particularly since many of the same assumptions were also used to justify the location of the Bhilai mill and have not yet proven correct.

My cost analysis assumes shadow prices for certain inputs. This is necessary because actual prices tend to understate the real costs of producing steel in the south. Were south Indian mills to be based wholly or in part on imported coal, the official rate of exchange would, in effect, understate the real cost of this coal to the Indian economy. Were south Indian mills based on north Indian coal, excessive telescoping of railway rates would understate the real costs of shipping this coal to south Indian mills by rail. Because I am interested in the real costs to the Indian economy of producing steel in the south, some adjustment in unremunerative factor prices is necessary.

Simply because south Indian mills would produce and distribute steel at higher costs than north Indian mills does not mean that they are unjustified. Possible external economies and noneconomic advantages from regional dispersal of the industry are not unimportant. Still, one wonders whether the regional dispersal of the steel industry is the most advantageous way to secure these objectives. Any externalities specific to the steel industry have, to some extent, already been secured by regional price equalization for steel. Although dispersal of industry in general seems to me to be a reasonable objective, I find it difficult to accept the notion that this objective must be defined restrictively to mean the dispersal of each industry.

There are advantages in regional specialization. If a region does not have a comparative advantage in steel, it will have a comparative advantage in some other industry that may serve as a more appropriate basis for its industrial growth. There is a real need for the Indian government to impress upon the states that steel is not all-important and to devise more meaningful alternatives that will stimulate the spread of industrial growth, satisfy the political objectives of planning, and still allow the efficient use of India's resources.

The Location of Existing Public Sector Steel Mills

The location of India's first four public sector mills in four different states has not resulted in mislocation of India's steel industry.[8] Real costs of production should be more or less the same at each of these mills. This is not too surprising since all four locations are conventional by Indian standards. Durgapur and Bokaro are coal-based whereas Rourkela and Bhilai, in addition to being ore-based, are both near their sources of limestone.

[8] The following discussion is a summary of a detailed analysis of the mills' locations included in the study upon which this book is based. See William A. Johnson, "India's Iron and Steel Industry: A Study of Planned Industrial Growth" (unpub. diss., Harvard University, 1964), pp. 236–265.

Bhilai is farther from its raw materials than the other three locations.[9] This disadvantage is offset by the slightly higher iron content, the greater hardness, and the lower alumina of the Dhalli-Rajhara ores upon which Bhilai is based. Primarily because of the better quality of Bhilai's ores, its consumption of principal raw materials is lower than that of other Indian mills.[10] This is an important advantage which should result in lower real costs of production at the Bhilai mill, all other things being equal.

The choice of Bhilai was a departure in the location of Indian steel mills. With the exception of the Mysore Iron and Steel Works, Bhilai was and remains the only Indian mill outside the "Ruhr of India," a region centered around the Bengal-Bihar-Orissa ore and coalfields. That location at Bhilai would necessitate additional haulage of raw materials was known at the time of its selection. However, for several reasons it was thought that any disadvantage resulting from Bhilai's relative distance from coal could be minimized. In particular, three assumptions were made by Indian planners that favored the Bhilai site. First, it was assumed implicitly that Indian railway rates on coal reflected the true costs to the economy of hauling coal over long distances. Second, it was assumed that Bhilai could blend coals from central Indian coalfields with coking coals obtained from West Bengal and Bihar. Third, it was assumed that a Bhilai mill, being nearer to southern and western India, could specialize on markets in these regions, thereby allowing lower total haulage of salable steel. All three assumptions were erroneous.

Several studies of alternative mill sites have used existing railway rates on coal.[11] In India, as elsewhere, goods rates are

[9] Table F-3

[10] Table F-1. See also reference 3, Chapter 3.

[11] Shortly after Independence three firms were contracted by the Government of India to study proposed new steel mills. All three firms concluded that two new mills should be erected, one each in Orissa and

"telescoped." The further a good is carried the less is the average rate charged per ton-mile. The ostensible reason for telescoped rates is an element in total costs of haulage that does not vary with distance, terminal charges such as the costs of the normal retention of wagons, operation of sidings, and the keeping of records. The rate on coal has long been excessively telescoped, with the result that coal hauled short distances has been charged slightly higher rates, and, conversely, coal hauled relatively long distances has been charged considerably lower rates than other bulk commodities. The excessive telescoping of coal rates has borne little relationship to the costs of transporting coal, has existed for years, and has been retained, in effect, to subsidize the delivery of coal to regions distant from India's coal mines. For this reason, use of existing rates on coal to judge steel plant locations would understate the real costs of hauling coal to hypothetical mills located at greater distances from India's coal mines, mills at Bhilai and in south India.[12]

Second, it was assumed at the time the Bhilai mill was erected that it would blend coals from the Korba seam of

---

Madhya Pradesh, states relatively distant from India's coking coals. Each study used existing railway rates on coking coal. Arthur G. McKee & Company, Engineers and Contractors, Cleveland, Ohio, "General Plans for Increasing the Production of Iron and Steel in India" (unpub., January 1949); Koppers Company, Inc., Pittsburgh, Penn., *Indian Steel Report* (Pittsburgh: Koppers Company, 1948); and International Construction Company, Ltd., *Report on the Establishment of an Iron and Steel Works in India* (London: Waterlow & Sons, Ltd., January 1949). More recently, M. N. Dastur & Company of Calcutta and Hindustan Steel Limited of Ranchi have completed preliminary studies of proposed mills in southwestern and southeastern India respectively. Although I have not read either report, I understand that existing rates on coal have been used in both.

[12] At least two studies have attempted to estimate the actual costs of hauling Indian coal. One has been prepared for the World Bank. Coverdale & Colpitts, New York City, and Surveys and Research Corporation, Washington, "India Coal Transport Study" (unpub., June 1, 1964), esp. Vol. III, pp. 93–131. The other is Alan Carlin, *A Possible U.S. Policy Towards Indian Transportation: An Illustration of Improved Sectoral Policies* (Santa Monica, Calif.: The RAND Corporation, RM-4379-AID, June 1965), Appendix B.

Madhya Pradesh.[13] In fact, at that time Korba coals had not been surveyed thoroughly. It was only after Bhilai's coke ovens had been commissioned that it was found that the Korba coals were not suitable for use in these ovens. A rail line has been extended to the northern half of the Korba field where the coal is said to be of better quality. However, it is likely that coal from this field will at best be used as a steam coal at the Bhilai plant.

Third, it was thought that a relatively large proportion of the steel produced at Bhilai would be consumed in regions near the plant, central and western India.[14] In fact, this has not been the case. Were the steel produced at other actual or potential north Indian mills distributed to Bhilai's markets, total haulage of finished products would be no different than actual haulage from Bhilai.[15] Bhilai has thus far had no overall advantage in the distribution of its steel.

What are the merits of uncovering ghosts of the industry's past? Why discuss errors in the selection of the Bhilai location when, admittedly, they have not caused serious difficulties? Quite simply, the assumptions that have proved to be erroneous in the past are once again being made in support of locations in south India. False assumptions did not result in serious difficulties for Bhilai for two basic reasons. First, because of inadequate groundwork on the raw materials consumed by the Rourkela and Durgapur mills, the quality of these raw materials, notably iron ore, proved poorer than had been anticipated. However, Bhilai has had a major advantage in its consumption of a superior quality ore. Perhaps more important, Bhilai is not so distant from its sources of coal that the levy of appropriate rates on coal or the mill's inability to use Korba

[13] Bhilai's coke ovens were designed to consume 20 per cent Korba coals. Government of India, Ministry of Steel, Mines and Fuel, Department of Iron and Steel, *Report, 1958–59* (New Delhi: Government of India Publication, 1959), p. 21. See also *Indian Construction News*, Oct. 1959, p. 23.

[14] Ministry of Steel, Mines and Fuel, *Report, 1958–59*, p. 15.

[15] Tables F-5 and F-6.

coals would result in a serious cost disadvantage. Bhilai's central location also permits reasonable access to all major Indian markets for steel. Bhilai's failure to concentrate on nearby markets has not placed the mill at a disadvantage. In short, one crucial advantage of the Bhilai site was the fact that the consequences of false assumptions made in its behalf were not severe. This may not be true of proposed south Indian mills.

The Location of Future Indian Steel Mills

Two general regions are commonly mentioned for locations of future conventional steel mills. The first is southwestern India. A steel plant would be located either on the coast in Goa or nearly 300 miles inland in the vicinity of the Bellary-Hospet ore deposits of Mysore. The second is southeastern India, and again two potential sites have been mentioned, one near Vishakhapatnam, a port in Andhra Pradesh, the other 300 miles inland in the vicinity of the Bailadilla ore deposits of southern Madhya Pradesh. Plants at these sites would consume south Indian ores and fluxes and coking coal shipped from northern India or from abroad. Erection of one mill is scheduled to begin early in the Fourth Plan period; erection of another by the end of the period.

A steel mill in the south Indian state of Madras has been under consideration for years. This mill would employ an alternative method to the blast furnace. Its economics are highly suspect and, primarily for this reason, its erection by the Government of India is doubtful. Discussion of this mill is reserved to Appendix H.

Many arguments have been made in favor of the regional dispersal of India's steel industry:

1. If south Indian mills are based upon imported coal, they would not draw upon India's already "limited" reserves of coking coal.

2. Coal found near several of the proposed locations, notably in northern Andhra Pradesh and Madhya Pradesh, could be blended with north Indian or imported coal to lower the fuel costs of south Indian mills.

3. South Indian mills would also consume a better quality of ore and limestone. Some south Indian deposits of iron ore have a relatively low alumina content which would enable production of iron at lower costs than in northeastern India.

4. Goa, Bellary, and Bailadilla ores are now or will eventually be exported, principally to Japan. Under the terms of agreements with the Japanese, small particle ores called fines are rejected. It is suggested that these fines could be utilized with no additional costs of mining.

5. Although coking coal would be imported at high cost, its use at a south Indian mill might actually reduce overall costs of production. First, imported coal would have a lower ash content which would allow lower costs of producing iron. Second, ships carrying iron ore from Goa and Vishakhapatnam could return with imported coking coal, thus reducing costs of delivering coal to India. Third, railway wagons carrying exported iron ore from the interior to the sea could return filled with imported coal, thus lowering the costs of assembling coal at the Bellary-Hospet and Bailadilla plants.

6. Consumption of coal could be reduced by smelting a greater proportion of scrap obtained from such scrap-producing centers as Bombay and Madras City and by adopting recent developments in iron production such as pelletization, sintering, and oil and solid fuel injection.

7. Additional expenditures of foreign exchange incurred by importing coal could be offset by the allocation for export of iron ore or some of the iron and steel produced by these mills.

8. The dispersal of the steel industry would stimulate the economic development of a wider area of India than would its concentration in northeastern India.

9. Dispersal of the steel industry would also ease already substantial burdens on Indian railways near existing steel mills. It would facilitate delivery of finished steel to southern and western India by circumventing rail bottlenecks that have hindered shipment of steel to these regions in the past. Because south Indian mills would produce primarily for southern and western India, these mills would allow a reduction in the total costs of delivering steel to Indian markets.[16]

Unfortunately, many of these arguments have been too readily accepted at face value. Although some are valid, many are not. The remaining sections of this chapter consider these arguments one by one and, going beyond this, examine the implications of dispersal of India's steel industry for the development of her economy.

Costs of Production at Proposed Indian Mills

TISCO has shown interest in expanding across the Kharkai River to Adityapur, possibly developing this site into an integrated steel mill having an eventual capacity of approximately four million ingot tons.[17] A number of potential north Indian locations have been suggested by M. N. Dastur & Company.[18]

[16] Each of these arguments has at one time or another been made in numerous discussions with individuals associated with the Indian steel industry. The interested reader may wish to consult two printed sources: Dr. K. S. Gill, "Suggestions Regarding Major Projects of Iron and Steel Development in the Fourth Plan" (unpub., Indian Planning Commission, August 1962), pp. 14–19; and Sir Jehangir Ghandy, "Outlook on Steel," *Iron and Steel Review* (March 1963), pp. 20–22.

[17] In 1957 TISCO made a preliminary study of the Adityapur site which concluded that not only would it be feasible but also that it would entail lower costs of assembling raw materials than all other potential sites considered, Bokaro, Sindri (Bihar), Bailadilla, Hirakud (Orissa), and Panagarh (West Bengal), and all but two existing sites, Rourkela and Jamshedpur. Conversations with TISCO officials early in 1963 indicated continuing interest in an Adityapur mill.

[18] M. N. Dastur & Company, Private, Ltd., "Preliminary Report to Hindustan Steel Limited on the Establishment of an Integrated Steel Works at Bokaro" (unpub., December 1959), Appendix 7.

There is no shortage of suitable mill sites in northeastern India. Although India's coking coals are of poor quality and their amounts small relative to her reserves of iron ore, they are sufficient to sustain the erection of anywhere from two to six new north Indian steel mills.[19] Moreover, new deposits of coal have recently been uncovered. It is likely that India's reserves of fluxes are also adequate.[20] Therefore, the dispersal of India's steel industry is not necessitated by an absence of potential sites or limited supplies of raw materials. Whether or not dispersal is desirable will depend upon how advantageous production of steel in the south will be relative to production in the north. This will in turn depend primarily on the relative costs of producing finished steel and delivering it to markets.

The fuel costs of some south Indian mills could conceivably be reduced were these mills to blend Andhra Pradesh or Madhya Pradesh coals. However, this is reminiscent of a claim once made on behalf of the Bhilai plant. Bhilai was supposed to blend Korba coals from Madhya Pradesh, but has not because these coals are too inferior in quality. Thorough tests on proposed blending coals should be undertaken before it is assumed that south Indian mills will be any more fortunate.

There are, of course, other prerequisites for the location of a steel mill. The ground structure of a mill site must be capable of bearing the mill's weight. It must also be reasonably level and, preferably, uninhabited. Adequate supplies of fresh water are also mandatory, a prerequisite that gives some cause for concern about one of the proposed south Indian locations, Vishakhapatnam. There is an inadequacy of fresh water at or near this port city that will require the costly diversion of a stream sixty miles from the mill site. If not, a Vishakhapatnam mill could become a modern Fatehpur-Sikri.[21]

[19] Appendix A. [20] See Chapter 3.

[21] Fatehpur-Sikri is an ancient fort twenty miles west of Agra. Built by the Mogul Emperor, Akbar, it was abandoned shortly after its completion because of a shortage of water.

Several cost advantages claimed for south Indian steel mills are questionable. The use of sintered or pelletized fines may result in lower costs of mining per ton of iron. However, it will also necessitate additional operating and capital charges incurred in preparing the blast furnace burden. Were the use of sinter or pellets to result in improved blast furnace performance, these additional costs might be more than offset by lower overall costs of production. Unfortunately, India's experience with sintering thus far has been less than satisfactory, and, partly for this reason, fines are accumulating in the north. India's ores can be mined relatively inexpensively with unskilled labor. Therefore, in the absence of conclusive evidence that agglomerated fines are as satisfactory as lump ore, it is questionable that their use will be beneficial at this time. In any event, because there are also fines in the north, this is not an advantage specific to proposed south Indian locations.

The argument that a south Indian plant could use a greater proportion of market scrap is equally questionable. Relatively long haulage of scrap from scrap-producing centers would be necessary. Scrap purchased in Calcutta could also be used in a north Indian plant. Once again, the use of scrap is an advantage that is not specific to a south Indian mill.

The argument that wagons carrying ore to the sea could return with coal to an inland south Indian mill also applies equally to north Indian mills. Existing north Indian mills do not have the equipment to handle the types of wagons that are returning empty from other north Indian mills. There is no reason why lack of coordination in plant design should be repeated.

Australia, Poland, West Germany, the Union of South Africa, and the United States have been mentioned as possible sources of imported coal. Because the bulk of the ore shipped from Goa and Vishakhapatnam will be carried to Japan, it is difficult to see how ships would be able to stop in these countries advantageously on their return to India. A bilateral trade arrangement with several countries is possible, Indian ore exchanged for non-Indian coal. It is claimed that such an arrangement could allow the use of freighters that might otherwise return to coal exporters empty. However, exports of Indian ore to these countries, with the possible exception of West Germany, would have to be increased substantially. Moreover, because iron ore can be purchased from a number of other nations, India may have to export her best ores, deposits low in alumina and high in iron. If the remaining ores were to be decidedly inferior in quality, the costs of production at south Indian mills would suffer.

Both the purchase of foreign coal and its shipment to India would necessitate expenditures of scarce foreign exchange and would intensify India's foreign exchange difficulties. Exports of ore or, perhaps, some of the iron and steel produced by the south Indian plant, it is argued, could offset increased expenditures of foreign exchange. However, this is begging the issue. If exports can be increased, then India should consider doing so regardless of whether or not she needs to import coal. The export of iron ore and steel would earn needed foreign exchange. Only if coal can be imported without expenditure of convertible currencies, perhaps under a bilateral trade agreement with a country that is unable or unwilling to export anything else of importance to India, could the import of coal be considered no drain on India's actual or potential sources of foreign exchange.

This is not to say that India should embark upon a policy of autarky. The possession of reserves of coking coal is not sufficient reason for India's exploitation of them. Rather, in judging whether or not coal should be imported or mined domestically Indian policy-makers should use a rate of exchange that reflects India's special need for foreign exchange and the purchasing power of the rupee.

It is claimed that regional dispersal of the steel industry would allow circumvention of rail bottlenecks that have hindered the assembly of raw materials and the distribution of finished steel. In particular, it would allow expansion of steel capacity without increasing burdens on lines near existing steel mills. In reality, were a south Indian mill to obtain its coal from north India, either by rail or sea, substantial traffic in the vicinity of existing steel mills would still be necessary. Moreover, Bailadilla and Vishakhapatnam are north of the primary bottleneck that has inhibited shipment of finished steel to south India, Vijayawada in Andhra Pradesh. Perhaps most important, the railways are a decreasing cost industry; it is cheaper to expand the railway capacity in high density areas. The laying of additional track beside existing track will enable the provision of rail services at lower average costs. A large volume of traffic will also enable the profitable adoption of electric traction. In short, additional traffic in northeastern India, far from intensifying India's rail difficulties, may facilitate many needed improvements on India's railways.[22]

It is one thing for India to utilize existing railway facilities as much as possible. Such a policy has had precedent in Soviet economic planning and would serve to minimize investment of scarce resources in a capital-intensive industry. It is another thing for India to mislocate her industry to avoid necessary improvements in her transportation system and to circumvent bottlenecks that are partly a result of past mistakes. Many of these improvements would be necessary regardless of an expansion of northeastern India's steel industry. In fact, some of the industry's rail difficulties have been adjustments to recent changes in India's rail system. In time these difficulties will be overcome without the need for unconventional locations of

[22] I am especially indebted to Alan P. Carlin for this last observation and for many others that have enriched my discussion of the industry's transportation problems.

new industrial units. Far larger steel industries are operating satisfactorily elsewhere in areas as compact as northeastern India and without benefit of water transportation to facilitate their assembly of raw materials. With proper planning, some investment, a revision of policies, and a little patience, India's current transportation difficulties will be overcome.

India's coastal trade in general and methods of handling cargo in particular may be tactfully described as underdeveloped, but better described as primitive.[23] Ships are in many instances manually loaded and unloaded. Although some satisfaction may be taken in this use of labor-intensive methods in a "labor rich" economy, this satisfaction is hardly merited. These methods are slow and tie up costly ship and wharf facilities. They lessen the productivity of the limited amount of capital India has already invested in coastal shipping. At present only a minor proportion of Indian traffic is by sea. Were sufficient attention given to the development of coastal shipping this proportion might be increased significantly. Accordingly, it has been suggested that north Indian coal could be shipped by sea to Goa and Vishakhapatnam to supply south Indian steel mills.

Coastal shipment of coal would not be satisfactory under all circumstances. First, the feasibility of the massive shipment of coal necessitated by a south Indian steel mill could depend on the creation of the deep-water port of Haldia in West Bengal. Work on Haldia has been delayed because the World Bank has had doubts about sponsoring the project.[24] Second, the coastal shipment of coal to a south Indian mill would necessitate more efficient methods of handling ships and more appropriate

[23] For a description of some of the present difficulties involved in moving coal by sea, see Carlin, *A Possible U.S. Policy Towards Indian Transportation . . .*, pp. 32–36; and Coverdale & Colpitts, "India Coal Transport Study," Vol. III, pp. 68–84.

[24] It was reported in mid-1965 that the World Bank has now decided to finance the Haldia project.

vessels than are now employed. Barring major improvements in India's shipping industry, the difficulties that have hampered delivery of raw materials to steel mills by rail will probably be repeated for steel mills that receive part of their raw materials by sea. Transshipment would be necessary at Goa and Vishakhapatnam for inland south Indian plants. If wagons carrying ore to the sea are also to carry coal inland, existing methods may not allow the orderly delivery of coal to south Indian plants. It would probably be better to ship coal to inland mills by rail rather than to transship coal from rail to sea and then back to rail. Finally, Vishakhapatnam is not so distant from Haldia that the coastal shipment of coal to Vishakhapatnam would be advantageous. In short, of all suggested mill sites, only Goa would appear to benefit from the efficient coastal shipment of north Indian coal.

Several advantages can be claimed for hypothetical south Indian mills. Were these mills to consume imported coal, the lower ash content of this coal would enable lower costs of production, all other things being equal. The import of coal would also allow less domestic haulage of raw materials. Similarly, the consumption of south Indian ores with relatively low alumina contents would also enable lower costs of production. Offsetting these cost advantages would be the higher real cost of imported coal, allowing for a suitable revaluation of foreign exchange, and the greater haulage of raw materials were south Indian mills based on north Indian coal.

Whether hypothetical south Indian mills would enjoy a net production cost advantage is a question considered in Table 16. I estimate that costs of production would be lower in hypothetical north Indian plants at Adityapur and Purulia under all circumstances. Were hypothetical south Indian mills to consume imported coal, cost disadvantages resulting from the higher real cost of imported coal would more than offset cost advantages resulting from the better quality of this coal. Were

Table 16. Production Cost Advantages Accruing to Hypothetical Indian Steel Mills
(Rs. per ton of iron)

	Goa	Bellary	Bailadilla	Vishakhapatnam	Adityapur	Purulia
North Indian mills based on north Indian coal; south Indian mills based on imported coal						
Cost advantage resulting from:						
Better quality coal	44	44	44	44	0	0
Lower real cost of coal	0	0	4	4	84	84
Better quality iron ore	16	16	22	22	0	0
Greater proximity to raw materials:						
Through traffic assumed	0	6	7	4	3	0
Closed-circuit traffic assumed	0	6	7	2	5	3
Net cost advantage:						
Through traffic assumed	0	10	21	18	31	28
Closed-circuit traffic assumed	0	10	21	16	33	31
All mills based on north Indian coal						
Cost advantage resulting from:						
Better quality iron ore	16	16	22	22	0	0
Greater proximity to raw materials:						
Through traffic assumed	0	7	35	31	70	67
Closed-circuit traffic assumed	0	14	35	31	62	60
Net cost advantage:						
Through traffic assumed	0	7	41	37	54	51
Closed-circuit traffic assumed	0	14	41	37	46	44

This table is a compilation of information presented in Appendix G.

south Indian mills to consume north Indian coal, lower costs resulting from the consumption of better quality ore would not offset the higher costs of assembling raw materials at south Indian mills.

Costs of Distributing Steel from Hypothetical Steel Mills

Demand for salable steel is concentrated in two Indian states, West Bengal and Maharashtra, or, more particularly, the metropolitan areas of Calcutta and Bombay City. Together these two states account for nearly half of India's demand for steel, although only one-sixth of her population.[25] There are other lesser markets for steel in Uttar Pradesh, the Punjab, Bihar, and Delhi in northern India, and Madras and Andhra Pradesh in southern India.

To determine the costs of distributing finished steel from hypothetical Indian mills, I assume that present patterns of steel distribution are not only economically justified, but will remain unchanged in the future. In fact, the concentration of demand in Bombay and, to a lesser extent, Madras is in part a consequence of an artificial price system in force prior to Indian Independence, the levy of a base price at major ports plus freight inland. Initially, this price policy enabled Indian producers to compete with imported steel. However, since the 1930s Indian costs of production have generally been lower than comparable import prices, assuming a meaningful devaluation of the rupee, and Indian producers have supplied most of India's demand for steel. By the 1950s this price system was an anachronism that had resulted in some mislocation of steel-consuming industries in major port cities relatively distant from Indian mills.

In 1956 this policy was succeeded by regional price equalization which, considering costs alone, is equally unjustified. This new price system may have encouraged additional demand in regions relatively distant from existing mills, southern, western,

[25] Table F-9.

and northwestern India. The establishment of steel prices equal to costs at mills plus freight would, in the long run, probably result in greater concentration of steel demand in northeastern India, where costs of production are the lowest. Although the actual regional distribution of steel demand has almost certainly been distorted by past and present price policies, I still use it to determine the costs of distributing steel produced in hypothetical Indian mills. Any bias introduced should favor locations in southern India.

Proponents of south Indian mills also argue that even though costs of production may be greater in southern India, present demand for steel by both southern and western markets is capable of supporting south Indian mills specializing in production for these regions. Higher costs of production could be offset by lower costs of delivering finished steel to markets.

The locations of several steel mills erected during this century have been market oriented. The Kaiser plant at Fontana, California, the United States Steel Corporation plant at Morrisville, Pennsylvania, and the Bethlehem Steel plant at Sparrows Point, Maryland, are instances of mills situated in relative proximity to markets rather than raw materials. However, it must be stressed that the circumstances that have encouraged market-oriented location elsewhere are relatively unimportant or nonexistent in India.

Historically, the industry has been located near raw materials because of its dependence on large tonnages of coal and iron ore. Over time its consumption of raw materials, particularly coal, has been reduced by improved coke oven and blast furnace techniques. Consumption of coal per ton of iron in Indian plants exceeds consumption of coal elsewhere. This is partly a result of the limited application of recent advances in technology. It is also a result of undesirable impurities in Indian raw materials, the high ash content of India's coal and the high alumina content of her ore. Therefore locations relatively distant from sources of coal will be more disadvantageous in India than elsewhere.[26]

Locations such as Morrisville and Sparrows Point were also selected because of their proximity to the sea, which facilitates receipt of imported iron ore, as well as their proximity to markets for finished steel. Although a coastal-based plant has been considered for India, it is not a necessity. India's raw materials are sufficient to support several new steel mills; conditions of raw materials supply that exist elsewhere and encourage market-oriented location do not exist in India.

Large markets for steel generate large amounts of scrap. In the United States, scrap constitutes 30 to 40 per cent of the charge of open hearth furnaces. The scrap consumed by furnaces has been increasing but is still only slightly more than 20 per cent, and almost all of this scrap is produced in the plants themselves. Relatively little scrap is purchased from the market for two basic reasons. Abundant and well-located ore deposits have made their conservation less necessary than in such countries as the United States, where reserves of high grade ore are nearly depleted. In addition, the ability of a nation to generate scrap is largely a function of its level of economic development. India's is still an underdeveloped economy and her production of market scrap is limited. There are no large centers of scrap production in India of the magnitude of those that exist in Europe, America, and Japan.

Market-oriented location has also been encouraged by market conditions governing the sale of steel. With the exception of the war and immediate postwar years, the steel industries of

[26] Indian consumption of coke per ton of iron was 900 kg in 1960. By use of improved techniques it is thought that this rate could be brought down to 650 kg. Even so, it would still be above the maximum 570 kg obtained in the United States and Canada in 1959. M. N. Dastur, *Steel in India—Economic and Technological Possibilities*, The fourth Sir M. Visvesvaraya Lecture, delivered at the 41st Annual Convention of the Institution of Engineers (India) (Calcutta: *The Statesman*, Commercial Printing Department, 1961), p. 19.

Europe and America have been plagued by continued overcapacity. Even so, price competition in steel has been limited by a steel cartel in Europe and the basing point system and, more recently, price leadership in America. Competition has generally assumed other forms, one being service to customers. The location of mills near their markets has enabled rapid delivery of steel with less need for maintaining large inventories. There is no evidence of long-run overcapacity in India's steel industry. Nor need there be with judicious planning.

Finally, it is usually more profitable for a mill with a capacity of 1.5 million ingot tons, the tentative initial capacity of each of the proposed south Indian plants, to produce only one of several broad categories of steel. Also, it is more profitable for all mills to produce relatively large tonnages of few sections rather than smaller tonnages of many sections. A steel mill is able to locate near Detroit specializing in the production of sheets for the Detroit market. India may be unique among underdeveloped economies in that her market for various broad categories of steel is sufficient to sustain production of each major category of steel at economic levels. However, it may be questioned whether this demand is so concentrated in any one consuming center, let alone in southern and western India, that both minimization of costs of producing steel and of costs of delivering steel to customers would be possible.

Despite shortcomings in the argument that the locations of south Indian mills would benefit from the proximity of markets, I assume that these mills will distribute their steel only to southern and western India. The estimated average costs of distributing steel from these mills to their markets are presented in Table 17. These estimates yield several important conclusions.

First, if a steel mill is to produce rails and heavy structurals for southern and western markets, considering costs of distribution alone it would be better to locate a new mill in northeastern India and to allow Bhilai to specialize on these markets.

Table 17. Average Costs of Distributing the Product of Proposed South and North Indian Steel Mills to Markets[a]
(Rs. per ton of salable steel)

	Product distributed to seven southern and western states			Product distributed to all of India		
Mill site	Rails and heavy sections	Bars and light structurals	Flat products	Rails and heavy sections	Bars and light structurals	Flat products
Goa	62[b]	61	59	94	91	93
Bellary	57[b]	55	55	87	85	88
Bailadilla	77[b]	94	96	91	92	95
Vishakhapatnam	69[b]	77	79	74	75	79
Adityapur	55[c]	93	92	62	65	66
Purulia	55[c]	95	95	62	66	66

[a] Computed from data presented in Tables F–4, F–9 and F–11, Appendix F, assuming the average cost of transporting a ton of finished steel equal to the weighted average of rates actually charged from July 1962 until April 1964. These rates are presented in Indian Railway Conference Association, *Goods Rate Tables in Force from 1st July, 1962*, Goods Tariff—No. 31-A, Part II (New Delhi: Government of India Publication, 1962), pp. 6–14, Col. 65-B. For assumptions underlying data presented in this table, see Appendix G.

[b] Arithmetic average assuming Bhilai to produce for northern and eastern markets.

[c] Arithmetic average assuming Bhilai to produce for southern and western markets.

Second, location of a steel mill at Bailadilla would confer no advantage and at Vishakhapatnam relatively little advantage in the distribution of steel to southern and western markets. It is unfortunate that, although both sites would allow lower costs of production than Goa and Bellary, both would also necessitate higher costs of distributing finished steel to assumed markets. Third, the shipment of finished steel from Goa by rail would in most instances require either transshipment from meter to broad gauge track or construction of additional broad gauge track to the plant site. Finally, should south Indian mills distribute their steel throughout India, all mills would be placed at a substantial disadvantage in the distribution of their steel. Location of a mill at Vishakhapatnam would be less disadvantageous, an important benefit of this mill site.

Total Cost Advantages Resulting from the Location of New Mills in South India

Will advantages accruing to south Indian mills because of their proximity to assumed markets offset disadvantages resulting from their higher costs of production? An answer to this question is indicated in Table 18. Assuming the products of new Indian steel mills to be distributed only to southern and western markets, it would appear that only under certain circumstances would south Indian locations be justified by costs alone. South Indian mills would have to produce bars and light structurals or flat products and not rails and heavy sections. The Bellary mill would appear to be preferable were a new south Indian mill based on imported coal, the advantage of the Bellary site for the most part deriving from its proximity to assumed markets. Even so, the maximum difference between the total costs of production and distribution at Bellary and Adityapur would be Rs. 14 per ton of salable steel, only 2 per cent of the official selling price in force in 1962. Vishakhapatnam would be preferred were south Indian mills based on

Table 18. Cost Advantages Accruing to Hypothetical Steel Mills Whose Output Is Distributed Only to Southern and Western Markets[a]
(Rs. per ton of salable steel)

	Goa	Bellary	Bailadilla	Vishakhapatnam	Adityapur	Purulia
North Indian mills based on north Indian coal; south Indian mills based on imported coal						
Through traffic of raw materials:						
Rails and heavy sections	0	16	9	13	42	39
Bars and light structurals	9	26	0	13	12	7
Flat products	13	28	0	13	15	9
Closed-circuit traffic of raw materials:						
Rails and heavy sections	0	16	9	11	44	42
Bars and light sections	9	26	0	11	14	10
Flat products	13	28	0	11	17	12
All mills based on north Indian coal						
Through traffic of raw materials:						
Rails and heavy sections	0	13	31	35	68	64
Bars and light sections	0	14	13	26	29	23
Flat products	0	12	9	22	28	21
Closed-circuit traffic of raw materials:						
Rails and heavy sections	0	21	31	35	59	57
Bars and light sections	0	22	13	26	20	16
Flat products	0	20	9	22	19	14

[a] Computed from data presented in Tables 16 and 17. Production costs per ton of iron have been converted to costs per ton of salable steel on the assumption that on average .88 tons of iron are consumed per ton of ingots and 1.28 tons of ingots per ton of salable steel.

north Indian coal and were closed-circuit traffic of raw materials possible. However, once again the maximum cost advantage accruing to a mill at Vishakhapatnam would be minor, less than one per cent of the official selling price for steel. *For all practical purposes, south Indian mills would have no cost advantage over north Indian mills.*

Barring adequate information, I have made assumptions that, if anything, tend to bias cost estimates against proposed north Indian plants. For example, were the real cost of distributing a ton of steel lower than that assumed, cost advantages possessed by south Indian mills in the distribution of their steel could disappear. Were the assumed value of the rupee still lower, the apparent cost advantages of south Indian mills based on imported coal would vanish.[27] Perhaps most important, if it is assumed that south Indian mills, following the example of Bhilai, distribute their product throughout India, there would be no economic justification for their existence. In short, evidence suggests that the location of new mills in south India would confer little or no cost advantage to the Indian economy; it may, in fact, inflict a substantial cost disadvantage on the economy.

Prospects for Regional Specialization in Distribution as well as Commodity Specialization in Production

One assumption made in the foregoing section can be relaxed. It has been assumed that south Indian plants, in addition to specializing in broad categories of rolled steel, would distribute their entire output to southern and western India. The implicit assumption has been made that it would be at least as advantageous for a mill to produce many different sections as it would

[27] Were the rupee assumed equal to 10.5 cents, rather than 14 cents, the costs of imported coal would increase by Rs. 36 per ton. This would result in an increase in production costs at south Indian mills based on imported coal of at least Rs. 42 per ton of salable steel.

be to produce large tonnages of a few sections within a broad category of products. This assumption may be incorrect. At present Bhilai produces only billets, heavy rails, and larger cross-section structurals. On the other hand, TISCO, IISCO, and Durgapur also produce lighter rails and smaller structurals. There is some specialization in the specific types of steel rolled in a mill, although such specialization is by no means complete.

Specialization in production allows lower operating and capital costs. It eliminates the necessity for duplicating rolls for low tonnage sections. It also allows longer rolling periods per section which in turn enables fuller utilization of plant and manpower. However, lower production costs would be partially offset by higher costs of distributing finished steel. Barring regional concentration of demand for a specific section, the more of a specific section produced by a plant the further that section will have to be distributed.

It is for this reason, primarily, that neither Bhilai nor any other mill has concentrated on nearby markets. Prior to decontrol, rolling schedules were determined by the Office of the Iron and Steel Controller in Calcutta. Since decontrol they have been determined by the steel mills through the Joint Plant Committee. Both parties have had incentives to establish longer rolling programs for specific sections, the Office of the Iron and Steel Controller because they would enable a more rapid reduction in the backlog of demand for scarce sections, the Joint Plant Committee because they would result in greater output and profits. Neither party has had an incentive to minimize costs of distributing steel because these costs are borne by consumers. Barring some change in the method of determining rolling schedules, it is possible that future south Indian steel mills, like Bhilai originally justified by their proximity to nearby markets, will in fact distribute much of their steel to northern and eastern India. If so, this will be still another instance of lack of coordination between planners in New Delhi and administrators in Calcutta.

Costs of distributing steel have been recomputed on the assumption that steel produced at all hypothetical mills will be sold throughout India. Were this to happen, data presented in Table 19 indicate that all south Indian mills would be placed at a cost disadvantage with respect to hypothetical north Indian mills. The economics of south Indian mills depend critically on the distribution of their steel to nearby markets.

Conclusion

The economic justification of south Indian steel mills will depend upon the correctness of a number of assumptions made on their behalf. Judging from the recent experience of the industry, these assumptions may prove incorrect. The steel produced by a south Indian plant may be distributed throughout India and not to southern and western India alone. The raw materials consumed by a south Indian plant may, like some raw materials consumed by mills erected in northeastern India, prove less satisfactory than is now anticipated. Bottlenecks, delays, and lapses in planning may hinder the development of India's coastal trade or the erection of essential rail lines. The consequences of Bhilai's failure to fulfill the expectations of Indian planners, Bhilai's inability to use Korba coals and its seeming inability to distribute a large percentage of its steel to southern and western India, have not been serious. However, the failure of south Indian mills to fulfill the expectations of India's planners could place these mills, with the possible exception of Vishakhapatnam, at a substantial cost disadvantage with respect to potential north Indian mills.

Proponents of the industry's dispersal often claim that it will enable more rapid growth in all regions of India, a benefit not measured by a simple cost analysis of alternative mill sites. In other words, dispersal would result in external economies that would justify the erection of a steel mill in south India.

I am skeptical about this claim. The erection of a machine tools, aluminum, or power plant in south India may provide

Table 19. Cost Advantages Accruing to Hypothetical Steel Mills Whose Output Is Distributed Throughout India[a]
(Rs. per ton of salable steel)

	Goa	Bellary	Bailadilla	Vishakhapatnam	Adityapur	Purulia
North Indian mills based on north Indian coal; south Indian mills based on imported coal						
Through traffic of raw materials:						
Rails and heavy sections	0	18	27	40	67	64
Bars and light structurals	0	17	23	36	61	57
Flat products	0	16	22	34	62	59
Closed-circuit traffic of raw materials:						
Rails and heavy sections	0	18	27	38	69	67
Bars and light structurals	0	17	23	34	63	60
Flat products	0	16	22	32	64	62
All mills based on north Indian coal						
Through traffic of raw materials:						
Rails and heavy sections	0	15	49	62	93	89
Bars and light structurals	0	14	45	58	87	82
Flat products	0	13	44	56	88	84
Closed-circuit traffic of raw materials:						
Rails and heavy sections	0	23	49	62	84	82
Bars and light structurals	0	22	45	58	78	75
Flat products	0	21	44	56	79	77

[a] Computed from data presented in Tables 16 and 17. Production costs per ton of iron have been converted to costs per ton of salable steel on assumption that on average .88 tons of iron are consumed per ton of ingots and 1.28 tons of ingots per ton of salable steel.

as much stimulus to the region's industrial growth as a new steel mill and may also be justified by the region's factor endowments. Moreover, steel is not an essential or at least a primary input for most industries; other inputs or perhaps market considerations may be more important determinants of an industry's location. Even if it is assumed that a region is a high cost producer of all commodities, factors of production would have to be completely mobile were the law of comparative advantage to be totally inoperative. In any event, regional price equalization for steel and the Indian government's attempts to license new industrial capacity in relatively underdeveloped regions have already stimulated much of the industrial growth that would, presumably, result from the regional dispersal of the steel industry. All in all, I fail to see how external economies would favor the location of new steel mills in as many states as possible.

Economists tend to be purists about the intrusion of non-economic objectives into economic policy decisions. Indian planning is also a political process and some adherence to non-economic objectives in planning is inevitable. There is frequent mention in India of "fissiparous tendencies" rooted in intense regional loyalties.[28] There are also contrary forces tending toward union, and no doubt India must maintain and strengthen these forces even at some cost of growth of the Indian economy. One of these forces is the planning process itself. One way the Congress Party has maintained its strength in all regions of India has been its allocation of major plan projects to each region. By performing its essential function of interest satisfaction, Congress has also contributed, in some measure, to the strengthening of the Indian union.

Does the political and ideological imperative, the regional dispersal of each industry necessarily mean the dispersal of

[28] For example, see Selig S. Harrison, *India, the Most Dangerous Decades* (Princeton, N.J.: Princeton University Press, 1960).

each industry, or, at least, each industry considered basic to the Indian economy? I do not think so. It is possible for south India to specialize on those industries for which it is well endowed. Given an integrated economy in which trade between regions is possible, there is no reason why any one region of India cannot specialize in industries for which it has a comparative advantage, trade the goods produced by these industries with other regions, and thereby contribute to the maximization of India's national income. Indian policy-makers might make more effective use of their skills were they to cease attempting to justify south Indian steel mills and instead seek to determine how regional dispersal of industry can best be reconciled with the most efficient use of India's resources. Regional dispersal need not and probably should not mean the erection of a steel mill in as many states as possible.

10 | Small Pig Iron Plants: The Use of Unconventional Methods of Producing Iron

The blast furnace is almost universally used for smelting ore because it is normally the lowest cost process. However the range of raw materials consumed by the blast furnace is limited. Because it is a relatively large and indivisible unit, reserves of iron ore must be ample for a furnace life that allows an adequate return on capital. In addition, the blast furnace demands a porous coke relatively low in ash and other impurities and sufficiently hard to withstand the weight of the furnace burden. Only a small proportion of the world's coals can be converted into coke possessing these specifications.

Although iron ores are distributed throughout the Indian subcontinent, coking coals are found only in West Bengal and Bihar. Therefore the regional dispersal of iron production in blast furnaces will be limited unless coking coal is imported or hauled over long distances. To overcome this obstacle to dispersal, the government has either sanctioned or is considering the erection of a number of alternative types of furnaces or small blast furnaces both in the public and private sectors. These furnaces may use as their source of heat such fuels as noncoking coal and lignite briquettes, or as an alternative to fuel, electricity. All but one would produce pig iron for sale on the market. The exception, a proposed mill in Madras, would produce iron for conversion to steel.

This chapter considers India's experiment with small pig iron plants because it illustrates how plan objectives for the private sector must be supported by meaningful incentives if these objectives are to be met. The Madras steel mill, although interesting for some purposes, is not directly relevant to my discussion and is examined in Appendix H.

India's Experiment with Small Pig Iron Plants

Not all iron is converted to steel. Some is sold on the market primarily to foundries for the manufacture of castings. At present most of India's salable iron is produced by IISCO and two public sector plants, the output of the former reserved almost entirely for that company's pipe plant at Kulti. A small amount of salable pig iron has been produced in what are called "small pig iron plants," and if present plans come to fruition, the output of these plants will increase substantially during the next decade.

Small pig iron plants were originally licensed up to a capacity of 15,000 tons per year. Because this was thought too low to encourage their erection, the upper limit was raised to 100,000 and, more recently, 300,000 tons. As another incentive to their establishment, small pig iron plants were exempted from price and distribution controls governing India's integrated steel mills. For over a decade there was a severe shortage of foundry grade iron. Therefore, freedom to sell iron at the market price was thought to be a considerable incentive for the erection of small pig iron plants.

Originally all pig iron plants were to be established in the private sector. However, since 1963 the governments of at least three states, Andhra Pradesh, Orissa, and the Punjab, have either purchased or have plans to build small pig iron plants. State government entry into the pig iron industry is a departure of great importance.

Small pig iron plants that have been licensed by the government are indicated in Table 20. Of twelve plants approved by March 1963 only three have been erected, and one of the three has suspended operations. By 1963 licenses of at least four of the twelve plants were surrendered or revoked because the firms sponsoring them took no action toward their erection. The establishment of all but one of the remaining plants is now in doubt. At least eight additional plants are reported to have been licensed since March 1963. It is still too soon to know whether most of these plants will be erected or, as in so many instances in the past, whether they will progress no further than their licensing. However, it is certain that the Third Plan target for small pig iron plants has failed. Slightly less than half of increased production of pig iron during the period was to have come from these plants.[1] In fact, their contribution was negligible by the end of the period.[2]

Perhaps the best place to begin an appraisal of India's small pig iron plants is with the three that have been erected. The plant at Barbil, Orissa, was originally owned by private interests, including a former chief minister of Orissa. In 1963 it was sold to the Orissan State Government. Not only was the government eager to establish a state sector in the industry, the Barbil plant allegedly had not proved overly profitable despite its sales at the market price and not the controlled price established by the Government of India. The plant at Coimbatore, Madras,

[1] India's output of salable pig iron was to increase from 1.14 million tons in 1961 to 1.53 million tons in 1965–66. Bokaro was to supply an additional .36 million tons; small pig iron plants, .31 million tons. The output of existing steel mills was expected to fall. Government of India, Planning Commission, "Steel in the Third Five Year Plan: Requirements, Availability and Allocation," (mimeograph, New Delhi, 1962), p. 30.

[2] In 1964, the most recent year for which production data are available, India produced 1.13 million tons of salable iron; small pig iron plants produced .04 million tons. Government of India, Ministry of Steel and Mines, Department of Iron and Steel, *Report, 1964–65* (New Delhi: Government of India Publication, 1965), p. 1.

Table 20. Small Pig Iron Plants Licensed by Mid-1964[a]

Location of the plant	Firm erecting the plant	Year licensed	Licensed capacity (tons)	Status of the plant
Licensed as of March 1963				
Barbil, Orissa	Kalinga Industries, Ltd.	1955	15,000[b]	In operation. Transferred to the Government of Orissa in 1963.
—	(expansion of same)	1960	100,000[c]	Expansion originally scheduled for completion in 1966 is being sponsored by the West German government.
Coimbatore, Madras	Textool Co., Ltd.	1957	15,000	Ceased operations in April 1960, six months after operations were begun.
Salem, Madras	Soundarajan & Co., Madras	1958	15,000	No action; license revoked.
Bombay, Maharashtra	Sepulchre Bros., Bombay	1958	15,000	No action; license revoked.
Salem, Madras	Kalinga Industries, Ltd.	1959	15,000	License surrendered
Calcutta, West Bengal	Todi Steel Corp., Ltd.	1959	15,000	No action; license revoked.
Khapoli, Maharashtra	Acme Pig Iron and Centrifugal Pipe Works, Ltd., Bombay	1959	15,000	In operation since late 1962.
—	(expansion)	1961	30,000[c]	Expansion reported to be underway in 1963.

Location of the plant	Firm erecting the plant	Year licensed	Licensed capacity (tons)	Status of the plant
Chanda, Maharashtra	Hind Traders, Bombay	1960	96,000	Firm was serious but no action was taken; project has been canceled.
Chanda, Maharashtra	Birla Gwalior (P) Ltd.	1962	100,000	Firm was serious and initial preparations were made; however, firm now plans another plant in Bihar.
Udaipur, Rajasthan	Kamani Engineering Corp., Ltd., Bombay	1962	100,000	Firm was serious and initial preparations were made; however, firm now plans another plant in Maharashtra.
Khammam, Andhra Pradesh	Kalinga Industries, Ltd.	1962	100,000	Erection is doubtful.
Kothagudem, Andhra Pradesh	Government of Andhra Pradesh, Industrial Development Corp.	1963	100,000	State government is serious; preparations are said to be underway.
Some plants reported to have been licensed subsequent to March 1963[d]				
Hissar, Punjab	Government of the Punjab	1963	100,000	State government appears serious; foreign participation is being sought.
Bihar	Birla Gwalior (P) Ltd.	1964	300,000	Loan application to World Bank is pending.

(*Table 20 continued on next page*)

Table 20 (*cont.*)

Location of the plant	Firm erecting the plant	Year licensed	Licensed capacity (tons)	Status of the plant
Goa	V. S. Dempo and Co., Goa	1964	300,000	Foreign collaboration is being sought.
Goa	V. M. Salgaocar E. Imrao, Ltd., Goa	1964	300,000	Preliminary work is said to be underway.
Ratnagiri Dt., Maharashtra	P. D. Chowgule and Company, Bombay	1964	200,000	Application for a loan was rejected by the World Bank.
Goa	The Asian Industries Corp., Bombay	1964	200,000	Foreign collaboration is being sought.
Talcher, Orissa	Orissa (Government) Industrial Development Corporation, Ltd., Bhubaneshwar	1964	180,000	Initial preparations have been made.
Maharashtra	Kamani Engineering Corp., Ltd., Bombay	1964	100,000	No information available.

[a] This table is based on information obtained from the Indian Foundry Association and Ministry of Steel and Heavy Industries, Department of Iron and Steel, in early 1963. It is also based on articles published subsequently in the Indian press and trade journals. In particular, see, *Iron and Steel Review,* June 1964, pp. 11–12; August 1964, p. 27; September 1964, p. 23; and October 1964, p. 23.

[b] Actual initial capacity, 30,000 tons.

[c] Total capacity after expansion.

[d] In addition there have been incomplete and, in some instances, contradictory reports of the licensing of other plants in West Bengal, Goa, and Madras.

was a misadventure. Although distinguished by the fact that it was built with discarded equipment assembled entirely from within India, it was defectively designed, poorly situated, and could produce pig iron only at a very high cost. When a part of its equipment was destroyed in April 1960, six months after it began production, the plant's management chose to suspend operations rather than replace the equipment. The plant at Khapoli, near Bombay, employs a hot blast cupola to melt scrap. It is atypical because it does not smelt iron ore, and its success or failure is no measure for other small pig iron plants. In short, the experience thus far has not been particularly encouraging.

The advantages claimed for small pig iron plants are the same or similar to those claimed for the dispersal of India's steel industry.[3] In general small pig iron plants would be located near deposits of iron ore and, in a few instances, deposits of coal unsuitable for use in blast furnaces. These locations would be doubly advantageous. First, because of their small capacities, the plants could draw upon reserves that are too limited to sustain larger blast furnaces. Second, because many of these plants would use alternative processes to the blast furnace, they could consume poorer quality raw materials, particularly nonmetallurgical coals.

The exploitation of scattered deposits of iron ore and coal may not be advantageous if these deposits need not be used. Once again, India's reserves of coking coal in the Bengal and Bihar coalfields and probable reserves of iron ore and limestone are adequate for much greater iron production than is contemplated from existing and proposed mills in northeastern India.[4] Whether or not lesser deposits of raw materials should be exploited can be determined only by a comparison of pro-

[3] For a discussion of the merits of small pig iron plants, see B. R. Nijhawan, "Iron and Steel Industry in India," *Symposium on Iron and Steel Industry in India, Jamshedpur, 1959* (Calcutta: Technical Journals of India, Private, Ltd., 1959), p. 334.

[4] See Chapter 3 and Appendix A.

duction costs of small pig iron plants with production costs of conventional blast furnaces.

It is also claimed that small pig iron plants can be erected more quickly than large blast furnace units. This may be true in theory; it has not happened in fact. Most plants that have been licensed have never been built. The Barbil plant was licensed in 1955 but did not begin production until 1959, the same period of time in which the first HSL blast furnaces were erected. The Khapoli plant was licensed in 1959 but was not completed until the end of 1962. Only the Coimbatore plant was set up in a considerably shorter period of time than is needed to establish a blast furnace unit, and that plant has been closed, in part because of mistakes resulting from its too hasty erection.

A small pig iron plant would use one of four processes: electric reduction; the low shaft furnace; the small blast furnace; or a combination of electric reduction and prereduction in a kiln. Electric furnaces are operating in a number of countries, including India. However, these furnaces cannot produce a competitive pig iron unless they consume exceedingly low cost power. The Mysore Iron and Steel Works uses electric reduction and is situated near cheap hydroelectric power. Yet it has been a substantially higher cost producer of iron than north Indian steel mills. The outlook for the profitable use of electric reduction elsewhere in India is not bright.

The low shaft furnace is essentially a blast furnace in which the ratio of height to diameter is unusually small. Although this furnace is capable of using such inferior fuels as lignite briquettes and nut coke, its fuel consumption is substantially greater than that of the blast furnace. The Barbil low shaft or small blast furnace (opinions differ about its correct designation) was sold to the Orissa government because it was not profitable. A West German prototype of the Barbil furnace was closed down because its iron could not compete with iron produced in conventional blast furnaces. The outlook for the profitable use of low shaft furnaces in India also is not very bright.

Perhaps the greatest hope for small pig iron plants lies in electric reduction combined with prereduction in a kiln, if for no other reason than because such processes are relatively new and have had little commercial application elsewhere. Before entering an electric furnace, the charge is passed through a kiln for prereduction. A number of prereduction processes have been developed since World War II. Only one, the Strategic-Udy process, was in commercial operation by 1965, at a steel mill in Venezuela.

It is generally conceded that the operating costs of small pig iron plants would be higher than those of the large blast furnace, a rough estimate of the difference being Rs. 75 per ton.[5] The principal advantage of the large blast furnace lies in its efficient consumption of fuel. However, it is often claimed that the higher operating costs of small pig iron plants would be offset by lower capital charges and savings in the distribution of iron to nearby markets. The validity of this claim is open to question.

[5] In 1961–62 the actual works costs at the three integrated steel mills that produce significant amounts of foundry grade iron, IISCO, Bhilai, and Durgapur, ranged from Rs. 120.84 to Rs. 123.45 per ton. Indian Tariff Commission, *Report on the Fair Ex-Works Retention Prices of Pig Iron for the Period 1st April 1960 to 31st March 1962* (New Delhi: Government of India Publication, 1962), pp. 5 and 9. A reasonable minimum estimate of works costs at small pig iron plants is Rs. 200 per ton. An informant familiar with the Barbil furnace declared in 1963 that its operating costs were at least Rs. 220 per ton. These should be reduced when its expansion program is completed. The consultant for the company proposing to erect an electric furnace at Udaipur, Rajasthan, has, in his project report, predicted works costs equal to Rs. 234 per ton including depreciation, or slightly more than Rs. 200 per ton excluding depreciation. The company that controls the Strategic-Udy process claims that this process is capable of producing iron at Khammam, Andhra Pradesh, at works costs equal to Rs. 175.25 per ton. This projection was considered exceedingly optimistic by an Indian engineer familiar with the process.

Whether or not investment in a small pig iron plant would be lower than investment in a large blast furnace unit is debatable.[6] Even so, lower capital charges incurred by a small pig iron plant would at best amount to Rs. 25 per ton.[7] The cost of shipping pig iron produced at existing steel mills to the furthest small pig iron plants would be approximately Rs. 50 per ton. Clearly, only under the most favorable assumptions would the costs incurred by a small pig iron plant be comparable to those incurred by a blast furnace unit. Were these assumptions less than favorable, small pig iron plants would be placed at a cost disadvantage.

In fact, the Indian market for pig iron is overwhelmingly concentrated in regions nearest India's existing steel mills. The actual regional distribution of pig iron is indicated in Table 21. Eastern and north central India, including West Bengal, consume 76 per cent of India's salable iron; West Bengal alone consumes 66 per cent. Unless there are major changes in regional patterns of iron consumption, advantages resulting from the regional dispersal of pig iron manufacture will be limited.

Under normal circumstances iron produced in small pig iron plants could not compete with iron produced in large blast furnaces located in northeastern India. Private interests have considered erecting small pig iron plants only because circumstances have not been normal. Until recently Indian demand for foundry grade iron was well in excess of supply, and the

[6] In 1962 average investment in a new blast furnace unit, including ancillary facilities, was slightly more than Rs. 500 per annual ton. Anticipated investment in a small pig iron plant licensed for erection in Maharashtra was Rs. 500 per annual ton. *Iron and Steel Review* (September 1961), p. 46. The consultant for a firm planning to erect a plant at Udaipur, Rajasthan, placed the plant's cost at Rs. 460 per ton. The company that developed the Strategic-Udy process predicted a capital cost of Rs. 400 per ton for a plant at Khammam, Andhra Pradesh. This last estimate was thought somewhat optimistic by an Indian engineer familiar with the process.

[7] I assume that a blast furnace unit would cost Rs. 525 per annual ton; a small pig iron plant, Rs. 400. I also assume that return on investment is estimated at 15 per cent and depreciation at 5 per cent.

Table 21. Regional Distribution of Salable Pig Iron in India, April 1961 through November 1962[a]

	Distribution of pig iron (thousand tons)	(per cent)
Total	*1,654.7*	*100.0*
Exports	87.0	5.3
Eastern and north central India excluding West Bengal (Assam, Bihar, NEFA, Madhya Pradesh, Orissa, Tripura, and Uttar Pradesh)	159.7	9.7
West Bengal	1,089.4	65.8
Northwestern India (Delhi, Himachal Pradesh, Jammu and Kashmir, Punjab, and Rajasthan)	134.4	8.1
Western India (Maharashtra and Gujarat)	118.3	7.2
Southern India (Andhra Pradesh, Kerala, Andaman Islands, Madras, Mysore, and Pondicherry)	65.9	4.0

[a] Data on the distribution of iron are estimated from Government of India, Ministry of Steel and Heavy Industries, *Iron and Steel Control, Monthly Bulletin* (Calcutta: Government of India Publication, various months).

quality of foundry iron produced by India's integrated steel mills was not altogether satisfactory. Both circumstances encouraged consumers to search for alternative sources of foundry iron. A ready market developed capable of bearing prices substantially in excess of controlled selling prices and of sustaining an artificially high level of profits for small pig iron plants.[8]

[8] In early 1963 the Barbil plant allegedly sold its foundry iron at approximately Rs. 300 per ton, Rs. 50 per ton higher than the controlled selling price in force at that time.

Some plants have been promoted by companies that are themselves consumers of iron and are willing to pay a higher price for the iron they need in terms of its higher production costs. Several state governments have also supported private schemes, notably by offering to charge low electricity rates for plants that would be wholly or partially dependent on electric smelting. Therefore, the willingness of private parties to consider erecting small pig iron plants is no indication of their economic soundness.

Several small pig iron ventures were never serious proposals. License collecting has been encouraged by the complexity of India's licensing procedures. Moreover, even serious proposals have foundered because of the inability of their promoters to arrange foreign collaboration. Some of the processes to be used by these plants have been little used elsewhere. The profitability of these processes is open to question, and the future policies of the government are in doubt. Therefore foreign business interests have not been willing to participate in the erection of small pig iron plants. Moreover, small pig iron plants would be profitable only if India's shortage of high quality, foundry grade pig iron persists. The elimination of this shortage by the erection of small pig iron plants already licensed could substantially reduce the earnings of these plants. Its elimination by an increase in the pig iron output of India's integrated steel mills, which I am told has happened during the mid-1960s, and an improvement in the quality of the pig iron produced by India's integrated mills could make it impossible for small pig iron plants to earn any profit at all. Thus, a paradoxical situation has arisen. The possible elimination of India's pig iron shortage has discouraged an important means by which this is to be achieved.[9]

[9] For a brief discussion of some of the reasons given by the government for the slow progress in erecting small pig iron plants, see Government of India, Ministry of Steel, Mines and Heavy Engineering, Department of Iron and Steel, *Report, 1963–64* (New Delhi: Government of India Publication, 1964), p. 17.

The Significance of the Experiment's Failure

There is growing disillusion with India's experiment with small pig iron plants. Realizing that the program has failed, and that foundry iron shortages will continue, the government has decided to expand facilities for the production of salable iron at its integrated mills. Moreover, proposed small pig iron plants are no longer small. Originally a plant's maximum capacity was 15,000 tons per year. The limit is now 300,000 tons, the capacity of a small blast furnace. Finally, the government has begun to license small blast furnaces in the private sector. One result of these policy revisions is a partial retreat from two important objectives of small pig iron plants: the regional dispersal of the pig iron industry and the establishment of small units in the private sector to avoid concentrations of economic power.

Although small pig iron plants would produce iron at higher costs than large blast furnaces, it has been argued that the regional dispersal made possible by the erection of these plants would yield external economies. It would contribute to the more widespread diffusion of modern technologies, work practices, and patterns of behavior, and thereby make a larger cross-section of the Indian population susceptible to industrial growth.

The dispersal of the pig iron industry could also result in external diseconomies. If pig iron plants based partly or entirely on electric reduction are located in regions that suffer from power scarcities, they may force a curtailment in the activities of other industries.[10] Similarly, if the spread of small pig iron plants requires a relatively large number of skilled technicians, the result of this spread may be the intensification of skill scarcities suffered by other public and private sector enterprise.

[10] The possibility of power shortages resulting from the erection of the Madras steel mill is discussed in Appendix H.

India's experience with small pig iron plants demonstrates the need to internalize external economies if development plans are to be based upon private sector expansion of an industry. If a new plant is considered laudable on social grounds, but is unprofitable, it would be nonsensical to expect a businessman to erect the plant. The government allowed small pig iron plants to sell their products at market prices rather than the lower controlled prices allowed integrated steel mills. However, this concession was not sufficient to encourage meaningful private sector entry into the industry. One result was the failure of India's plan targets for small pig iron plants and continued scarcities of foundry iron until the mid–1960s.

Alternative methods of producing iron suggested for India have not had successful commercial application. It is questionable that India should use these methods. This is not to say that advantages do not accrue to developing economies from their ability to copy recent technological innovations elsewhere. India might profitably adopt such accepted advances in the iron and steel industry as continuous casting and the use of oxygen in the manufacture of steel. The argument here is that alternative processes to the blast furnace are still relatively unknown and not widely accepted. Until it can be shown conclusively that they are commercially feasible, Indian planners would do well to be wary of them. One advantage to a nation possessing a relatively underdeveloped economy is its ability to benefit from research, experimentation, and commercial application elsewhere. This allows more of the nation's limited resources of skilled manpower and savings to be utilized in the erection of productive enterprises of well-known commercial advantage rather than experimental laboratories, pilot plants, and establishments of unknown or doubtful commercial advantage. Plants based upon alternative processes for manufacturing iron would be gambles. Although a contribution to mankind's knowledge of these processes, these plants could be decidedly less beneficial to India.

11 | The Planned Growth of India's Steel Industry: A Summary

This study finds relatively little theoretical reason to question the existence of an Indian steel industry. India possesses a long history of iron and steel manufacture that, aside from providing her policy-makers with a measure of her ability to produce steel at low cost, has equipped her with a basis of expertise upon which to build her industry. Moreover, India has all major raw materials necessary for the manufacture of steel and, although some reservations about their quality are justified, these raw materials possess other attributes that commend their exploitation. Present aggregate Indian demand for steel is adequate for existing steel mills, and future demand will probably be sufficient to support much of the increased steel capacity contemplated by Indian planners. Finally, assuming any realistic rate of exchange, a rate that adequately values foreign exchange to the Indian economy, Indian steel could be produced at a total real cost competitive with the landed price of imported steel. In theory, at least, India might plan for some expansion of her steel industry.

Admittedly, these conclusions are only as good as the many assumptions upon which they are based. They are subject to at least five major qualifications. First, India's comparative advantage in the production of steel is less evident if this production is to take place in mills located in southern and western India. Whether these mills will be as advantageous as mills located at alternative sites in northeastern India will depend upon the validity of several assumptions made on their behalf. Similar assumptions have proved to be incorrect in the past. Second, economic advantages accruing from the production of iron by use of alternative methods to the blast furnace are not obvious. Both the dispersal of the industry and the use of alternative methods to enable this dispersal are motivated by political and ideological considerations and appear to have doubtful economic bases. Third, the argument favoring the production of steel in India is less compelling insofar as the price mechanism and controls governing the production and distribution of steel encourage output of the wrong types of steel and its allocation for the wrong uses. Fourth, this argument is also less compelling insofar as the public sector mills' operations fall far short of expectations, nullifying assumptions made about the value of the mills' output, their costs of production, and the long-run investment in their plant and equipment. Finally, although most estimates of aggregate demand support India's plan targets for steel, demand for specific categories of steel do not. There was excessive emphasis on rails, bars, and structurals during the Second and Third Plan periods. It now seems likely that there will be excessive emphasis on flat products during the Fourth Plan period.

It is from these qualifications that there is, perhaps, much to learn about the process of industrialization, not only in India, but also in underdeveloped economies in general. It is not unfair to say that Indian planners have restricted themselves too exclusively to the establishment of targets for the industry and to obtaining the financial resources necessary to achieve these targets. They have not given due consideration to the problems of insuring that new capacity is utilized in ways most beneficial to the industry and the Indian economy. As a consequence, the performance of India's steel mills has been considerably less satisfactory than it should be. Moreover, through the possible mislocation of the industry, Indian planners may well increase the likelihood of continued difficulties in years to come. In short, industrial growth is a complex process that involves more than the installation of new capacity. The government's controls over the industry, its pricing and distribution of steel, its choice of locations and methods of producing iron, and its unwillingness or inability to rectify unsatisfactory practices at its mills all have a crucial bearing on this process and ultimately on the success of Indian planning itself.

Of special significance is the failure of the government in the past to secure qualified persons to direct the operations of its steel mills, the managerial and technical expertise that is, perhaps, the industry's scarcest resource. The industry's need for expertise has either not been recognized by persons responsible for the industry or, if recognized, appears to have had only limited influence upon their decisions. The notions that a distinguished career as a civil servant qualifies a person to administer any organization and that, in any event, administrative talents necessary for managing a steel mill can be developed on the job appear to be widespread. Both beliefs are mistaken. The successful management of a steel mill demands specialized skills derived from long experience in the industry and an administrative organization appropriate to the industry. A steel mill is a complex industrial undertaking in which no less than five separate units must operate in synchronization with one another. Failure to secure a management able to coordinate the activities of these units has resulted in a number of the difficulties suffered by India's public sector mills.

The creation of both managerial and technical expertise appropriate for the steel industry may take decades. Until such time as sufficient Indian expertise can be created, available Indian skills must be considered a scarce resource to be employed in the most efficient manner possible. For example, in selecting plan projects the government might weigh alternatives that permit the most productive use of available Indian expertise, perhaps allowing some relaxation of controls over pricing and distribution, the policy of regional dispersal, and restrictions upon private sector entry into the industry. If these alternatives are not acceptable to the government, expertise might be freely imported from nations with longer experience in the manufacture of steel.

Not a few economists concerned with the problem of economic development have tended to emphasize scarcity of investable funds and the need for capital formation in underdeveloped economies, an emphasis apparently shared by the Indian planning authorities. Yet the history of India's steel industry would indicate that rupee savings, at least, have not been a serious obstacle to the growth of the industry unless as a result of various government policies. Personal and corporate income disparities, business reputations, and communal identifications have created imperfections in Indian capital markets that have enabled the mobilization from within India of funds sufficient for the growth of India's steel industry. On the contrary, Indian steel mills have not, as a rule, been able to circumvent shortages of expertise without initial recourse to the employment of foreign personnel.

There also seems to be a tendency among some economists to think of capital as a uniformly scarce factor and labor as a uniformly abundant factor of production in underdeveloped economies. It is evident from a study of India's steel industry that the factor endowments of an underdeveloped economy are more complex than is generally presumed, and the optimum factor proportions used in investment may be far different than is often suggested. Highly automated methods of production may be most suitable for an underdeveloped economy, despite the fact that these methods may also be highly capital-intensive, if they minimize the need for human decision based on specialized skills. This is not to say that the use of more capital-intensive methods or investment in more capital-intensive industries in underdeveloped economies should be encouraged. Capital, both domestic and foreign, is still a scarce factor of production to underdeveloped economies as a whole. Rather, the selection of plan alternatives is a complex decision for which there can be no one fully satisfactory yet simple criterion. The alternatives to the production of steel in India are the curtailment of the activities of user industries or the import of steel from abroad. Even though the industry is highly capital-intensive, the production of steel in India would appear to be the most desirable of these alternatives.

Indian planning for the expansion of the steel, ancillary, and user industries has aimed at balanced growth. It has resulted in, or at the very least has not forestalled, the creation of imbalances among the steel and other Indian industries. Unplanned imbalances have not encouraged a more rapid growth of India's economy. Rather, because of the operation of the price system governing steel, the persistence of a shortage of steel throughout the late 1950s allowed inordinate profits to accrue to middlemen and some users and not to producers of steel. Because of both the price system and government controls over entry into the industry, this imbalance was not rectified until the commissioning of the new public sector mills early in the 1960s. Shortages of washed coal have decreased the productivity of Indian blast furnaces and increased the costs of producing iron in India. Yet, once again, this imbalance has not been rectified as soon as possible because of government restrictions upon entry into the coal washing industry. Aside from the stimulus given to the government itself, imbalances could persist indefinitely in the institutional setting governing India's steel industry.

The elimination of impediments to the fullest use of Indian resources might require further changes in the government's controls over the private sector and policies for locating new mills. Ultimately, it would require some sacrifice of noneconomic objectives that influence Indian planning, such as the ideological and political desires to limit the expansion of the private sector and to allocate iron and steel mills to as many states as possible. The noneconomic motives of Indian planning cannot be dismissed out of hand. The location of a steel mill, no matter how uneconomic, may in its own way help to mollify regional interests. Whether or not noneconomic motives are to outweigh economic considerations is a welfare question that has to be determined by Indian policy-makers, the economist confining himself to assessing the costs of satisfying these motives. However, judging from the recent experience of India's steel industry, these costs have been significant and threaten to become still greater in the future.

Appendixes | Bibliography | Index

Appendix A | Indian Reserves of Coking Coal

I assume that India's reserves of washed coking coal were at least 1,600 million tons as of March 31, 1963.[1] If existing mills and the proposed Bokaro plant are expanded to their maximum capacities, and all coking coal is allocated to India's steel industry, these reserves would be sufficient to support at least two new steel mills after the Bokaro plant, each having an ultimate capacity of four million ingot tons.

To prepare this estimate I made the following assumptions:

1. India's ingot steel production from April 1963 until March 1966 will average 5.9 million tons per year.

2. Bhilai will expand to a capacity of 2.5 million ingot tons by 1966–67, to 3.5 million ingot tons by 1970–71 and to 4.0 million ingot tons by 1975–76.

3. Rourkela will expand to a capacity of 1.8 million ingot tons by 1967–68 and to 2.5 million ingot tons by 1971–72.

4. Durgapur will expand to a capacity of 1.6 million ingot tons by 1967–68, to 3.0 million ingot tons by 1971–72 and to 3.2 million ingot tons by 1976–77.[2]

5. TISCO will expand to a capacity of 3.0 million ingot tons by 1970–71.

[1] M. N. Dastur, *Steel in India—Economic and Technological Possibilities*, the fourth Sir M. Visvesvaraya Lecture, delivered at the 41st Annual Convention of the Institution of Engineers (India) (Calcutta: *The Statesman*, Commercial Printing Department, 1961), p. 17.

[2] Durgapur's tentative Fourth Plan capacity has been set at 3.5 million tons since the preparation of this appendix.

6. IISCO will expand to a capacity of 2.0 million ingot tons by 1970–71.[3]

7. Bokaro will begin with an initial capacity of 1.5 million ingot tons in 1970–71, will expand to a capacity of 2.5 million ingot tons by 1975–76 and 4.0 million ingot tons by 1980–81.

8. India's capacity for salable pig iron production using coking coal was .92 million tons in 1963–64; will become 1.77 million tons in 1966–67, 3.0 million tons in 1970–71, and 4.0 million tons in 1975–76.

9. It will take three years for each plant to achieve full capacity after an expansion program is completed, output rising by one-half of increased capacity during the first year and by three-fourths during the second year.

10. 1.35 tons of washed coal will be consumed per ton of iron, and 1.30 tons per ton of ingot steel.[4]

11. Steel mills and blast furnace units must operate for at least thirty years after their last expansion programs have been completed.[5]

On the basis of these assumptions I estimate that slightly over 1.1 billion tons of washed coal will be consumed by existing mills and the proposed Bokaro plant *at present rates of washed coal consumption.* The rest of India's known reserves of washed coal, approximately 0.5 billion tons, would be sufficient to support at least two new steel mills with eventual capacities of four million tons each, assuming a total con-

[3] Private sector expansion programs were indefinite as of mid-1965.

[4] These are approximate coefficients achieved at present. The lower coefficient corresponding to ingot steel is the result of the consumption of scrap in steel manufacture.

[5] A suitable life expectancy for a new steel mill was discussed with several persons associated with India's steel industry. In general, it was thought that raw materials should allow the operation of a mill for about 30 years following its last expansion, after which the plant will have paid for itself, the technology of producing iron will probably have changed radically, and India may have discovered new coal deposits or means of exploiting known deposits far below the earth's surface. This figure is supported by the average lifetime generally assumed for steel mill plant and equipment, 20 to 25 years. Of course, life expectancy varies from facility to facility. However, few facilities other than road beds, buildings, and other structures possess lives greater than thirty years.

sumption of washed coal equal to that projected for the Bokaro plant, 188 million tons.

It has been assumed that there will be no future change in present input coefficients for washed coal. In fact, blast furnace and coke oven techniques have improved in recent years and are expected to continue to improve in the future. Coal washing techniques have been adopted in India. Other recent developments—improved burden preparation, greater use of self-fluxing sinter or pellets, generation of high blast temperatures, and injection of oil, solid fuel, and oxygen into blast furnaces—may be adopted with advantage at some future date, and, if so, it is certain that future input coefficients for coal will be lower than those achieved at present. It has been suggested that the coke rate in Indian blast furnaces could be reduced from 900 kg to 650 kg by use of improved techniques.[6] This would correspond to a reduction in the consumption of washed coal to approximately .97 tons per ton of iron and .94 tons per ton of ingot steel. In addition, as India's economy develops it will generate far more market scrap than at present. The scrap rate at India's steel mills has been increasing over time. It is now .20 to .24 tons per ton of ingots and is expected to rise to .30 tons by the end of the Fourth Plan period.[7]

Improved blast furnace and coke oven techniques and increased utilization of scrap would lengthen the life of India's coking coal reserves. If future average input coefficients for washed coal are assumed to be 1.16 tons per ton of iron and 1.12 tons per ton of ingots, allowing for improved techniques only, then future consumption of washed coal by existing mills and the proposed Bokaro mill would fall from 1.1 billion tons to 957 million tons, 175 million used in the production of pig iron for sale and 782 million in the production of basic iron for

[6] Dastur, *Steel in India*, p. 19.

[7] Government of India, Planning Commission, Perspective Planning Division, "Iron and Steel, Advance Action for the Fourth Plan" (mimeograph, 1962), pp. 11–12. The percentage of scrap may not increase if there is widespread adoption of the LD process in India. At present a typical LD furnace consumes only 15 per cent scrap.

conversion to steel. If it is also assumed that scrap will be consumed at an average rate of 30 per cent, total future consumption of coking coal could fall to as low as 879 million tons.[8] The remaining reserves of washed coal would then be sufficient to support as many as six new steel mills the size of the proposed Bokaro mill, each consuming 117 million tons of washed coal during its lifetime.

India's potential supplies of washed coal, although limited relative to her reserves of iron ore, are nonetheless sufficient to support at least two new steel mills with eventual four million ton capacities assuming continuation of existing rates of coal consumption. If recent advances in blast furnace and coke oven techniques are adopted and greater amounts of scrap are consumed, India's potential supplies of washed coal would support at least six new steel mills. Clearly, the quantity of India's coking coal reserves need not yet prevent an expansion of India's steel industry based upon indigenous supplies of metallurgical coal.

[8] It is assumed that the current scrap rate is 22 per cent. If so, the proportion of ingot steel produced from basic iron would fall from 78 to 70 per cent and washed coal consumed in manufacturing ingot steel from 782 million to 704 million tons.

Appendix B | The Financial History of the Indian Steel Industry prior to 1939

The Tatas first attempted to interest British investors in an Indian steel mill in 1906. Their efforts failed because the London money market was depressed and those who were interested demanded more control than the Tatas were willing to cede. The Tatas then turned to India. In August 1907 they issued a prospectus in Bombay asking for Rs. 23 million, which at that time corresponded to about $7.5 million. Within three weeks this amount was subscribed by over 8000 persons, almost all Indians.[1]

Tata's success may be startling at first sight, particularly to the economist trained in the belief that capital scarcity is a principal obstacle to industrial development in underdeveloped economies. It should not be. There were at least four major reasons why TISCO was able to attract Indian capital without difficulty and why capital scarcity in India was not particularly applicable to the Tatas and, perhaps, to many other Indian business ventures.

In 1907 India was in the midst of the Swadeshi movement, an early expression of Indian nationalism. Fundamental to this

[1] For accounts of the initial sale of TISCO's shares, the reader may wish to consult Verrier Elwin, *The Story of Tata Steel* (Bombay: Tata Industries Private Ltd., 1958), pp. 35–37; and Frank Harris, *Jamsetji Nusserwanji Tata, A Chronicle of His Life,* second ed. (Bombay: Blackie & Son (India) Limited, 1958), pp. 188–191. The latter source consists of chapters written for the most part by Lovat Fraser which were published separately as a book. Fraser, *Iron and Steel in India* (Bombay: The Times Press, 1919), pp. 52–55.

movement was the belief that Indian resources should be developed by Indians themselves and that this would be encouraged by "buying Indian." Because of Swadeshi it is likely that some savings were attracted to TISCO that could not have been obtained at another time.[2]

There were other more enduring reasons for Tata's success. A large percentage of TISCO's capital came from the Parsee community, a closely knit social and religious minority in India to which the Tata family belongs.[3] I have classified TISCO's early shareholders according to their religious communities. The results of this classification are summarized in Table B-1. Including members of the Tata family, Parsees accounted for at least 36 per cent of TISCO's share capital in 1911; excluding members of the Tata family, 26 per cent. Yet in 1911 Parsees constituted only .03 per cent and 5.2 per cent of the populations of India and Bombay City respectively. Clearly, the contribution of the Parsee community to TISCO's capital was disproportionate to its numbers.[4]

This is not very surprising. Some Parsees are prominent industrialists and large merchants. Many others are small merchants, professionals, and white collar workers who, although of modest means, are nevertheless reasonably well-to-do by Indian standards. Whether the per capita income of the Parsee community is higher than the per capita incomes of most other Indian religious communities is a moot question. Almost certainly, the spread in Parsee incomes is greater with the result that upper and middle income members of this community probably enjoy a higher per capita income and rate of savings

[2] Fraser, *Iron and Steel in India*, pp. 52–53; Elwin, *The Story of Tata Steel*, p. 36.

[3] The Parsees are Zoroastrians whose ancestors fled conversion to Islam by migrating from Persia to Gujarat in India during the eighth century. In 1911 there were only 100,000 Parsees in India, approximately half living in Bombay City.

[4] The distribution of TISCO's shareholders and the population of Bombay City by community, presented in columns 7 and 10 of Table B–1, have been subjected to chi-square analysis. The resultant chi-square statistic is 110, which at 5 degrees of freedom indicates a highly significant difference between the two distributions.

than the average Indian. The social cohesion of the Parsee community and the Tatas' membership in it helped to channel some of these savings to TISCO whereas they might not have been so readily available to non-Parsee ventures. Imperfections in India's capital markets are based in part on communal divisions. Although restricting the flow of capital within the economy as a whole, these imperfections also serve to circumvent India's basic shortage of capital for those few who are fortunate enough to belong to reasonably populous and well-to-do communities.

Because, in 1911, 64 per cent of the value of TISCO's shares were held by approximately 10,000 non-Parsees, it is evident that communal identifications were not the only or perhaps the primary reason for TISCO's success in marketing its initial share capital. By 1907 the Tatas were a prosperous and highly respected business house known for competence in management. It was for this reason primarily that the Tatas were able to attract substantial amounts of capital from outside their own social community. Risk is an important consideration for the Indian investor. The risk associated with investment in a Tata venture was far less than that associated with many alternative investments.

Finally, the Tatas were assisted by political stability in India. Indian savings could be attracted to industrial enterprise without guarantee of extraordinary rates of return because investments were secure from destruction by war and arbitrary expropriation by those in political power. Moreover, encouragement was given to the Tatas' steel mill by the government, notably by its agreement to purchase much of TISCO's initial output for India's railways. A minimum of governmental support was necessary and received.

Although over 11,000 persons held TISCO's shares in 1911, ownership was highly concentrated in the hands of a few individuals. Sixty-three persons, four of them members of the Tata family, owned 43 per cent of the total value of the company's stock. Less than 400 persons owned 63 per cent of TISCO's securities. Among the largest of TISCO's shareholders were

Table B–1. TISCO's Shareholders in 1911 Classified According to Community and Size of Holding[a]
(Percentage of the value of all shares owned in each size class)

	Shares held by individuals equivalent in value to rupees:									
					75,000 and over		Total		% of population[b]	
Community	Less than 1,500	1,500 to less than 7,500	7,500 to less than 30,000	30,000 to less than 75,000	Without Tatas	With Tatas	Without Tatas	With Tatas	India	Bombay City
Parsee	18	32	38	22	20	51	26	36	.03	5.2
Hindu, Jain, Sikh	68	49	42	68	64	39	57	50	70.8	69.9
Muslim	8	6	8	4	8	5	7	6	21.3	18.3
British and Anglo-Indian	4	10	10	6	2	1	6	5	0.1	1.6
Jewish	c	1	1	c	6	4	2	2	c	0.7
Others[d]	2	2	1	c	c	c	1	1	7.8	4.3
Total	100	100	100	100	100	100	100	100	100.0	100.0
Number of investors	over 10,000	789	315	37	22	26	over 11,000			
Value of shares[e] (thousand rupees)	3,984	2,915	3,874	1,722	3,896	6,397	16,391	18,891		
Percentage of total, including Tatas	21	15	21	9	c	34	c	100		

NOTES TO TABLE B–1

[a] Registrar of Companies, Maharashtra State, Bombay. The 1911 list of shareholders was censused for persons owning more than the equivalent of 20 ordinary shares in value (Rs. 1,500 per person) and sampled for those holding less. A sample size of 80 and a table of random numbers were used. It was not always possible to determine the total amounts of shares owned by families since TISCO's shareholders were listed in rough alphabetical order according to first, not family, names. It is possible that some shares were owned by several members of the same family, which would not affect the communal breakdown of shareholders but would cast some doubt on the size breakdown. The possibility that shares may have been registered in the names of fictitious persons or second parties, perhaps minor employees of a firm, has been suggested by one informant.

Because TISCO's shares were subject to call until May 1, 1911, there is good reason for having selected the list of 1911 rather than an earlier year. However, the choice of the 1911 list was primarily motivated by circumstances. It was the earliest available list not in such an advanced state of deterioration as to make its use impossible.

Shareholders have been classified according to their religious communities by Hariant Thanawala and Rasesh Thakkar of Bombay City.

[b] Population data have been taken from the 1911 *Census of India.*

[c] Not applicable.

[d] Includes Portuguese Indians and persons whose religious affiliations could not be determined from their names.

[e] Total value of shares held excludes shares forfeited and preference shares authorized but not sold to the public.

several rulers of princely states and some of Bombay's foremost businessmen, many like the Tatas having amassed their fortunes in the cotton textile industry.[5]

TISCO had less success in raising capital during the early 1920s. Extensions initiated in 1917 were to be financed primarily by the sale of new shares, and an additional Rs. 80 million of shares, roughly four times the amount marketed initially by the company, were sold by 1923. However, because these extensions were initiated at a time of inflated prices for capital goods and were under way when a worldwide depression in the steel industry brought TISCO near to collapse, revenue from the sale of new shares proved inadequate and additional sources unequal to the company's needs. TISCO's shortage of funds was overcome by the sale of debentures,[6] a loan from the government, and reserves accumulated during the war. Even so, limited funds along with the comparatively high rate of interest the company had to pay during the early 1920s resulted in the paring of planned expenditures on extensions.[7]

[5] TISCO's most important shareholders came from every major religious community in India. The largest shareholder outside the Tata family was Cowasjee Jehangir, a prominent Parsee merchant. Other important shareholders were Gordhandas and Mulraj Khattau, merchants and industrialists, and the Marahajas of Baroda, Mysore, and Bhavnagar, all Hindus; Fazulbhoy Currimbhoy Ebrahim, a Muslim merchant; Manekchand Hirachand, a Jain businessman; Sassoon David, a prominent Jewish merchant; and C. S. Clarke, a British banker. Parenthetically, fifteen maharajas and feudatory princes accounted for 13 per cent of TISCO's share capital, a rather good showing for a group much criticized for not having used its wealth to further India's economic growth.

[6] One series of debentures was sold in England in 1923 and retired in 1938, the only time prior to Indian Independence that TISCO ever obtained capital from abroad.

[7] These extensions and the availability of finances for them have been fully documented by the Indian Tariff Board which conducted several inquiries on the grant of protection to the Indian steel industry during the interwar period. The interested reader is directed to the following sources prepared by the Indian Tariff Board: *Evidence Recorded During Enquiry Into the Steel Industry* (Calcutta: Government of India Publication, 1924), Vol. I, pp. 88–89; *Report of the Indian Tariff Board Regarding the Grant of Protection to the Steel Industry* (Calcutta: Government of India Publication, 1924), pp. 36 and 42–43; and *Statutory Enquiry, 1926, Steel Industry* (Calcutta: Government of India Publication, 1927), Vol. II, pp. 29 and 335–336 and Vol. III, pp. 152–153, 278, and 285.

This was a temporary shortage of funds resulting from TISCO's postwar difficulties, not a fundamental scarcity of savings generated by the Indian economy.

Between 1924 and 1939 there were only minor additions to TISCO's share capital and a substantial decrease in its debt capital. Yet TISCO's capacity was doubled, an achievement made possible by drawing upon the company's depreciation reserve. TISCO's depreciation was based on the purchase cost of its plant and equipment at a standard rate allowed by Indian tax laws. Because most of TISCO's plant and equipment was new and not in need of replacement and was purchased at exceptionally high prices during and immediately after the First World War, the company was able to accumulate a reserve greater than that necessary for normal replacement. This excess reserve was used for expansion. Between 1924 and 1933 TISCO declared dividends on ordinary shares in only one year and on deferred shares in none. Use of TISCO's depreciation reserve for extensions in effect allowed expansion first call on profits, much to the discomfort of some of TISCO's shareholders but almost certainly to the benefit of India's economy.[8]

[8] During the 1920s TISCO's management had to contend with continued shareholder unrest because of its refusal to declare dividends. On June 4, 1925, R. D. Tata told his company's shareholders:

> We are like men building a wall against the sea. It would be the height of folly on our part to give away any part of the cement that is required to make the wall secure for all time. That is why we and you have to use this money . . . to build up this great industry . . . And we should not think of dividends until we have done that . . .
>
> Make no mistake about this point. We hold this money in trust for you. But you yourselves hold it in trust for the Indian Nation . . .

The Indian Tariff Board's reports once again offer the researcher a wealth of information about corporate finance during the interwar period. TISCO's use of depreciation reserves for expansion was deliberate and not only coincident with normal replacement expenditures. The interested reader is directed to: *Statutory Enquiry, 1926* . . . , p. 35; Vol. II, pp. 12–13; Vol. III, pp. 137–140; *Statutory Enquiry—1933—Steel Industry* (Delhi: Government of India Publication, 1934), Vol. II, pp. 87–88 and 90–91; and *Report of the Indian Tariff Board on the Iron and Steel Industry* (Delhi: Government of India Publication, 1934), pp. 12 and 41. Major items of TISCO's annual balance sheets are reproduced in any *Annual Report* of the company prior to 1959–60.

The rate of interest paid by TISCO was remarkably low. In 1916 the company paid between 5 and 5½ per cent on its debentures; in 1923, between 7 and 8 per cent. These rates were rarely more than two percentage points higher than rates charged steel companies in the United Kingdom at the same time, a surprisingly low differential considering India's alleged shortage of capital and the precarious financial position of the Tata Company during the early 1920s.[9]

IISCO was founded for the most part by British and Anglo-Indian interests and its shares first sold in Calcutta and London in 1918. No less than 71 per cent of the value of the company's shares were purchased by Britons, Anglo-Indians and British institutions in India. Only 11 per cent were purchased by Indians, and the remainder by other non-Indian interests.[10] IISCO is operated by the Anglo-Indian managing agency, Martin Burn Ltd. of Calcutta. In recent years it has increasingly been taken over by Indian interests.

The Mysore Iron and Steel Works was erected by the state of Mysore, for years ruled by one of India's more enlightened maharajas. The works has never issued shares to the public, but instead was financed entirely from the revenues of the state.

It is evident that India's first steel mills were able to draw upon very different sources for their financial capital. TISCO obtained much of its original finances from the Parsee and Gujarati business communities of Bombay, IISCO from Anglo-Indian business interests in Calcutta and London, and MISW from the revenues of the state of Mysore. None of the three mills suffered from a long-run shortage of funds during the interwar period. Although costly ventures, all three were able to overcome problems involved in mobilizing savings.

[9] *Evidence Recorded . . .* , Vol. I, p. 316. See also Robert Spiegelman, "Protection in India During the Interwar Period with Special Reference to the Steel Industry" (unpub. diss., Columbia University, 1960), pp. 283ff.

[10] Members' lists for IISCO are available for inspection at the Office of the Registrar of Companies, State of West Bengal, Calcutta. Unfortunately, members' lists for SCOB in 1939 and subsequent years either do not exist or, if they do, were inaccessible.

Appendix C | Assumptions Underlying the Estimation of Full Cost Prices for Indian Steel in Chapter 5

In a market economy the long-run price of an industry's product should at least equal the minimum average costs of the industry's highest cost producer. For several reasons, new Indian steel mills will probably be higher cost producers than established mills. Therefore, a long-run price for Indian steel should at least equal the minimum costs of new Indian mills.

Unfortunately, because I am attempting to measure a price for steel to be used as a norm for the Indian industry, I cannot simply adopt the actual average production costs of India's newest steel mills, her public sector plants. These costs have been substantially in excess of what they should be, in part because of problems resulting from the mills' newness, but also because all three have, for various reasons, been unable to reduce their current costs of production to reasonable levels. Competition has not spurred cost minimization. To the contrary, it seems to have encouraged production at high cost.[1]

[1] Costs of production are discussed at length in Chapter 8. One important reason for unduly high costs of production at India's public sector mills is excessive emphasis placed on output by a mill to match or more than match output records established by another mill. Some output above effective capacity is possible, but only at substantially higher costs of production. Additional employment of labor and overtime worked by existing labor are two examples. Perhaps more important has been the sacrifice of maintenance at two of the government mills, at least prior to 1963,

Therefore, I must look elsewhere to estimate a price based on the standard costs of a new steel mill. I assume the investment costs of a new mill to be comparable to those of India's public sector plants. However, I assume its operating costs to be comparable to those of TISCO, the higher cost producer of the two private sector mills.

Because of the incidence of substantial fixed or nearly fixed costs, a steel mill's average costs should decrease until the mill operates at or near full capacity.[2] Hence, the minimum price that would justify the existence of a new mill operating over a long period of time is assumed to be equal to the mill's average costs of production when it is operating at or near full capacity. This would approximate both the mill's and the industry's long-run marginal costs of production at this level of output and would represent the classical equilibrium, were the classical assumption of a competitive market valid.

The use of TISCO's average works costs as a norm for production costs at a new mill is far from ideal. It is certain that the actual capital costs of a new Indian plant will exceed the historical capital costs of an established plant because of price inflation over time. However, the relationship between operating costs at the two plants can only be conjectured. The new plant will be able to install more modern and efficient methods of production, notably such relatively recent innovations as the

---

in part to avoid unproductive downtime in their plants. This has contributed to the premature replacement of machinery and some reduction in the plants' effective capacities.

[2] Not only are capital costs a large proportion of the industry's total costs of production, but also many other costs that are normally considered variable costs elsewhere but are more properly treated as fixed costs in India. For example, most labor costs are for all practical purposes fixed in all but the very long run as a result of wage determination and restrictions upon dismissals by state and central governments. Even barring these controls it is likely that the companies would maintain much of their labor force during periods of slack because of possible labor unrest and difficulties in rehiring skilled and semiskilled personnel. Rough estimates place the industry's fixed costs of production at as high as eighty to ninety per cent.

use of oxygen in steel making, improved methods of preparing blast furnace burdens, and continuous or semicontinuous processes. On the other hand, existing mills have important cost advantages in their accumulation of skills through years of experience in the manufacture of steel and, particularly in the case of TISCO, in their access to better quality ores and closer proximity to all raw materials. By and large, in the opinion of persons associated with India's steel industry, the operating costs of new and established plants should not differ significantly, even though, to date, actual operating costs at the new government plants have been substantially higher. If anything, India's established steel mills should enjoy slightly lower costs of production until new mills have created organizations, skills, and work practices comparable to those of established plants.[3]

The private sector mills' operating costs were reasonably well covered by retention prices. Primarily out-of-pocket expenditures, most of these costs were reimbursed, retroactively if necessary, simply by establishing that these expenditures did, in fact, take place. However, TISCO's works costs reflect the measured and not the true costs of producing steel in India. Because the prices of several of the industry's inputs have been kept unduly low, real production costs to the Indian economy, if not to steel mills, should be somewhat higher than TISCO's measured costs during the early 1960s.

An adjustment may have to be made in the prices of at least four of the industry's principal inputs: coal obtained from independent collieries; power obtained from external sources; purchases in foreign exchange; and the haulage of raw materials, particularly coal, over long distances. The incidence of unduly low production costs resulting from unduly low prices for these factors varies from mill to mill. For TISCO, whose costs are used as a norm, this incidence is probably at a minimum.

India's railway rates for bulk materials have not always cov-

[3] This contention is based on discussions with cost accountants and other officials of Indian public and private sector mills.

ered all costs of haulage, the rate on coal, in particular, having been excessively "telescoped."[4] In general, the further a commodity is hauled, the lower will be its rate per ton-mile. For years India's rates on coal have fallen more rapidly with distance than rates on other bulk materials, bearing little relationship to the actual costs of hauling coal and, in effect, providing a subsidy to consumers distant from coal mines. Because TISCO's mill is situated only slightly more than one hundred miles from its mines, it has not benefited from telescoped rates on coal. In fact, rough computations indicate that in 1962 the costs of hauling coal to Jamshedpur were slightly lower than rates charged by the railways. Were haulage of TISCO's other principal raw materials also charged at cost, there would be no significant change in TISCO's total costs of production.[5]

In 1960 approximately half of TISCO's power was obtained from the Damodar Valley Corporation, the remainder produced by the plant itself. Although Indian power rates often do not reflect all costs of generating electricity, it was claimed by a Tata official that rates charged by the DVC do. Superficial analysis indicates the correctness of this claim.[6] Therefore, I also make no adjustment in TISCO's electricity costs.

Prices of Indian coal are controlled by the government. A

[4] At least two recent studies have examined India's raw materials and, particularly, coal transport costs: Coverdale and Colpitts, New York City, and Surveys and Research Corporation, Washington, "India Coal Transport Study" (unpub. June 1, 1964); and Alan P. Carlin, *A Possible U.S. Policy Towards Indian Transportation: An Illustration of Improved Sectoral Policies* (Santa Monica, Calif.: The RAND Corporation, RM–4379–AID, June 1965), Appendix B.

[5] Railway rates are published in Indian Railway Conference Association, *Goods Rate Tables in Force from 1st July, 1962, Goods Tariff—No. 31–A*, Part II (New Delhi: Government of India Publication, 1962). I have used Carlin's revised India Coal Transport Study cost estimates to approximate the actual costs of hauling all principal raw materials consumed by the TISCO mill: Carlin, *A Possible U.S. Policy Towards Indian Transportation*, Appendix B, p. 64.

[6] Actual charges for hydroelectric power by the State Electricity Board of Bihar, the state in which TISCO's mill is located, approximate estimated costs of generating this power. Planning Unit, Indian Statistical Institute, "Price Policy for Electricity Undertakings" (mimeograph, Indian Planning Commission, 1962), esp. p. 29.

recent Planning Commission study concluded that, on average, a 20 per cent increase in coal prices would be warranted and that this would result in an increase in the price of steel of about one per cent. My own computations substantiate this estimate, and, therefore, I have adjusted TISCO's works costs accordingly.[7]

An element of the total costs of production of all Indian steel mills involves the expenditure of foreign exchange. At TISCO this is incurred almost solely in the purchase of imported plant and machinery, although at all other mills fairly large numbers of foreign technicians are still employed. To estimate a price for Indian steel that reflects the value of this steel to the Indian economy, some adjustment is necessary to account for an overvalued rupee and, hence, undervalued costs of production.

The official value of the Indian rupee was 21 cents prior to devaluation in June 1966. For many years it was apparent to most observers that this rate was far too high, although a more appropriate rate remained a matter of speculation. Free market buying and selling rates fluctuated between 11 and 14 cents during 1964, but these rates were influenced by circumstances not directly associated with the overvaluation of the rupee, notably the risk with which gold is smuggled into India. One student of India's economy has suggested 14 cents as the rate of exchange that would assume a minimum justified devaluation.[8] This rate is used to compute full cost prices for Indian steel. It is supported by the new rate established by the Indian government in June 1966, 13.33 cents.

I have assumed that 50 per cent of the actual investment in

[7] Planning Unit, Indian Statistical Institute, "Price Policy for Coal Undertakings" (mimeograph, Indian Planning Commission, 1963), pp. 50–51. During 1960–62 TISCO obtained roughly half of its coal from outside collieries in the Jharia coalfields at an average price of Rs. 21.88 per ton of coal. Adjusting this price on the basis of estimates prepared by the Planning Unit and assuming coking coal to bear the same price relationship to non-coking coal after a revision in coal prices, I estimate that the price of Jharia coal should be increased by Rs. 6.11 per ton. This corresponds to Rs. 6.4 per ton of salable steel.

[8] Wilfred Malenbaum, "Comparative Costs and Economic Development," *American Economic Review*, LIV (May 1964), 397.

new Indian steel mill is in foreign exchange and, accordingly, have revalued half of a new plant's capital costs at the revised "shadow" rate of exchange. For the most part TISCO obtains all of its other inputs from within India. There are a few minor exceptions, such as petroleum products derived from imported crude oil and machinery and equipment of foreign origin used indirectly in the manufacture of the mill's inputs. No attempt is made to adjust TISCO's works costs for a revision in the foreign exchange costs of these inputs. Rough computations indicate that any adjustments would be minor.

However, India's other steel mills still employ substantial numbers of foreign technicians, IISCO partly out of choice, the public sector mills out of necessity. A new Indian mill will also be obliged to import some of its skilled personnel from abroad to assist in its operations until Indian technicians are trained to take their places. Employment of foreign technicians will necessitate an additional expenditure of foreign exchange which should be costed at a more appropriate value for the rupee. I assume that the true costs of this imported personnel are additive to TISCO's works costs because by 1963 TISCO employed only one foreign technician. I also assume employment of imported foreign personnel at a new mill to cost an average of Rs. 84 per ton of salable steel during the mill's first stage and Rs. 12 per ton during its second stage.[9]

Return on investment in the steel industry should at least approximate the marginal rate of return on Indian capital. Measures of the marginal rate of return on Indian capital vary, particularly from one sector of the Indian economy to another,[10] being as high as 20 per cent on relatively risk-free investment

[9] These figures are estimated from projected costs of foreign personnel employed at the proposed Bokaro steel mill. U.S. Steel Corporation, "A Techno-Economic Survey of a Proposed Integrated Steel Mill at Bokaro, Bihar State, India (unpub. report submitted to the U.S. Government, Agency for International Development, March 1963), Vol. II, p. 146.

[10] For a more detailed discussion, see Alan P. Carlin, "An Evaluation of U.S. Government Aid to India" (unpub. diss., Massachusetts Institute of Technology, 1964), pp. 27–31. The rate of return referred to includes taxes but excludes depreciation.

in modern private industry[11] and as low as 3 per cent on investment in agriculture.[12] Most analysts have chosen rates of return equal to 10 or 12 per cent. I assume arbitrarily that 10 per cent is a minimum marginal rate of return and 15 per cent a maximum marginal rate of return appropriate for India.

[11] Louis Lefeber and M. Datta Chaudhuri, "Transportation Policy in India," *Pricing and Fiscal Policies, Studies in the Economic Development of India*, P. N. Rosenstein-Rodan, ed. (London: George Allen and Unwin, Ltd., 1964), pp. 99–100.

[12] W. David Hopper, "Allocation Efficiency in a Traditional Indian Agriculture," *Journal of Farm Economics*, 47 (August 1965), p. 622. Three per cent is the author's estimate of the marginal product of land in an Indian village.

Appendix D | Internal Social Rate of Return and Present Value of Return from Investment in a Representative Indian Steel Mill

The internal rate of return, *r*, of a particular investment alternative covering a period of *n* years is given by the expression:

$$\sum_{i=0}^{n} \frac{b_i}{(1+r)^i} = \sum_{i=0}^{n} \frac{c_i}{(1+r)^i}$$

where b_i is the total revenues and c_i total costs of a project in year *i*. In theory, the internal rate of return for a project must be independent of investment in other projects. In practice this condition rarely holds. For this reason, it is assumed that there will be all necessary investment in other complementary industries, such as mining, coal washing, railways, and electricity generation, and that investment in potentially competitive industries, such as aluminum, would not affect the profitability of the steel industry.

As a first approximation, it is estimated that a *minimum* internal social rate of return earned by a representative Indian mill is 3.2 per cent. The data from which this estimate is derived are presented in Table D-1. The following assumptions have been made:

1. The mill will be erected in two stages. At the end of its first stage it will have an annual capacity of 0.77 million tons of salable steel; at the end of its second stage, 1.50 million tons.

Table D–1. Revenues and Costs of a New Indian Steel Mill Assuming Two Stages and a Constant Rate of Replacement (Rs. million)

Year (i)	Total revenues (b_i)	New investment	Replacements	Operating costs	Total costs (c_i)
0	—	12	—	—	12
1	—	287	—	—	287
2	—	876	—	—	876
3	—	845	—	—	845
4	319	351	101	302	754
5	639	63	119	337	519
6	711	—	122	345	467
7	793	—	122	354	476
8	793	183	122	354	659
9	793	428	122	354	904
10	793	428	122	354	904
11	1,092	183	174	542	899
12	1,390	—	183	558	741
13	1,473	—	183	576	759
14 to infinity	1,545	—	183	582	765

Sources of data contained in Table D–1 are indicated in the text of Appendix D. A dash indicates zero revenues or costs.

2. The original capital cost of the mill's first stage will be Rs. 3,161 per ton; of its combined first and second stage, Rs. 2,438 per ton.

3. At the end of its first stage the mill's total costs, excluding depreciation and return on investment, will be Rs. 460 per ton; at the end of its second stage, Rs. 388 per ton. Rs. 9 per ton has been allowed for interest on working capital.[1]

4. The mill's initial construction will take six years; its expansion four years.[2] It is assumed arbitrarily that investment will be incurred at the beginning of each year.

[1] For a justification of the first three assumptions, see Table 8.

[2] The proportion of initial capital invested each year is assumed to be the same as that anticipated for the Bokaro project by U.S. Steel, Bokaro's

5. The mill will receive an average price of Rs. 1,030 per ton, the revalued average landed import price of the steel it would produce.[3] The actual import price has been revalued at one rupee equal to 14 cents in an attempt to measure the social, not the actual cost of imported steel.

6. The mill will produce at 40 per cent of new capacity in the first year after its initial plant and extensions are commissioned; 80 and 90 per cent in the following two years and 100 per cent in each subsequent year.[4]

7. At each stage operating costs (total costs less depreciation and return) will be 75 per cent fixed and 25 per cent variable costs of production. In addition, the arbitrary assumption is made that the real cost of foreign personnel, valued at one rupee equal to 14 cents, will in the eleventh year of production fall from Rs. 84 per ton to Rs. 12 per ton as the result of the replacement of foreign technicians with Indians.

8. Replacement will be 5 per cent of installed plant and equipment each year after new production begins.

9. Continued replacement will allow the plant to operate *ad infinitum.* In other words, n is assumed equal to infinity.[5]

---

foreign exchange component revalued at one rupee equal to 14¢. U.S. Government, Agency for International Development, "Background and Summary of Techno-Economic Survey of a Proposed Integrated Steel Plant at Bokaro, Bihar State, India," press release, April 28, 1963, p. 9. The mill's expansion program is assumed to take four years, 15 per cent of its capital costs incurred during the first and fourth years, 35 per cent during the second and third years.

[3] The average landed import price has been estimated from trade data for 1961 and 1962. See Table 7.

[4] This time schedule for phasing in new capacity is the same as that assumed by U.S. Steel. U.S. Steel Corporation, "A Techno-Economic Survey of a Proposed Integrated Steel Mill at Bokaro, Bihar State, India" (unpub. report submitted to the U.S. Government, Agency for International Development, March 1963), Vol. III, Exhibit C-3.

[5] This assumption contradicts one made in Appendix A, that a new mill will produce steel for 30 years after completion of its last expansion program. An infinite lifetime is assumed for computational convenience. It permits an estimate of the internal rate of return without accounting for scrap value or costs of disposing of steel mill plant and equipment at the end of their lives. For the representative mill the assumption in Appendix

10. There are no external economies or diseconomies or noneconomic benefits from investment in a steel mill. Therefore, the revalued price of imported steel can be used to measure the benefits derived from the mill.

Some of the assumptions upon which this computation is based are unduly stringent. The actual internal rate of return should be higher, but by how much it is not known. Two extreme assumptions can be relaxed. First, it has been assumed that the plant will not be expanded beyond its second stage. In fact, the plant would, in all probability, be expanded to an ultimate capacity of about 2.5 million tons of finished steel. Second, it has been assumed that replacement would be incurred at 5 per cent of plant and equipment once a plant begins production. In fact, in its first years the plant's replacement needs would be far less, 5 per cent more properly being its long-run rate of replacement. In the short run, actual return on its investment would be somewhat higher than has been assumed in this first and very crude approximation.

A second internal rate of return has been computed relaxing these assumptions. The data upon which this rate is based are presented in Table D-2. It is assumed that the mill will produce 2.50 million tons of salable steel after completion of its third stage, earning a crude social rate of return of 28.4 per cent. It is also assumed that the mill's new plant and equipment will have to be replaced at a rate of one per cent during its first year of operation and that this rate will increase by one percentage point each year until the mill's fifth year of operations, after which its rate of replacement will remain constant at 5 per cent. This last assumption is no more than an educated guess. All other assumptions remaining unchanged, it is estimated that the internal social rate of return on investment in an Indian steel mill would be 14.9 per cent. This is, perhaps, a more realistic estimate of the true internal rate of return on investment in the industry.

A is equivalent to a 43 year lifetime. Given the high rate of discount appropriate to India, discounted returns on a new mill after 43 years are for all practical purposes negligible.

Table D–2. Revenues and Costs of a New Indian Steel Mill Assuming Three Stages and an Increasing Rate of Replacement (Rs. million)

Year (i)	Total revenues (b_i)	New investment	Replacements	Operating costs	Total costs (c_i)
0	—	12	—	—	12
1	—	287	—	—	287
2	—	876	—	—	876
3	—	845	—	—	845
4	319	351	24	302	677
5	639	63	49	337	449
6	711	—	73	345	418
7	793	—	98	354	452
8	793	183	122	354	659
9	793	428	122	354	904
10	793	428	122	354	904
11	1,092	183	132	542	857
12	1,390	—	146	558	704
13	1,473	—	159	576	735
14	1,545	—	171	582	753
15	1,545	—	183	582	765
16	1,545	186	183	582	951
17	1,545	433	183	582	1,198
18	1,545	453	183	582	1,218
19	1,957	186	194	884	1,264
20	2,369	—	208	921	1,129
21	2,472	—	220	931	1,151
22	2,575	—	233	940	1,173
23 to infinity	2,575	—	245	940	1,185

Sources of data contained in Table D–2 are indicated in the text of Appendix D. A dash indicates zero revenues or costs.

The computation of an internal rate of return requires no assumptions about the rate of discount appropriate for a particular economy, an advantage when the rate of discount is open to question. Unfortunately, this criterion can be misleading or fundamentally incorrect. Among its faults, under certain circumstances it is possible to compute not one but several internal rates of return. Under other circumstances there may be no internal rate of return at all. For this reason, the internal rate of return should not be used in exclusion of other investment criteria as a sufficient test of a project's worth. More to the point, this criterion should only be used if the theoretically different but more acceptable present value criterion is also satisfied.

The present value (P.V.) of return on an investment is the difference between its discounted revenues and costs for all years. In particular:

$$\text{P.V.} = \sum_{i=0}^{n} \frac{b_i - c_i}{(1 + \rho)^i}$$

where ρ is equal to an appropriate discount rate. It is assumed here that this rate is constant for all years. This need not be the case. In theory, projects should be accepted if they yield a positive present value when discounted at the theoretical market rate of interest, the marginal rate of return on investment. If the rate of discount is equal to the internal rate of return, present value will equal zero. The internal rate of return is an acceptable measure of a project's worth if the project's present value is positive for discount rates lower than the internal rate of return and negative for discount rates greater than the internal rate.

Descartes' rule of signs indicates either one or three positive real solutions for the internal rate of return on investment in an Indian steel mill. There is, in fact, only one. Present values for the two approximations, based on discount rates ranging from 1 to 30 per cent, are presented in Table D-3. For both approximations, present values decrease uniformly as discount rates in-

Table D–3. The Present Value of Return on Investment in an Indian Steel Mill Given Rates of Discount Ranging from 1 to 30 Per Cent

ρ (per cent)	First approximation[a] (Rs. million)	Second approximation[b] (Rs. million)	ρ (per cent)	First approximation[a] (Rs. million)	Second approximation[b] (Rs. million)
1	68,080	117,739	16	−477	−225
2	29,565	49,831	17	−592	−377
3	17,013	28,071	18	−684	−499
4	10,927	17,737	19	−758	−597
5	7,411	11,900	20	−818	−676
6	5,166	8,262	21	−866	−739
7	3,640	5,846	22	−904	−790
8	2,555	4,168	23	−934	−830
9	1,758	2,964	24	−958	−862
10	1,159	2,077	25	−976	−887
11	701	1,412	26	−989	−906
12	344	905	27	−998	−921
13	64	513	28	−1,004	−931
14	−158	207	29	−1,008	−939
15	−335	−34	30	−1,009	−943

[a] Computed from data presented in Table D–1.
[b] Computed from data presented in Table D–2.

crease, switching from positive to negative signs when the discount rates are equal to the estimated internal rates of return. Parenthetically, for rates of discount greater than 30 per cent, this trend in present values reverses itself. However, for both approximations, estimated present values for high discount rates are in all instances negative, becoming asymptotic to -12 as ρ approaches infinity.

In conclusion, the internal rate of return would seem to be a suitable criterion for investment in India's steel industry. As long as the rate of discount appropriate for India is less than 13 to 15 per cent, investment in the industry would, in theory at least, appear justified.

Appendix E | Application of Regression Analysis to a Study of Indian Demand for Steel

In Appendix E, I present an explanation of the analysis used in Chapter 7 to separate past and projected Indian demand for steel that is a function of India's level of economic activity from demand that is spurious, a function of unduly low steel prices. The statistical method used is multiple regression analysis. At the outset it should be noted that it is possible to find several demand estimates for one year, all in seemingly reputable sources and all purported to measure the same phenomenon. As is indicated below, computed coefficients may vary significantly depending on which of these estimates is accepted. Moreover, because of the small number of observations and intercorrelation between several of the independent variables, not all meaningful variables can be included in the model. Estimated coefficients also differ depending on which variables are included. However, one conclusion remains the same throughout. There is a significant negative relationship between steel demand and steel prices. Elementary economic theory would appear to be vindicated. Yet it must be stressed that specific estimates of regression coefficients, although statistically significant, may nonetheless be suspect. This analysis should, perhaps, be considered demonstrative only, a caveat that I do not always heed in subsequent use of the model.

The relationship between steel demand and various independent variables is assumed at first to have the linear form:

$$Y = \alpha + \Sigma\beta_i X_i + u$$

where Y is the dependent variable, steel demand, each X_i an independent variable and u the error term. The data used in this analysis are time series for the ten years ending March 31, 1962. Observations for an eleventh year, 1951–52, were available but were discarded because of an extreme observation for one independent variable.

The dependent variable, demand for steel, is measured by the indents placed on controlling authorities in any one fiscal year. Unlike data ordinarily used in demand studies, they do not measure actual consumption, the result of the simultaneous determination of supply and demand. Rather they indicate responses by consumers to steel prices established exogenously by the Government of India and, as such, measure actual demand for steel at various prices.[1] Estimates of demand for the ten years ending March 31, 1962, are presented in Table E-1.

Data on Indian demand are far from ideal. As already indicated, it is possible to find different measures for the same year in equally reputable sources. Of particular note are the higher alternatives for the last two years. The larger observations would indicate a substantial jump in demand which belies the fact that Indian demand for steel and the rate of growth of the Indian economy, on which increases in demand for steel depend, are thought to have been relatively stagnant during the early 1960s. Where alternative data vary widely I have exercised my own best judgment. Those observations used in the analysis discussed in Chapter 7 are indicated in the first column of Table E-1. Nevertheless, regression coefficients have also been estimated using alternative observations.

Because steel is a heterogeneous commodity, the use of aggregate demand data is not ideal. Consumers may not easily substitute one type of steel for another. Moreover, the ability of consumers to substitute steel for other commodities varies from type to type. Steel sheets can be used in place of tile, thatch, asbestos, and other roofing materials. However, rail-

[1] However, this analysis is not completely free from problems of identification. As indicated below, demand has to some extent been a function of its own relation to supply.

Table E–1. Estimated Indian Demand for Finished Steel Based on Indents Placed on Controlling Authorities, 1952–1962 (millions of tons)

Year[a]	Demand (Y)	Alternative estimates		
1952–53	2.20[b,c]			
1953–54	1.49[b,c]			
1954–55	1.51[b,c]			
1955–56	2.04[b,c,d]			
1956–57	3.99[b,d]	3.49[e]		
1957–58	4.14[b,d,e]			
1958–59	4.27[e]	4.18[d]		
1959–60	4.79[e]	4.06[d]	4.10[f,g]	
1960–61	5.07[e]	5.06[f]	5.60[g]	5.10[h]
1961–62	5.40[h]		6.20[g]	

[a] Fiscal year, April 1 through March 31.
[b] Srilekha Basu, "India's Iron and Steel Industry," *AICC Economic Review*, Jan. 15, 1958, p. 96.
[c] Incomplete enumeration.
[d] Government of India, Ministry of Steel, Mines and Fuel (Department of Iron and Steel), *Report, 1959–60* (New Delhi: Government of India Publication, 1961), p. 6.
[e] Government of India, Planning Commission, *Programmes of Industrial Development, 1961–66* (New Delhi: Government of India Publication, 1962), p. 6.
[f] Government of India, Ministry of Steel, Mines and Fuel (Department of Iron and Steel), *Report, 1960–61* (New Delhi: Government of India Publication, 1961), p. 6.
[g] Government of India, Ministry of Steel and Heavy Industries (Department of Iron and Steel), *Report, 1961–62* (New Delhi: Government of India Publication, 1962), p. 5.
[h] Unpublished information supplied by the Office of the Iron and Steel Controller, Calcutta.

ways have little alternative to the use of steel rails. For this reason, demand for all steel taken as a function of the average selling price for all steel may be a comparatively meaningless concept. It would be far better, were adequate data available, to estimate demand relationships for individual forms of steel such as sheets, plates, rails, and bars.

Changes in steel prices have not always been made at the beginning of fiscal years. For this reason, measures of demand collected on an annual basis in some instances indicate responses of consumers to two or more average prices. Again, were satisfactory data available, it might be better to analyze demand for shorter time periods, perhaps for quarters or even months.

Finally, demand estimates collected from indents on controlling authorities are understated for the first four years considered. Because of slack demand, control over the distribution of heavy structurals and heavy rails used in construction was ended in July 1952. Decontrol was extended to bars and rods six months later. Not until November 1955, when demand for these sections began to increase relative to supply, was control over their distribution reimposed. Thus annual demand for these sections would not be included in estimates for the second and third years considered, whereas roughly half of the annual demand for these sections would be included in estimates for the first and fourth years. An adjustment for these discrepancies is attempted by inclusion of two dummy independent variables in the model. X_1 is set equal to zero for the first and fourth years and to one for all others, and X_2 is set equal to zero for the second and third years and equal to one for all others. For the inclusion of the dummy variables in the model to be justified, it must be assumed that the three sets of data come from the same population, that is, that their regression coefficients do not differ significantly from each other. Unfortunately, too few degrees of freedom prohibit a test of this assumption. It is expected that the coefficients of the dummy variables are positive.

The third independent variable of the model, X_3, is a measure of the level of India's economic activity. Three variables were considered: national income at constant 1961–62 prices; plan expenditures at constant 1952–53 prices; and the official index of industrial production. Demand would in theory be a positive function of any one or more of these variables. All three measures provide excellent explanation of variation in Indian demand for steel, with the last, industrial production, providing slightly better explanation than the other two.

The choice of industrial production as an explanatory variable is not ideal. Steel output is included in the official index of industrial production. However, the dangers of spurious correlation are probably not very great because steel represents only one relatively small component of the index. More serious, steel is used for two purposes, construction and the manufacture of goods, primarily investment goods and consumer durables. These uses account for approximately 40 and 60 per cent of total Indian demand for steel, respectively. Although the index of industrial production, presented in Table E-2, should provide reasonably good explanation for demand for steel needed in the production of goods, it may not for demand associated with construction. Demand for construction encompasses steel needed

Table E–2. Official Revised Index of Indian Industrial Production and a Computed Index of Real Plan Outlay, 1952–1961

Year	Official index of industrial production[a] (1951 = 100) (X_3)	Index of real plan outlay[b] (1952 = 100)
1952	103.6	100.0
1953	105.6	125.6
1954	112.9	182.4
1955	122.4	256.1
1956	132.6	235.5
1957	137.3	310.3
1958	139.7	344.3
1959	152.1	334.0
1960	169.7	332.4
1961	181.2	342.7

[a] The Index of Industrial Production refers to calendar years and is obtained from Department of Statistics, Central Statistical Organization, *Monthly Statistics of Production of Selected Industries of India* (Calcutta: Government of India Publication, various months). A more recent index has been adopted since completion of this appendix. This index has a base year of 1956 and a different set of weights from the old index.

[b] Computed from data presented in Government of India, Planning Commission, *Third Five Year Plan* (New Delhi: Government of India Publication, 1961), pp. 733 and 738–739. Actual plan outlay has been deflated by the official wholesale price index also presented in this source.

for the railways and other means of transportation and communication; the development of irrigation, mining and power; the erection of buildings; and most of the steel needed for Indian agriculture. An index of real plan outlay primarily for these sectors, also indicated in Table E-2, was one of the independent variables used to explain variation in Indian demand for steel. Unfortunately, there is substantial intercorrelation between this variable and both the index of industrial production and the two dummy variables. As a result, its inclusion in the model does not add significantly to explanation of the total variance of the dependent variable, even though alone there is a significant positive relationship between demand for steel and plan outlay.

Real plan outlay, unlike industrial production, has increased discontinuously over time. It rose steadily during the first four years and then again in the sixth year under consideration. However, since 1957 real plan outlay has remained virtually constant. To some extent the substantial increase in India's demand for steel during the mid-1950s may have been associated with this discontinuous increase in plan outlay, not simply under-enumeration of demand during earlier years. Indeed, it would appear that the dummy variables do, in fact, adjust for something other than under-enumeration.[2] Therefore, the computed regression coefficients used in subsequent analysis, in effect, assume continuation of constant or nearly constant real plan expenditures in the future. Given the relative stagnation of the Indian economy and substantial inflation during the Third Plan period, this would seem to be a realistic assumption for this period. *However, use of the regression analysis for prediction of demand beyond the Third Plan period, when real plan outlay may once again increase, could prove misleading.*

The fourth independent variable considered is the ratio of the average selling price for steel to the wholesale price index during the ten year period. This ratio is presented in Table E-3.

[2] The computed regression coefficients for the dummy variables, X_1 and X_2, are substantially greater than any reasonable estimate of under-enumeration of demand as a result of partial decontrol.

Table E–3. The Average Selling Price for Steel, the Wholesale Price Index and Consumption of Finished Steel, 1952–1962

Year	Average selling price for steel[a] (Rs./ton)	Price index[b] (revised series) (1952–53 = 100)	Selling price divided by price index (X_4)	Consumption of steel[c] (millions of long tons) (Y–X_5)
1952–53	354	102.3	3.460	1.249
1953–54	404	104.1	3.881	1.352
1954–55	418	99.6	4.197	1.641
1955–56	444	91.5	4.852	2.135
1956–57	541	102.6	5.273	2.855
1957–58	612	108.7	5.630	2.616
1958–59	612	111.0	5.514	2.216
1959–60	612	115.5	5.299	2.798
1960–61	612	122.9	4.980	3.821
1961–62	619	125.8	4.921	4.078

[a] Steel prices refer to the average selling prices in force for all or most of the fiscal year or, barring this, during the mid-year period. These prices have been reproduced from or computed from information presented in two sources: Indian Tariff Commission, *Report on the Fair Ex-Works Retention Prices of Steel for the Period 1st April 1960 to 31st March 1962, Bombay, 1962* (New Delhi: Government of India Publication, 1962), p. 76; and, Government of India, Planning Commission, *Programmes of Industrial Development, 1956–61* (New Delhi: Government of India Publication, 1956), p. 7.

[b] The official wholesale price index (revised series) may be found in Department of Statistics, Central Statistical Organization, *Monthly Abstract of Statistics* (Calcutta: Government of India Publication, various months). The index refers to calendar years.

[c] Consumption is assumed equal to domestic production plus imports less exports of finished steel. For sources of the data used to compute consumption of finished steel, see the notes to Table 2. Data for consumption presented in the two tables differ. Data in Table 2 refer to salable steel; data in Table E–3, finished steel.

It has been included in the regression analysis, rather than the absolute price itself, for two reasons. First, it makes economic sense to say that the demand for steel is a function of the relative rather than the absolute level of steel prices. If all prices were changed proportionately there would be no incentive for consumers to alter their consumption of steel relative to other commodities unless there is a corresponding change in real incomes and some income elasticity of demand for steel, a money illusion, or a change in real balances that affects steel demand. The sole purpose for the inclusion of this variable in the model is to attempt to measure the extent to which substitution of steel for other commodities has been encouraged by an unduly low level of steel prices and this, it is presumed, is also a function of other Indian prices. Second, inclusion of the ratio, rather than steel prices and the wholesale price index as two separate independent variables, reduces the statistical problem of multicollinearity or intercorrelation with other independent variables. It is expected that the relationship between Y and X_4 will be negative.

The last independent variable, X_5, is the difference between demand for steel and actual consumption of steel, a measure of the extent to which demand has been satisfied each fiscal year during the decade under consideration. The hypothesis to be tested is that when there is a large amount of unsatisfied demand for steel, indentors will inflate their orders to obtain the steel they actually want and, in so doing, will exaggerate estimates of demand based on indents. Two problems arise from the use of this variable. First, some time lag is to be expected because it takes a while for consumers to become aware of changes in the relationship between the supply and demand for steel in India. This lag is partially a result of delays in publishing information about the distribution of steel. Perhaps more important, it is also a result of administrative delays. In the past it has taken at least three or four months, and perhaps many more, for controlling authorities to process an indent. However, a lag of a full year would be excessive and, in fact, provided comparatively poor explanation when included in the model.

Another difficulty with this procedure arises from the fact that the dependent variable is, in effect, taken to be a function of itself along with the other variable used in computing X_5, Indian consumption of steel. The identification problem and resulting biases, so neatly avoided because of the Indian government's price controls, enters into the model through the back door, as it were, because of the government's methods of distributing steel. The basic linear structural form of the equation is:

$$Y = \alpha + \sum_{i=1}^{4} \beta_i X_i + \beta_5 (Y - C) + u$$

where X_5, equal to demand (Y) minus consumption (C) of steel, is separated from the other independent variables. The reduced form of the equation is:

$$Y = \frac{\alpha}{1 - \beta_5} + \sum_{i=1}^{4} \left(\frac{\beta_i}{1 - \beta_5} \right) X_i - \left(\frac{\beta_5}{1 - \beta_5} \right) C + u$$

where each of the independent variables is now exogenous to the model.[3] Structural form coefficients are computed from estimates of the reduced form coefficients.

A constant elasticity logarithmic model for steel demand is also projected. The structural form of this model is:

$$\log Y = \alpha + \sum_{i=1}^{2} \beta_i X_1 + \sum_{i=3}^{4} \beta_i \log X_i + \beta_5 \log \left(\frac{C}{Y} \right) + u$$

where the coefficient of log X_4 is the price elasticity of demand. In this model X_5 is defined as the ratio of consumption to demand, a change made for computational convenience. The reduced form of the equation is:

$$\log Y = \frac{\alpha}{1 + \beta_5} + \sum_{i=1}^{2} \left(\frac{\beta_i}{1 + \beta_5} \right) X_i + \sum_{i=3}^{4} \left(\frac{\beta_i}{1 + \beta_5} \right) \log X_i$$

$$+ \left(\frac{\beta_5}{1 + \beta_5} \right) \log C + u.$$

[3] It should be noted that consumption of steel in the current year, which may be thought of as the supply of steel, is by and large exogenous and unrelated to demand in the current year. Prior to March 1964 the prices received by producers and paid by consumers differed and, as noted in Chapter 5, bore little relation to each other.

Here, too, it is possible to estimate the structural from the reduced form coefficients.

Estimates of all coefficients are highly significant despite the small number of degrees of freedom provided by the data. All coefficients are positive and negative as anticipated. Unfortunately, one of the assumptions underlying regression analysis appears to be violated. Tests on residuals indicate a high degree of negative autocorrelation,[4] a finding that casts doubt upon the significance of these estimates.

That there is autocorrelation is itself an interesting economic finding. It indicates that demand for steel in any one year is not independent of demand in previous years. In other words, as far as consumers of steel are concerned, one year would appear to be too short a time horizon for planning indents on controlling authorities.

To eliminate autocorrelation of residuals, the same regression coefficients are estimated using two-year rather than annual observations of the dependent and independent variables, a variation on moving averages. The dummy variables are still assumed to equal one or zero. However, an additional dummy variable, X_6, is now required. The new structural equation for the linear regression has the form:

$$Y' = \alpha + \sum_{i=1}^{2,6} \beta_i X_1 + \sum_{i=3}^{5} \beta_i X'_i + u$$

where:

$$Y' = Y(t) + Y(t-1)$$

and:

$$X'_i = X(t)_i + X(t-1)_i$$

X_1 is now equal to zero for the first and third observations, X_2 is equal to zero for the second observation, and X_6 is equal to zero for the fourth observation. The reader can easily de-

[4] Von Neumann's ratio was used to test autocorrelation of residuals. For a presentation of this test see Mordecai Ezekiel and Karl A. Fox, *Methods of Correlation and Regression Analysis: Linear and Curvilinear,* third ed. (New York: John Wiley & Sons, Inc., 1959), pp. 337–340.

duce the structural equation for the logarithmic regression and the reduced form equations for both linear and logarithmic regressions.

Although the use of two-year observations results in the loss of two degrees of freedom, it eliminates the negative autocorrelation associated with the model based on annual data. Estimated reduced form coefficients using two-year data are also highly significant at two degrees of freedom,[5] are negative or positive as anticipated, and, except for the dummy variables, which change in meaning when two-year observations are used, are very little different from coefficients obtained using annual data. Computed linear regression coefficients using two-year data are presented in Table E-4; computed logarithmic regression coefficients in Table E-5.

The proportion of total variance in steel demand explained by the six independent variables, R^2, is .999 for both the linear and logarithmic equations. The size of R^2 is not too surprising given the inclusion of three dummy variables which together explain well over 90 per cent of the total variance of each model. Even so, the other three independent variables explain over 99 per cent of the remaining variance. This is a surprisingly high degree of explanation and accounts for the fact that even at only two degrees of freedom all the regression coefficients appear to be significantly different from zero.

The estimates presented in Tables E-4 and E-5 are based upon demand data reproduced in the first column of Table E-1. Alternative data are also presented in Table E-1. Were other observations used, most regression estimates would still be significant. However, most estimated price elasticities of demand would be greater, particularly if the higher observations for the last two years are adopted. Similarly, substantially higher price elasticities would result if other measures of India's economic growth during the decade considered were substituted for the index of industrial production. The purpose of this analysis is to determine to what extent demand estimates and,

[5] The exception is the coefficient for X_5' which, although not highly significant, is nonetheless significantly different from zero at more than 95 per cent confidence.

Table E–4. Computed Regression Coefficients, Standard Errors of Estimates, and t-Values Using Data Measured on a Two-Year Basis and the Linear Model[a]

	Variable[b]	Reduced form			Structural form
		Regression coefficient	Standard error	t	Regression coefficient[c]
X_1	First dummy variable ($X_1 = 0$ for the first and third observations; $X_1 = 1$ for all others)	4.65841	0.20762	22.44	3.54682
X_2	Second dummy variable ($X_2 = 0$ for the second observation; $X_2 = 1$ for all others)	5.25791	0.22342	23.53	4.00327
X_6	Third dummy variable ($X_6 = 0$ for the fourth observation; $X_6 = 1$ for all others)	2.03761	0.13129	15.52	1.55140
X'_3	Index of industrial production	0.03418	0.00333	10.28	0.02602
X'_4	Ratio of steel prices to the wholesale price index	−0.39675	0.05534	−7.17	−0.30208
X'_5	Consumption of steel	−0.31340	0.08465	−3.70	0.23862[d]
Constant term		−7.02221			−5.34657

[a] Computed by means of the regression analysis discussed in Appendix E using demand data indicated in the first column of Table E–1.

[b] $X'_4 = X_4(t) + X_4(t-1)$.

[c] Structural form coefficients are estimated from reduced form coefficients. For example, $b_4 = (1 - b_5)\ (-0.39675)$.

[d] Regression coefficient corresponding to demand (Y') less consumption (C') of steel.

Table E–5. Computed Regression Coefficients, Standard Errors of Estimates, and t-Values Using Data Measured on a Two-Year Basis and the Logarithmic Model[a]

	Variable[b]	Reduced form: Regression coefficient	Reduced form: Standard error	Reduced form: t	Structural form: Regression coefficient[c]
X_1	First dummy variable ($X_1 = 0$ for the first and third observations; $X_1 = 1$ for all others)	0.36274	0.01146	31.66	0.30455
X_2	Second dummy variable ($X_2 = 0$ for the second observation; $X_2 = 1$ for all others)	0.44260	0.01224	36.17	0.37159
X_6	Third dummy variable ($X_6 = 0$ for the fourth observation; $X_6 = 1$ for all others)	0.12494	0.00809	15.45	0.10490
X'_3	Index of industrial production	1.09343	0.12729	8.59	0.91801
X'_4	Ratio of steel prices to the wholesale price index	−0.46275	0.06974	−6.64	−0.38851
X'_5	Consumption of steel	−0.19109	0.05961	−3.21	−0.16043[d]
Constant term		−2.05775			−1.72763

[a] Computed by means of the regression analysis discussed in Appendix E using demand data indicated in the first column of Table E–1. Logarithms are to the base 10.

[b] $X'_i = X_i(t) + X_i(t-1)$.

[c] Structural form coefficients are estimated from reduced form coefficients. For example, $b_4 = (1 + b_5)\ (-0.46275)$.

[d] Regression coefficient corresponding to consumption (C') divided by demand (Y') for steel.

Table E–6. Projections of Indian Demand for Steel in 1965–66 and 1970–71, Based upon the Linear and Logarithmic Regression Models[a]
(millions of tons per year)

	Linear model	Logarithmic model
1965–66		
Assuming an 8 per cent rate of industrial growth during the Third Plan period and an average real price of steel equal to:		
Rs. 619 per ton[b]	6.80	6.88
Rs. 822 per ton[c]	6.32	6.18
Rs. 948 per ton[c]	6.02	5.84
Assuming an 11 per cent rate of industrial growth during the Third Plan period and an average real price of steel equal to:		
Rs. 619 per ton[b]	7.54	7.61
Rs. 822 per ton[c]	7.06	6.83
Rs. 948 per ton[c]	6.76	6.46
1970–71		
Assuming an 11 per cent rate of industrial growth during the Fourth Plan period on top of an 8 per cent rate of growth during the Third Plan period and an average real price of steel equal to:		
Rs. 619 per ton[b]	11.19	11.11
Rs. 822 per ton[c]	10.71	9.98
Rs. 948 per ton[c]	10.41	9.44
Assuming an 11 per cent rate of industrial growth in both the Third and Fourth Plan periods and an average real price of steel equal to:		
Rs. 619 per ton[b]	12.44	12.29
Rs. 822 per ton[c]	11.96	11.03
Rs. 948 per ton[c]	11.66	10.44

(*Notes on next page*)

NOTES TO TABLE E-6

[a] Computed from the linear and logarithmic regressions discussed in Appendix E. Full satiation of indents for steel has been assumed. In theory, because the observations used to compute these regressions had to be aggregated on a two year basis, only two year projections are possible. Since other demand projections are usually presented on an annual basis, this results in a nuisance in making comparisons. For convenience, annual demand is projected assuming that the rate of growth in steel demand between the last two years of a plan period and the two years straddling plan periods is the same as the rate of growth in steel demand from year to year.

[b] Average selling price for steel in 1961–62. See Table 7.

[c] Full cost prices estimated in Table 6 plus Rs. 60 per ton, the average cost of hauling finished steel to markets. Rs. 822 is based on a long-run rate of return on investment of 10 per cent; Rs. 948 on a long-run rate of return of 15 per cent.

---

hence, plan targets are exaggerated because of the failure of Indian planners to give due regard to unduly low steel prices. For this reason, the use of observations of demand presented in the first column of Table E-1 and the index of industrial production gives Indian planners the maximum benefit of the doubt. Their use prejudices the results of this analysis against the hypothesis that a substantial proportion of steel demand would disappear given an appropriate increase in steel prices.

The price elasticity of demand for steel is constant and equal to the coefficient of the price variable in the logarithmic model.[6] Elasticity varies with demand in the linear model, but for later years is, in general, lower than the log elasticity. In both instances, demand is relatively inelastic. Therefore, there would appear to be very little reason to choose one form of the model over the other. In fact, the linear model is preferred because, as is indicated in Table E-6, demand projections based on it are biased against the conclusion that an increase in steel selling prices would result in a disappearance of demand sufficient to allow a meaningful reduction in future steel targets.

[6] For the logarithmic model, the price elasticity of demand is equal to b_4 or −0.39.

Appendix F | Data Pertaining to the Locations of Actual and Hypothetical Steel Mills—A Statistical Appendix to Chapter 9

This appendix presents data essential to the analysis contained in Chapter 9 but not readily obtained from published sources. Two hypothetical mills in northeastern India and four in south India are considered in addition to Bokaro and the five major iron and steel mills already in existence. Adityapur is adjacent to Jamshedpur in Bihar. Purulia is north of Adityapur in West Bengal. The four hypothetical south Indian plants are Mormugao in Goa on the western coast of India, Bellary in Mysore, approximately 300 miles inland from Goa, Vishakhapatnam in Andhra Pradesh on the eastern coast of India, and Bailadilla in Madhya Pradesh, approximately 300 miles inland from Vishakhapatnam.

Table F–1. Actual or Probable Consumption of Principal Raw Materials by Indian Steel Mills
(tons of raw material consumed per ton of iron produced)[a]

	Iron ore	Coking and noncoking coal	Fluxes		
			Limestone	Dolomite	Total
Bhilai	1.419	1.457	.548	.101	.649
Rourkela					
Beneficiated ore	1.551[b]	1.526[c]			.583[c]
Unbeneficiated ore	1.669	1.717[d]	.590	.270	.860
Durgapur					
Beneficiated ore	1.522[b]	1.823[c]			.458[c]
Unbeneficiated ore	1.700[e]	1.930	.496	.133	.629
TISCO	1.564	1.678	.498	.095	.631
IISCO	1.694	1.829	.401	.141	.542
Bokaro[f]	1.613	1.547			.595

[a] Unless otherwise specified, data presented in Table F–1 represent actual input coefficients during the ten months ending October 31, 1962. These have been computed from Government of India, Ministry of Steel and Heavy Industries, *Iron and Steel Control, Monthly Bulletin* (Calcutta: Government of India Publication, various months).

[b] It is assumed that ore is beneficiated at mines by crushing, washing, wet screening, and concentration of both lumps and fines. P. H. Kutar and B. R. Nijhawan, "Some Problems of Iron and Steel-making in the Hindustan Steel Plants," *Symposium on India's Iron and Steel Industry, Jamshedpur, February 1963* (Calcutta: Technical Journals of India, Private, Ltd., 1963). pp. 2/4 and 2/5.

[c] *Ibid.*, pp. 2/4 and 2/5; and National Metallurgical Laboratory, *Annual* Report, 1961–1962 (Jamshedpur: National Metallurgical Laboratory, 1962), pp. 10–21. The following assumptions have been made. Existing alumina contents of ores consumed by Rourkela and Durgapur are taken to be a weighted average of: 11.34 per cent, Barsua; 6.30 per cent, Bolani; 4.00 per cent, Barajamda; and 2.00 per cent, Dhalli-Rajhara. Weights used are the percentages of total ores consumed drawn from various deposits indicated in Table F–2. The alumina content of Barsua ores after beneficiation is estimated to be 4.67 per cent, and of Bolani ores, 3.05 per cent. For each one per cent reduction in alumina content there is an estimated 85 pound reduction in the coke rate and a 135 pound reduction in the flux rate.

[d] Actual rate for the five months ending October 31, 1962.

[e] Actual rate for the three months ending October 31, 1962.

[f] Anticipated raw material consumption at Bokaro has been estimated from data presented in M. N. Dastur & Company, Private, Ltd., Consulting Engineers, Calcutta, "Preliminary Report to Hindustan Steel Limited on the Establishment of an Integrated Steel Works at Bokaro" (unpub., December 1959), p. 47 and Appendix 42.

Table F–2. Rail Distances between Existing and Potential North Indian Steel Mills and Sources of Their Principal Raw Materials[a] (kilometers)

Mill	Iron ore	Coal	Limestone	Dolomite
Bhilai	85 (Dhalli-Rajhara)	725 (Jharia 60) 736 (Kargali 40)	23 (Nandini)	161 (Hirri)
Rourkela				
Beneficiated ore	80 (Barsua)	287 (Jharia 25) 298 (Kargali 75)	32 (Purnapani)	32 (Purnapani)
Unbeneficiated ore	80 (Barsua 75) 219 (Barajamda 16) 523 (Dhalli-Rajhara 9)	(Same)	(Same)	(Same)
Durgapur				
Beneficiated ore	341 (Bolani)	110 (Jharia 50) 59 (Barakar 50)	367 (Birmitrapur)	367 (Birmitrapur)
Unbeneficiated ore	341 (Bolani 80) 316 (Barajamda 20)	(Same)	(Same)	(Same)
TISCO	126 (Noamundi 50) 64 (Gurumaishini 27) 90 (Badampahar 17) 64 (Sulaipet 6)	193 (Jharia)	187 (Birmitrapur)	177 (Panposh)
IISCO	282 (Gua 80) 274 (Barajamda 20)	63 (Jharia 82) 18 (Raniganj 18)	325 (Birmitrapur)	325 (Birmitrapur)
Bokaro	380 (Kiruburu)	6 (Bokaro)	341 (Shahabad)	341 (Shahabad)
Adityapur	126 (Keonjhar)	193 (Jharia 60) 204 (Kargali 40)	187 (Birmitrapur)	187 (Birmitrapur; possibly Shahabad)
Purulia	217 (Keonjhar)	56 (Jharia 60) 136 (Kargali 40)	243 (Birmitrapur)	243 (Birmitrapur; possibly Shahabad)

[a] Sources and percentages of total raw materials obtained from these sources are indicated in parentheses. This table is based upon unpublished information provided by the Tata Iron and Steel Company and the American Iron and Steel Delegation to India, 1960, and obtained from interviews with employees of all five steel mills. By early 1963 Shahabad limestones had not been developed and whether they will be of the requisite quality for use in a blast furnace was uncertain.

Table F–3. Haulage of Principal Raw Materials Incurred by Actual or Hypothetical North Indian Steel Mills[a]

(ton-kilometers per ton of iron)

Bhilai	1,212
Rourkela	
Beneficiated ores	593
Unbeneficiated ores	772
Durgapur	
Beneficiated ores	841
Unbeneficiated ores	965
TISCO	589
IISCO	752
Bokaro	825
Adityapur[b]	639
Purulia[c]	722

[a] Ton-kilometers have been computed from data presented in Tables F–1 and F–2.

[b] The actual performance of TISCO is assumed for a hypothetical plant at Adityapur.

[c] The actual performance of Rourkela with unbeneficiated ores is assumed for a hypothetical plant at Purulia.

Table F–4. Distances between Actual and Hypothetical North Indian Steel Mills and Major Indian States[a]
(kilometers)

	Bhilai	Durgapur	Rourkela	TISCO and Adityapur	IISCO	Bokaro	Purulia
Eastern India							
Assam[b]	1,727	1,032	1,289	1,179	990	1,119	1,072
Bihar	930	291	492	382	249	204	379
Orissa	901	545	591	427	503	577	461
West Bengal	852	158	414	250	200	331	284
Northern India							
Delhi	1,327	1,312	1,485	1,375	1,270	1,225	1,295
Punjab[c]	1,683	1,623	1,796	1,686	1,581	1,536	1,606
Rajasthan[d]	1,418	1,380	1,553	1,443	1,338	1,293	1,363
Uttar Pradesh	922	877	1,050	940	835	790	860
Western India							
Gujarat	1,236	2,015	1,674	1,838	1,973	1,974	1,891
Madhya Pradesh	669	1,448	1,107	1,271	1,406	1,407	1,324
Maharashtra	1,116	1,895	1,554	1,718	1,853	1,854	1,771

(*Table F–4 continued on next page*)

	Bhilai	Durgapur	Rourkela	TISCO and Adityapur	IISCO	Bokaro	Purulia
Southern India							
Andhra Pradesh	856	1,716	1,672	1,598	1,674	1,748	1,632
Kerala	1,869	2,333	2,379	2,215	2,291	2,365	2,249
Madras[e]	1,332	1,796	1,842	1,678	1,754	1,828	1,712
Mysore	1,633	2,097	2,143	1,979	2,055	2,129	2,013

[a] Distances have been computed from *Newman's Indian Bradshaw, A Guide for Railway Travelers in India* (December 1962). Rail distances are from various steel mills to Amingaon (Gauhati) in Assam, Patna in Bihar, Cuttack in Orissa, Calcutta in West Bengal, Delhi in Delhi, Ludhiana in the Punjab, Jaipur in Rajasthan, Kanpur in Uttar Pradesh, Ahmedabad in Gujarat, Bhopal in Madhya Pradesh, Bombay in Maharashtra, Hyderabad in Andhra Pradesh, Shoranur in Kerala, Madras City in Madras, and Bangalore in Mysore. Whenever possible, it is assumed that finished steel is distributed by broad gauge railroads.

[b] Manipur, Nagaland, NEFA, and Tripura are not considered separately from Assam.

[c] Jammu and Kashmir and Himachal Pradesh are not considered separately from the Punjab.

[d] Haulage via both broad and meter gauge lines.

[e] Pondicherry is not considered separately from Madras.

Table F-5. Regional Distribution of Steel Produced by Indian Mills for the Seven Months Ending October 31, 1962

(percentage of all steel distributed from plant)

	TISCO	IISCO	Bhilai	Durgapur	Rourkela
Total	100.0	100.0	100.0	100.0	100.0
Eastern India	38.2	56.1	39.7	67.9	45.2
Assam, Manipur, Nagaland, NEFA, and Tripura	1.0	1.8	0.4	0.2	0.6
Bihar	8.6	3.9	5.4	4.3	5.5
Orissa	1.6	1.5	3.1	3.6	6.9
West Bengal	27.0	48.9	30.8	59.8	32.2
Northern India	22.1	14.2	20.8	16.0	14.3
Delhi	3.3	3.4	2.6	1.8	2.9
Punjab, Jammu and Kashmir, and Himachal Pradesh	8.9	4.1	6.1	6.7	4.7
Rajasthan	3.0	3.0	1.3	0.6	1.5
Uttar Pradesh	6.9	3.7	10.8	6.9	5.2
Western India	21.5	18.3	24.4	8.8	29.6
Gujarat	3.3	3.0	4.2	0.7	1.4
Madhya Pradesh	4.2	3.5	5.4	2.6	4.1
Maharashtra	14.0	11.8	14.8	5.5	24.1
Southern India	18.3	11.4	14.9	7.5	10.9
Andhra Pradesh	5.0	1.5	2.8	1.0	2.4
Kerala	0.9	0.6	1.5	0.7	0.5
Madras and Pondicherry	9.4	7.4	8.0	4.2	6.1
Mysore	3.0	1.9	2.6	0.7	1.9

Note: Computed from unpublished information supplied by the Office of the Iron and Steel Controller, Calcutta.

Table F-6. Haulage of Finished Product from Existing or Hypothetical Steel Mills to Actual Markets of Existing Mills for the Seven Months Ending October 31, 1962 (kilometers per ton of steel)

Iron and steel produced at	Iron and steel distributed to actual markets of: Bhilai	Durgapur	Rourkela	TISCO (Jamshed-pur)	IISCO (Burnpur)
Bhilai	1,059	979	1,042	1,102	1,036
Durgapur	1,021	625	1,038	1,108	848
Rourkela	1,107	790	1,065	1,171	953
Adityapur and Jamshedpur	1,038	665	1,009	1,094	870
Burnpur	1,040	633	1,023	1,055	869
Bokaro	1,082	711	1,070	1,126	915
Purulia	1,051	681	1,029	1,102	877

Note: Weighted averages computed from data presented in Tables F-4 and F-5.

Table F-7. Estimated Input Coefficients of Hypothetical South Indian Steel Mills Consuming Imported and North Indian Coking Coal[a] (tons of raw materials consumed per ton of iron produced)

	Mill based on imported coal		Mill based on north Indian coal	
	Goa and Bellary	Bailadilla and Vishakhapatnam	Goa and Bellary	Bailadilla and Vishakhapatnam
Coal	1.081	1.025	1.519	1.457
Iron ore	1.442	1.419	1.442	1.419
Fluxes (limestone and dolomite)	.508	.439	.720	.649

[a] I have estimated input coefficients assuming an average ash content in imported coal of 10 per cent. I also assume that for every additional one per cent of ash content in coal there will be a 4.5 per cent increase in the coal rate and a 5 per cent increase in the flux rate. Bailadilla ores have more or less the same analysis as the Dhalli-Rajhara ores consumed by the Bhilai plant. Estimated consumption of imported coal at Bailadilla for each ton of iron produced using imported coal would then be:

$$1.025 = \frac{1.457}{(1.045)^8}$$

where 1.457 is the actual coal rate at Bhilai (Table F-1). The flux rate is estimated similarly.

I assume Bellary ores to have an alumina content of 3 per cent and an iron content of 63 per cent compared to 2 per cent and 64 per cent for Bailadilla ores. Each additional one per cent of alumina is assumed to result in increased coal consumption of 85 pounds and flux consumption of 135 pounds (Table F–1). The approximate coal rate at Bellary and Goa would then be:

$$1.081 = \frac{.64}{.63}\left(1.025 + \frac{85}{2204.6}\right)$$

where one metric ton is equal to 2204.6 pounds. The ore and flux rates are estimated similarly.

Were coal shipped from northern India, the input coefficients for Bhilai and Bailadilla, by assumption, would be identical. The coal rate at Goa and Bellary would be:

$$1.519 = \frac{.64}{.63}\left(1.457 + \frac{85}{2204.6}\right)$$

Ores and flux rates are computed similarly.

Table F–8. Distances between Hypothetical South Indian Steel Mills and the Sources of Their Principal Raw Materials[a]

(kilometers)

	Goa	Bellary	Bailadilla	Vishakhapatnam
Coal				
Imported from abroad	0	440	460	0
Transported from north India	b	2,066	1,386	984
Iron ore	440	10	32	492
Fluxes (limestone and dolomite)	650	210	137	323

[a] Distances imported coal would be hauled represent rail distances within India alone. Raw materials are assumed to be shipped to south Indian mills by the shortest broad gauge lines or, barring this, the shortest meter gauge lines in existence or under construction. No transshipment from one gauge to another is assumed. It is also assumed that a short broad gauge spur from Bellary to Guntakal, connecting Bellary with the main broad gauge line running from Madras to Bombay, will be constructed if the Bellary site is selected. Goa and Bellary plants are to draw their iron ore from mines near Bellary; Bailadilla and Vishakhapatnam plants from mines near Bailadilla. Goa and Bellary plants are to draw their limestone from Dhone, Andhra Pradesh; Bailadilla and Vishakhaptnam plants from deposits in Bastar District, Madhya Pradesh.

[b] Approximate distance, 3,500 kilometers by sea and 319 by rail.

Table F–9. Estimated Regional Demand for Finished Steel in 1960–61[a]

	Rails and heavy sections		Bars and light structurals		Flat products (sheets and plates)		Others[b]		Total	
	(thousand tons)	(per cent)	(thousand tons)	(per cent)	(thousand tons)	(per cent)	(thousand tons)	(per cent)	(thousand tons)	(per cent)
Total	1,214.1	100.0	2,018.7	100.0	1,498.4	100.0	365.2	100.0	5,096.4	100.0
Eastern India	488.6	40.3	711.4	35.2	513.4	34.3	154.9	42.4	1,868.3	36.6
Assam, Manipur, Nagaland, NEFA, and Tripura	21.3	1.8	23.2	1.1	46.8	3.1	7.8	2.1	99.1	1.0
Bihar	102.1	8.4	93.2	4.6	75.2	5.0	48.3	13.2	318.8	6.3
Orissa	27.8	2.3	40.0	2.0	27.4	1.8	8.4	2.3	103.6	2.0
West Bengal	337.4	27.8	555.0	27.5	364.0	24.3	90.4	24.8	1,346.8	26.4
Northern India	240.4	19.8	405.0	20.1	397.8	26.5	104.7	28.7	1,147.9	22.5
Delhi	37.3	3.1	99.7	4.9	88.8	5.9	15.6	4.3	241.4	4.7
Jammu and Kashmir, H.P. and Punjab	75.2	6.2	99.2	4.9	116.2	7.7	33.9	9.3	324.5	6.4
Rajasthan	26.1	2.1	20.9	1.1	46.4	3.1	5.8	1.6	99.2	1.9
Uttar Pradesh	101.8	8.4	185.2	9.2	146.4	9.8	49.4	13.5	482.8	9.5

	Rails and heavy sections		Bars and light structurals		Flat products (sheets and plates)		Others[b]		Total	
	(thousand tons)	(per cent)	(thousand tons)	(per cent)	(thousand tons)	(per cent)	(thousand tons)	(per cent)	(thousand tons)	(per cent)
Western India	300.0	24.7	581.3	28.8	433.3	28.9	63.8	17.5	1,378.4	27.1
Gujarat	28.9	2.4	93.9	4.7	40.5	2.7	5.0	1.4	168.3	3.3
Madhya Pradesh	62.0	5.1	69.1	3.4	48.3	3.2	15.9	4.4	195.3	3.8
Maharashtra	209.1	17.2	418.3	20.7	344.5	23.0	42.9	11.7	1,014.8	19.9
Southern India	185.0	15.2	321.0	15.9	153.9	10.3	41.8	11.4	701.8	13.8
Andhra Pradesh	53.2	4.4	70.8	3.5	50.6	3.4	18.8	5.1	193.4	3.8
Kerala	9.5	0.8	61.1	3.0	14.1	0.9	3.6	1.0	88.4	1.7
Madras and Pondicherry	95.2	7.8	142.9	7.1	70.1	4.7	14.1	3.9	322.3	6.4
Mysore	27.1	2.2	46.2	2.3	19.1	1.3	5.3	1.4	97.7	1.9

[a] Data on demand have been computed from unpublished information made available by the Office of the Iron and Steel Controller in Calcutta. Estimates of demand are based upon indents received by this Office. Geographic variation in demand by Indian railways was not indicated. I have estimated this by allotting total railway demand for various type of steel according to actual geographic distribution of rails during the seven months ending October 31, 1962, information also supplied by the Office of the Iron and Steel Controller.

[b] Intermediate sections, wire, and other products of steel.

Table F-10. Estimated Regional Demand for Steel in 1975[a] (thousands of tons)

	Flat products	Bars, light structurals	Rails, heavy sections	All steel
Total	6,960	4,481	3,820	17,000
Eastern India	2,387	1,577	1,539	6,222
(West Bengal)	(1,691)	(1,232)	(1,062)	(4,488)
Northern India	1,844	901	756	3,825
Western India	2,012	1,291	944	4,607
(Maharashtra)	(1,600)	(1,031)	(658)	(3,383)
Southern India	717	712	581	2,346
(Madras)	(326)	(318)	(300)	(1,088)

[a] The regional distribution of demand for steel in 1975 is assumed to be the same as that in 1960–61, indicated in Table F-9. I have used total demand estimates prepared by U.S. Steel and discussed in Chapter 7 in making regional demand projections.

Table F-11. Distances between Potential South Indian Steel Mills and Major Indian States[a] (kilometers)

	Goa	Bellary	Bailadilla	Vishakhapatnam
Assam	3,493[b]	3,053	2,323	1,921
Bihar	2,696[b]	2,256	1,726	1,324
Orissa	2,083[b]	1,643	914	512
West Bengal	2,608[b]	2,168	1,339	937
Delhi	2,163[b]	2,083	2,220	1,818
Punjab	2,514[b]	2,434	2,576	2,174
Rajasthan	2,174[b]	2,174[b]	2,311[b]	1,909[b]
Uttar Pradesh	2,072[b]	1,935	1,885	1,483
Gujarat	1,271[b]	1,374	2,130	1,728
Madhya Pradesh	1,562[b]	1,425	1,562	1,160
Maharashtra	779[b]	882	2,010	1,608
Andhra Pradesh	855[c]	415[c]	1,107	705
Kerala	1,290[b]	1,029	1,714	1,312
Madras	1,010[b]	492	1,177	775
Mysore	768[c]	328[c]	1,478	1,076

[a] Unless otherwise specified, wherever possible rail distances represent the minimum distances finished steel is hauled over broad gauge track.
[b] Meter and broad gauge. [c] Meter gauge only.

Table F–12. Haulage of Salable Steel from Hypothetical South and North Indian Steel Mills[a]
(rail-kilometers per ton of steel)

	Product distributed to seven southern and western states			Product distributed to all of India		
	Rails and heavy sections	Bars and light structurals	Flat products	Rails and heavy sections	Bars and light structurals	Flat products
Goa	972	967	922	1,893	1,797	1,868
Bellary	826	858	858	1,638	1,573	1,674
Bailadilla	1,662	1,738	1,779	1,679	1,702	1,783
Vishakhapatnam	1,260	1,336	1,377	1,277	1,300	1,382
Adityapur	647[b]	1,728	1,695	1,056	1,132	1,136
Purulia	634[b]	1,774	1,743	1,066	1,146	1,139
Bhilai	1,031[b]	c	c	1,123[d]	c	c

[a] Haulage has been estimated from data presented in Tables F–9 and F–11. I have assumed the actual pattern of regional demand for the three categories of steel in 1960–61.
[b] Delivery to northern and eastern India only.
[c] Not computed.
[d] Delivery to southern and western India only.

Appendix G | A Cost Analysis of Proposed Locations for New Indian Steel Mills

The purpose of this appendix is to assess the cost advantages and disadvantages possessed by hypothetical south Indian mills. Four south Indian locations are considered: Mormugao in Goa, Bellary in Mysore, Bailadilla in Madhya Pradesh, and Vishakhapatnam in Andhra Pradesh. Two alternative north Indian locations are also considered, Adityapur in Bihar and Purulia in West Bengal. Adityapur, adjacent to Jamshedpur, is a site that has been investigated by TISCO. Purulia is north of Adityapur and somewhat closer to the coalfields of the Damodar Valley. It is one of many sites, including Adityapur, thought suitable for new steel mills by M. N. Dastur & Company.[1]

A south Indian steel mill would benefit from its consumption of better quality raw materials. Existing Indian mills consume coal with an average ash content of 18 per cent. This percentage has increased in recent years, and it is possible that once all needed washeries have been erected and methods of mining have been improved that it will fall one or two percentage points.[2] The ash content of imported coal would depend on its country of origin, an average content of ten per cent being assumed here. If so, consumption of imported coal would re-

[1] M. N. Dastur & Company, Private, Ltd., "Preliminary Report to Hindustan Steel Limited on the Establishment of an Integrated Steel Works at Bokaro" (unpub., December 1959), Appendix 7.

[2] Indian Tariff Commission, *Report on the Fair Ex-Works Retention Prices of Steel for the Period 1st April 1960 to 31st March 1962* (New Delhi: Government of India Publication, 1962), pp. 16–19.

sult in lower costs of producing iron, all other things being equal, by an estimated Rs. 44 per ton.[3] See Table G-1.

In fact, all other things are not equal. The price of imported coal is much higher than the cost of Indian coal.[4] In addition, were India's rupee revalued at one rupee equivalent to 14 cents, the difference between a fully economic domestic and import price of coal per ton of iron would be Rs. 84 for plants in Goa and Mysore and Rs. 80 for plants at Bailadilla and Vishakhapatnam.[5]

Iron ore is exported from Goa. Barring verification of potential reserves or substantial new finds, Goa's high quality ores are not expected to last more than twenty years. A Goan plant using lump ores would require curtailment of ore exports and in any event would ultimately have to draw its ores from nearby deposits in Mysore. Reserves in Mysore and southern Madhya Pradesh are sufficient to support several integrated steel mills. However, geological samples made thus far indicate a wide variation in their analyses. By and large, it would appear that both Mysore and Bailadilla ores are of better quality than ores found in Bihar and Orissa, and, of the two, Bailadilla ores are probably of better quality than Mysore ores.[6]

[3] The ash content of typical North American bituminous coal is 11.4 per cent. U.S. Steel Corporation, *The Making, Shaping and Treating of Steel,* seventh ed. (Pittsburgh: U.S. Steel Corporation, 1957), p. 62. Lower ash coals are found elsewhere but, for obvious reasons, can command higher prices from consumers. The assumed rate of 10 per cent is based on conversations with metallurgists associated with the Indian industry.

[4] I am told that the landed price of imported coal was assumed to be Rs. 72 per ton by HSL in its recent preliminary report on proposed steel mills in southeastern India. The average price of TISCO's coal, a mixture of washed and unwashed coal obtained from company and noncompany collieries, was Rs. 23.83 per ton in 1961–62. Were adjustments made, so that coal prices cover all costs of coal mining, it is estimated that full cost of Indian coking coal, exclusive of transportation, would be Rs. 30 per ton. See footnote 7, Appendix C.

[5] These estimates are based on input coefficients presented in Table F–7, and prices of imported and Indian coal indicated in footnote 4.

[6] B. B. Engineer, "Principal Mineral Raw Materials for Iron and Steel Industry," *Symposium on Iron and Steel Industry in India* (Calcutta: Technical Journals of India, Private, Ltd., 1959), pp. 98–99. For an analysis of Bailadilla ores, see National Council of Applied Economic Research, *Development of Dandakaranya* (New Delhi: NCAER, 1963), p. 18.

Table G–1. Estimated Cost Advantages Resulting from the Consumption of Low Ash Coal (Rs. per ton)

	Actual costs of producing iron[a] (18 per cent ash coal)	Estimated costs of producing iron (10 per cent ash coal)
Coke	40.50	28.48
Limestone	9.60	6.50
Costs above materials	12.00	8.30
Capital charges	83.00[c]	57.42
Total of costs considered	145.10	100.70[b]
Difference	—	44.40

[a] M. N. Dastur, *Steel in India—Economic and Technological Possibilities*, the fourth Sir M. Visvesvaraya Lecture, delivered at the 41st Annual Convention of the Institution of Engineers (India) (Calcutta: *The Statesman*, Commercial Printing Department, 1961), p. 27. Only components of costs affected by the quality of coal are considered.

[b] Estimated by means of the formula:

$$\text{Total cost} = \frac{40.50}{(1.045)^8} + \frac{9.60}{(1.05)^8} + (.955)^8\ (12.00) + (.955)^8\ (83.00)$$

where each component of the equation represents one of the above components of total costs. An 8 per cent difference in ash contents is assumed. Coke consumption is also assumed to *increase* by 4.5 per cent, limestone consumption by 5 per cent and output of pig iron per tap to *decrease* by 4.5 per cent with each additional one per cent of ash content. These are average percentages taken from Indian Tariff Commission, *Report on the Fair Ex-Works Retention Prices of Steel for the Period 1st April 1960 to 31st March 1962* (New Delhi: Government of India Publication, 1962), p. 18.

[c] Investment in a blast furnace unit is approximately Rs. 442.50 per ton of basic iron at the rate of exchange prior to June 1966. Were the rupee revalued to equal fourteen cents, investment would instead be Rs. 553.12 per ton of basic iron. This assumes 50 per cent of the capital costs of producing iron to be incurred in foreign exchange. Return is computed at 10 per cent and depreciation at 5 per cent of capital block.

In the following pages I assume that run-of-the-mine Mysore ores have an average iron content of 63 per cent and an average alumina content of 3 per cent and that run-of-the-mine Bailadilla ores have the same analysis as the Dhalli-Rajhara ores consumed by Bhilai, an average iron content of 64 per cent and an alumina content of 2 per cent. On the basis of these assumptions, a mill consuming Mysore ores would have a cost advantage of Rs. 16 per ton of iron and a mill consuming Bailadilla ores a cost advantage of Rs. 22 per ton of iron over a new north Indian steel mill based on Bihar and Orissa ores.[7] Bailadilla ores have another important cost advantage, a smaller percentage of fines than other Indian deposits. I have made no attempt to estimate the magnitude of this advantage.

Sea shipment of north Indian coal to a south Indian plant would almost certainly be advantageous only for plants located on or near the coast. Because Vishakhapatnam is not very distant from Haldia, continued shipment of coal by rail through Orissa and northern Andhra Pradesh would probably be more

[7] It has been estimated that for every one per cent reduction in the alumina content of Indian ores there will be a Rs. 4 per ton reduction in the total cost of producing iron. P. H. Kutar and B. R. Nijhawan, "Some Problems of Iron and Steelmaking in the Hindustan Steel Plants," *Symposium on India's Iron and Steel Industry* (Calcutta: Technical Journals of India, Private, Ltd., 1963), p. 2/5. Because measured Indian costs of production are thought to be too low, this estimate may also be too low. Nonetheless, it is the best available and therefore is used here. Bihar and Orissa ores, properly assayed and mined, are assumed to have an average alumina content of 5 per cent. The real cost of producing iron in northern India in 1961–62 is estimated to be Rs. 169 per metric ton allowing for an appropriate revaluation of capital and computing return at 10 per cent and depreciation at 5 per cent. M. N. Dastur, *Steel in India—Economic and Technological Possibilities*, the fourth Sir M. Visvesvaraya Lecture, delivered at the 41st Annual Convention of the Institution of Engineers (India) (Calcutta: *The Statesman*, Commercial Printing Department, 1961), p. 27. See, also, Table G-1. North Indian ores are assumed to have an average ore content of 60 per cent. Therefore, Mysore ores would yield approximately 5 per cent and Bailadilla ores 6.67 per cent more iron per blast than south Indian ores. Real costs of production would then be reduced by Rs. 8 and Rs. 10 per ton respectively, all other things being equal. Altogether, lower alumina and higher iron contents would result in a savings of Rs. 16 per ton of iron at a plant based on Mysore ores and Rs. 22 per ton at a plant based on Bailadilla ores.

advantageous than transshipment at Haldia from rail to sea. Therefore, I have assumed that, of the four proposed locations for south Indian mills, only Goa would benefit from the coastal shipment of coal. Were a Goan plant to obtain its coal from northeastern India by sea via Haldia, rail plus sea shipment would cost an estimated Rs. 63 per ton of iron.[8]

The use of actual railway rates on coal would introduce a bias in favor of mills relatively distant from their sources of coal. To avoid this bias, I have adopted shadow rates that purportedly reflect the full costs of hauling coal, and also other raw materials, for all distances. A recent study for the World Bank has attempted to measure the actual costs of hauling coal in India.[9] However, the conclusions of this study have been questioned by an economist who has examined India's railway rate structure in depth. Capital charges allowed in the World Bank's coal transport study are thought to be too low primarily because historical, not replacement, costs were used to estimate the railways' capital stock, and this stock was assumed to be substantially more depreciated than is believed justified.[10]

It is no easy matter to decide which railway rates should be used in determining production costs at hypothetical steel mills. This decision will depend on a number of assumptions, some arbitrarily made, about the theoretical basis of rate determination, the allocation of capital charges to various commodities

[8] Assuming the creation of the Haldia port, the adoption of more efficient vessels, and substantial improvements in handling ships and cargo, it is estimated that ocean shipment of coal from Haldia to Goa would cost Rs. 28.66 per ton of coal. Coverdale and Colpitts, New York City, and Surveys and Research Corporation, Washington, "India Coal Transport Study" (unpub., June 1, 1964), Appendix B, Exhibit 73. To this have been added costs of hauling coal by rail from the Jharia coalfields to Haldia, an estimated Rs. 12.50 per ton of coal using railway costs discussed below. Costs per ton of iron have been computed with input coefficients presented in Table F-7.

[9] Coverdale and Colpitts, "India Coal Transport Study," Vol. III, pp. 93–131.

[10] Alan P. Carlin, *A Possible U.S. Policy Towards Indian Transportation: An Illustration of Improved Sectoral Policies* (Santa Monica, Calif.: The RAND Corporation, RM-4379-AID, June 1965), Appendix B.

hauled by the railways, the relative costs of shipping commodities over different gauge lines, and a host of other considerations confronting the analyst. Allowing a rate of return of 10 per cent, Alan Carlin has estimated that full cost terminal charges for hauling Indian coal by rail are Rs. 2.60 per ton and full cost line-haul charges Rs. .0236 per ton-kilometer for ordinary through traffic on broad gauge lines. These estimates are 25 per cent higher than those prepared for the World Bank.[11]

Although, strictly speaking, they apply only to coal traffic on broad gauge lines, Carlin's rates are also used to measure the costs of transporting ore, limestone, and dolomite, in some instances over meter gauge track. Total predicted costs of transporting raw materials to hypothetical north and south Indian steel mills are presented in Table G-2. The adoption of the lower transportation cost estimates prepared by the World Bank's coal transport study would not effect a substantive change in either the relative costs of transporting raw materials to hypothetical steel mills or my overall conclusions.

The most efficient method of hauling raw materials by rail is by unit or closed-circuit train. The same wagons would move in an entire trainload between a mill and its mines, resulting in lower terminal and line-haul charges than are incurred by ordinary through traffic.[12] Whether closed-circuit operations can or will be established for all raw materials consumed by new steel mills is somewhat problematic in view of the fact that large tonnages are mandatory and recent wagon shortages have encouraged the diversion of wagons consigned to existing steel mills. Even so, were lower closed-circuit costs of haulage charged to hypothetical steel mills, south Indian mills based on north Indian coal would still incur substantially higher

[11] Carlin, *A Possible U.S. Policy*, Appendix B, Table B-6. By "through traffic" is meant haulage on broad gauge lines without the need for transshipment to meter or narrow gauge track or breaking up a train until arrival at the plant.

[12] Coverdale and Colpitts, "India Coal Transport Study," Vol. III, pp. 130–131. The coal transport study estimates that were coal hauled in a closed-circuit rather than by ordinary through trains, terminal charges would be reduced by 78 per cent and line-haul charges by 23 per cent.

Table G–2. Costs to the Indian Economy of Transporting Raw Materials to Hypothetical Steel Mills[a]
(Rs. per ton of iron)

	Mill based on imported coal[b]		Mill based on north Indian coal	
Mill site	Through traffic	Closed-circuit traffic	Through traffic	Closed-circuit traffic
Goa	28	19	95[c]	76[c]
Bellary	22	13	88	62
Bailadilla	21	12	60	41
Vishakhapatnam	24	17	64	45
Adityapur	d	d	25	14
Purulia	d	d	28	16

[a] Estimated from data presented in Tables F–1, F–3, F–7 and F–8, assuming terminal charges equal to Rs. 2.60 per ton of raw material and line-haul charges equal to Rs. .0236 per ton-kilometer for through traffic and to Rs. 0.57 per ton and Rs. .0182 per ton-kilometer for closed-circuit traffic.

[b] Excludes costs of transporting imported coal to south Indian plants by sea. These costs are considered separately.

[c] Includes estimated cost of shipping north Indian coal to Goa by sea, Rs. 63 per ton of iron where coal is carried on rail by means of through traffic and Rs. 55 per ton where it is carried by means of closed-circuit traffic.

[d] Not applicable.

transportation costs than north Indian mills. The use of closed-circuit rates does not affect the ultimate conclusions of this study.[13]

It is evident that both north and south Indian mills would enjoy certain cost advantages. Therefore, before anything can be said about their relative economics, an attempt must be

[13] The assumption of closed-circuit rates favors south Indian mills only if they are based on north Indian coal. See Table G-2. The closed-circuit rates assumed, Rs. 0.57 per ton, terminal charges, and Rs. .0182 per ton-kilometer, line-haul charges, are based upon Carlin's through traffic rates and the percentage differences between Coverdale and Colpitts' through traffic and closed-circuit rates. Admittedly, these are rather crude estimates.

made to estimate the net cost advantages accruing to each alternative mill site. This is done in Table 16.

I also attempt to estimate costs of distributing steel to markets. For the sake of argument, I assume that a south Indian mill will supply markets relatively distant from existing mills in northeastern India. In particular, I assume that south Indian mills will supply steel to southern and western states in the same proportions as these states demanded steel in 1960–61.[14] Much of the demand for south Indian steel would be concentrated in Maharashtra and Madras, states some distance from the proposed locations of new steel mills. I also assume that the real costs of shipping finished steel to markets are given by actual railway rates charged finished steel between July 1962 and April 1964. The use of these rates is far from ideal. Rates on finished products not only reflect costs of haulage but also "what the traffic will bear," the value of the goods hauled. For this reason, it is probable that the real cost of shipping finished steel to markets may be somewhat lower for most if not all distances.[15] Despite their shortcomings, I have used these rates to estimate cost advantages accruing to various hypothetical steel mill sites because of their proximity to markets. Any bias introduced would be prejudicial to proposed north Indian mills.

The method used to compute costs of distributing the output of mills producing flat products and bars and light structurals is straightforward and requires no explanation. However, the

[14] Rough estimates of regional demands in 1975–76, presented in Table F-10, indicate that a new mill could be supported by probable markets in southern and western India.

[15] The average rate for salable steel is nearly double the rate I have used for raw materials. In fact, Carlin argues that the average cost of hauling bulk materials on Indian railways should not be too different from that of hauling finished goods. Carlin, Appendix B. See also, Alan P. Carlin, "An Evaluation of U.S. Government Aid to India" (unpub. diss., Massachusetts Institute of Technology, 1964), pp. 101–105. The principal reasons given for the small difference between the costs of hauling both types of freight are the comparatively short trains used to haul bulk materials in India, and, perhaps more important, the larger percentage of empties returning to the origin of shipment generated by bulk freight.

method used to estimate costs of delivering rails and heavy sections to markets is somewhat more complicated. Bhilai's relative nearness to southern and western markets ostensibly influenced its selection. Yet Bhilai, which produces mostly rails and heavy sections, has not restricted her sales to these markets.[16] If a similar plant is to be erected in south India to supply southern and western markets, there should be no reason why Bhilai cannot do so also. For this reason two alternatives are considered. Either a new mill producing rails and heavy sections might be erected at one of the south Indian locations, specializing in production for southern and western markets, Bhilai and other existing mills producing for the rest of India, or a new mill producing these sections might be erected in northeastern India specializing in production for northern and eastern markets, Bhilai supplying markets in southern and western India.

Estimated costs of distributing salable steel to assumed markets are presented in Table 17. Also presented in this table are estimated costs of distributing salable steel throughout India if south Indian mills are unable to specialize in southern and western markets. Both production and distribution costs are considered together in Chapter 9 in an attempt to measure the overall cost advantages or disadvantages possessed by hypothetical south Indian locations.

[16] Barring a change in current plans, after its Fourth Plan expansion program Bhilai will also produce some flat products.

Appendix H | A Steel Plant in Madras

Extensive deposits of magnetite ore are found near Salem in Madras. Approximately ninety miles to the east are the Neyveli lignite deposits now being developed by the government for the production of thermoelectric power, fertilizer, and domestic fuel. Both raw materials are unsuitable for the manufacture of iron in blast furnaces, and both would have to be beneficiated before use in alternative types of furnaces.

Regional interests have advocated a Salem iron and steel plant for many years. In the Third Five Year Plan, published in mid-1961, the Indian government made a tentative commitment to these interests.[1] Within the next two years Neyveli lignite and Salem ore were subjected to tests in East and West Germany, Norway, and the United States as well as at the National Metallurgical Laboratory in Jamshedpur. These tests indicated that it would be possible to produce iron with raw materials found in Madras if these raw materials were properly beneficiated. In mid-1962 the Indian government commissioned M. N. Dastur & Company of Calcutta to prepare a techno-economic report on the proposed Madras plant. Submitted in 1964, this report concluded that the plant would be feasible on both technical and economic grounds.[2] Yet opposition to the

[1] Government of India, Planning Commission, *Third Five Year Plan* (New Delhi: Government of India Publication, 1961), pp. 467 and 496. The Third Plan allotted Rs. 250 million for a Neyveli lignite high temperature carbonization plant and connected pig iron facilities.

[2] A summary of the Dastur report has been published by the Madras government. M. N. Dastur & Company, *Consulting Engineers' Report on the Neyveli-Salem Steel Project—A Summary* (Madras: Government of Madras Publication, 1964).

plant seems to have increased since 1964. By 1966 there was some talk about participation in the project by Japanese equipment suppliers or, alternatively, the Madras government's building the plant alone. Even so, its erection still seems doubtful.

Two general methods for smelting Salem ore have been suggested by advocates of a Madras plant. The low shaft furnace is essentially a blast furnace, the ratio of its height to its diameter considerably lower than usual. Although its consumption of fuel is substantially greater than that of the blast furnace, the low shaft furnace is capable of using a wider range of raw materials. Commercial application of a lignite-based low shaft furnace has been limited to a plant at Calbe, East Germany.[3] However, lignite briquettes now produced at Neyveli are too soft for consumption in a similar plant in Madras. The reprocessing of these briquettes or the erection of an additional plant to manufacture the proper type of briquettes would be necessary. In either event, any advantage derived from an anticipated surplus of certain types of Neyveli briquettes would be limited.

A more likely method of production at Salem is a combination of electric reduction and prereduction in a kiln, probably the Elektrokemisk process developed in Norway or the Strategic-Udy process developed in North America. The former is advocated by M. N. Dastur & Company. In prereduction processes the charge is first passed through a kiln prior to entry into an electric furnace, lignite char serving as a reducing agent and not a source of heat. Lignite char now produced at Neyveli is suitable for both processes. Unfortunately, the commercial application of these processes has been limited.[4]

Salem ore has an iron content of only 36 per cent. No matter which process is adopted, this ore would have to be beneficiated

[3] Several low shaft furnaces are based on other fuels. One is located at Barbil, Orissa, in India and is discussed in Chapter 10. An experimental low shaft plant is operated by the National Metallurgical Laboratory in Jamshedpur.

[4] The first commercial Strategic-Udy plant was commissioned in Venezuela in 1963. Its performance has not been satisfactory. An Elektrokemisk plant has been ordered by Yugoslavia, but has not yet been commissioned.

by grinding, extracting iron-bearing particles by magnetic separation, and agglomerating these particles by sintering or pelletization. The beneficiated ore concentrate would have a slightly higher iron content than unbeneficiated ores found elsewhere in south India.

It is claimed that the costs of producing steel in Madras would be as low as the costs of producing similar types of steel elsewhere in India. In addition, the raw materials used in a Madras plant would yield an iron low in phosphorous and sulphur. This is a superior grade that cannot be produced by existing mills and is especially well suited for the manufacture of special steels. The location of a steel mill at Salem would also allow lower costs of distributing steel to markets and would help to relieve India's transportation difficulties. Finally, it is claimed that the erection of a plant in Madras would provide a strong stimulus to the economic development of south India.[5]

Nations that have adopted alternative methods of producing iron suffer without exception from an absence of coking coal. South India has no coking coal. However, northeastern India possesses deposits that are sufficient to support continued expansion of the steel industry.[6] Therefore, although it may be beneficial, it is not essential that India emulate the few instances in which alternative methods of producing iron have been applied commercially if she is to expand her industry.

It is claimed that a Salem plan could produce steel at a cost competitive with north Indian mills.[7] Several objections to this claim seem justified. First, the economics of electric reduction will depend critically on the cost of electricity. Although the rate assumed by M. N. Dastur & Company, Rs. 0.03 per kwh, is equal to rates charged several large industrial undertakings by the Madras State Electricity Board, it is well below the estimated cost of thermoelectric power in India, Rs. 0.073 per

[5] For these arguments and several others, see M. N. Dastur & Company, *Consulting Engineers' Report*, various pages.

[6] Appendix A.

[7] M. N. Dastur & Company, *Consulting Engineers' Report*, pp. 39–42.

kwh, and slightly lower than the estimated cost of hydroelectric power, Rs. 0.038 per kwh.[8] Were a Madras plant to consume hydroelectric power alone, Rs. 0.03 per kwh might be a reasonable rate. However, because opportunities for hydroelectric power development in Madras are largely exhausted, most additional power is to be supplied by thermoelectric power projects, notably the Neyveli lignite scheme. There is a severe shortage of power in Madras which as recently as 1964 forced a curtailment in the activities of many of the state's industries.[9] The Salem plant would consume nearly 60 per cent of the increase in the state's power capacity anticipated by 1967.[10] Unless there is a reduction in demands by other users, or continued shortages, it is almost certain that the Salem plant would

[8] *Ibid.*, p. 27, and Planning Unit, Indian Statistical Institute, "Price Policy for Electricity Undertakings" (mimeograph, New Delhi, June 1962), p. 25. Chapters 3 and 4 and Table 8 in the Appendix are also relevant to a discussion of the Madras plant. The costs cited assume a 90 per cent load factor, slightly higher than that estimated for the Salem plant by Dastur.

[9] The following news report is especially relevant:

The power cut in Madras State came into force on June 15, and it was at first announced that all industries, excepting those adopting the continuous processes, would have to reduce their consumption by 50 per cent in the hydel areas and by 40 per cent in the thermal areas. But the Madras State Electricity Board had to decide on the imposition of even more drastic restrictions because the expectations regarding adequate rainfall in the catchment areas did not prove correct. Actually, the demand for power was so great that even on the restricted basis, the Electricity Board found it difficult to keep the industries functioning. There was confusion in Coimbatore for a time and the mills could not operate even on the restricted basis as there were frequent interruptions and breakdowns. It was felt that a total cut would enable them to lay off workers. The complete cut became effective from 18th June in the hydel areas while in the thermal areas the industrial consumers were allowed to operate at only 20 per cent of their capacity. The continuous process industries are, however, exempt from the cut. The fresh restrictions were necessitated by the precarious level of water storage in the various hydel reservoirs. For a few hours, one of the units in Neyveli thermal station also was out of commission on account of minor trouble. The authorities, therefore, got alarmed and decided to enforce drastic restrictions. *The Eastern Economist,* June 26, 1964, p. 1463.

[10] M. N. Dastur & Company, *Consulting Engineers' Report,* p. 26.

necessitate the erection of additional power capacity. For this reason, the cost that should be charged for the mill's power should more closely approximate the costs of additional thermoelectric power generated in Madras.[11]

It is frequently claimed that the erection of a Salem steel plant would provide a strong stimulus to the industrial development of Madras. I consider this claim suspect. Because steel prices are equalized throughout India, a steel consumer in Madras pays no more than a consumer at the gates of an existing mill. Presumably any stimulus to south Indian industries using steel because of lower steel prices has already been created through regional price equalization. In addition, erection of a Madras plant may discourage the development of other industries dependent on electricity. Unless there is a substantial increase in power production in or near Madras, a Salem plant would very likely intensify that state's power difficulties. If so, a Madras steel plant may actually hinder the state's industrial growth.

The Dastur report states that one of the principal reasons for favorable capital and operating costs of the Salem plant, relative to costs of existing north Indian mills, would be the adoption of the continuous casting process. The Salem plant would also benefit from the use of LD converters and pellets.[12]

[11] There is hydroelectric power potential in two South Indian states, Mysore and Kerala. Should this potential be developed and South Indian power grids interconnected, the costs of power at Salem may be lowered. If so, one might then ask why locations in Mysore have not been considered for prereduction and electric furnaces. Not only would the costs of transmitting power be reduced, but also Mysore power potential is in close proximity to several high quality ore bodies.

[12] M. N. Dastur & Company, *Consulting Engineers' Report*, pp. 4, 21, 22, and 40. Continuous casting involves the direct casting of liquid steel into intermediate sections. Before the development of this process, ingots had to be rolled into these sections in a blooming mill, a highly indivisible and expensive unit of a steel plant. This process allows lower capital costs per ton of output. Because it permits less production of scrap, it also allows lower operating costs. In the LD process, oxygen is injected into hot metal in converters. This method of producing steel, developed in Austria after World War II, also enables lower capital and operating costs. Pelletization is the agglomeration of ore fines into pellets, an artificial

Comparisons need not be odious. However, comparisons between what is and what can be frequently are. These processes were not adopted at north Indian mills because they were still largely experimental at the time these mills were erected.[13] They are now commercially tried and are included in many of the industry's expansion programs. There is no reason why they cannot also be used in new mills erected elsewhere in India.

Any cost advantage accruing to a Salem plant relative to a *new* mill elsewhere should be restricted by and large to facilities used in the production of coke, lignite char, and iron. Beyond these stages in steel production costs at the Salem plant need not differ significantly from costs at a comparable plant manufacturing iron in blast furnaces. What evidence exists indicates that the blast furnace is still far and away the most economical method of producing iron.[14]

Special steels would account for 32 per cent of the Salem plant's output. This is partly because these are high value types of steel and would be better able to absorb the high costs of Salem's iron. It is also because of the low phosphorus content of the plant's iron, which is advantageous but not necessary for the production of alloy, tool, and stainless steels. However, low phosphorus iron is already being produced in south India, at the Mysore Iron and Steel Works, and will soon be converted to special steels.[15] The works is installing facilities for the production of special steels for two reasons. First, special steels

---

furnace input that enables smelting of a higher grade iron-bearing input and better performance by the furnace. All three processes have been widely accepted since the late 1950s and represent major technological changes in the industry.

[13] One exception is Rourkela which installed LD converters in its initial plant.

[14] In Chapter 10 I discuss cost disadvantages suffered by small pig iron plants that use methods of producing iron similar to that proposed for the Salem plant.

[15] Low phosphorus iron, by definition, has a maximum phosphorus content of 0.1 per cent. Madras iron would have a phosphorus content of up to 0.07 per cent. In the past MISW's iron has contained an average phosphorus content of 0.1 per cent. M. S. Krishnan, *Iron Ore, Iron and Steel, Bulletins of the Geological Survey of India*, Series A, Number 9, second ed. (Delhi: Government of India Publication, 1961), p. 213.

are manufactured in electric furnaces well suited for using the relatively inexpensive power of Mysore. Second, special steels are the most costly of all types of steel. High cost iron produced in Mysore, as at Salem, would be a relatively small proportion of the plant's total costs of production. If a plant producing special steels must be located in south India, it might be better on purely economic grounds to make the best of the existing plant in Mysore, putting to more advantageous use the resources already invested by the Indian economy.

The Planning Commission has estimated India's demand for special steels in 1970–71 to be 0.42 million tons.[16] The proposed initial output of the Salem plant would account for one-third of projected demand. MISW and three private sector special steel plants, already licensed for erection in Madras, will have a combined capacity also equal to one-third of projected demand. Therefore, were the Salem plant built, south India would almost certainly produce much more special steel than she can consume.[17]

If the Salem plant must produce a relatively large proportion of highly specialized types of steel to be competitive, then an important advantage claimed for a Madras plant would be in question. In general, the more specialized the product of a mill, the more widespread its markets. Therefore, the location of a special steel production in Madras would probably confer little if any advantage in costs of distribution.

[16] Government of India, Planning Commission, Perspective Planning Division, *Special Steel Requirements, India: 1960–70* (mimeograph, New Delhi, 1961), p. 3. For reasons discussed in Chapter 7, this estimate is probably exaggerated.

[17] For a discussion of private sector units licensed for the production of special steels, see Government of India, Planning Commission, *Programmes of Industrial Development, 1961–66* (New Delhi: Government of India Publication, 1962), p. 33. Of fourteen units licensed in the private sector, only two with a combined capacity of 22,000 tons are said to have progressed toward completion. Both are in Madras. "Prospects for Making Alloy and Tool Steel Seriously Delayed," Supplement to *Capital,* June 28, 1962, p. 17. I do not have a regional breakdown of Indian demand for special steels. However, in 1960–61 south Indian demand for steel was only 13.8 per cent of total Indian demand. See Table F-9. If the regional distribution of demand for special steels is at all similar, the suggested output of special steels in south India would be excessive.

This long and technical discussion of the Salem plant not only points out many of the deficiencies of the plant site, but also indicates some of the difficulties involved in site selection in general. If a project report is meant simply to justify a location chosen for political or ideological reasons, with deliberate sleight of hand to conceal the project's economic and technical deficiencies, then there is little use in discussing it, unless, of course, it is taken seriously by planners. On the other hand, if the report is intended to be an accurate assessment of the project to guide planners, it should satisfy several criteria. First, it must be internally consistent. One cannot simply add up all arguments in favor of a project as if they were independent of each other. In the case of the Salem plant, there is a possible inconsistency between the plant's production of special steels and its concentration on regional markets. There is also a possible inconsistency between its use of electricity and its contribution to the industrial growth of Madras state. Second, a project report cannot be prepared in isolation of other developments in the industry. Whether the Salem plant will be justified in producing special steels will depend on the plans of other plants in the same region. Third, if comparisons are to be made, as they must, these comparisons should be meaningful. The alternative to the Salem plant is a new plant producing similar types of steel located elsewhere in India. The criterion for judging whether one of these plants is preferred on economic and technical grounds should be based on relevant differences between the two plants. All things considered, I am skeptical that the Dastur report has made a convincing case for the Madras plant.

Bibliography

This bibliography contains some of the more important sources concerned with India's iron and steel industry in particular and Indian industry and planning in general when relevant to the industry. Several sources are included that are not mentioned in the text. Most of these additional sources concern the Indian industry before Independence, labor relations, and technical subjects that I have touched upon only indirectly but that may be of more immediate interest to the reader. A few sources are included in the bibliography that were published too late to be used as a basis for my own research.

India's Industry and Economy Prior to Independence

Anstey, Vera. *The Economic Development of India,* fourth ed. London: Longmans, Green and Co., 1952.

Baldwin, George B. *Industrial Growth in South India, Case Studies in Economic Development.* Glencoe, Ill.: The Free Press, 1959.

Buchanan, Daniel. *The Development of Capitalist Enterprise in India.* New York: Macmillan, 1934.

Buchanan, Francis. *A Journey from Madras through the Countries of Mysore, Canara and Malabar,* Vols. I and II. No publisher or date indicated. Francis Buchanan, an agent for the East India Company, made this journey in 1800 and 1801. His observations include detailed accounts of indigenous methods of producing iron and are invaluable to the scholar concerned with India's manufacture of iron in antiquity.

Elwin, Verrier. *The Story of Tata Steel.* Bombay: The Tata Iron and Steel Company, Ltd., 1958.

Fraser, Lovat. *Iron and Steel in India.* Bombay: The Times Press, 1919.

Harris, Frank. *Jamsetji Nusserwanji Tata, A Chronicle of His Life,* second ed. Bombay: Blackie & Son (India) Ltd., 1958. This book contains Fraser's study as Chapters VIII–X.

Howard, George C. "Iron and Steel Industry and Trade in India," *United States Government Trade Information Bulletin #816*. Washington, D.C.: U.S. Government Printing Office, 1933.

Indian Tariff Board. *Applications Received by the Indian Tariff Board From the Tata Iron and Steel Company, Ltd.* Calcutta: Government of India, Central Publication Branch, 1926.

——— *Evidence Recorded During Enquiry Into the Steel Industry.* Calcutta: Superintendent of Government Printing, 1924, Vols. 1, 2 and 3.

——— *Evidence Recorded During Enquiry on Additional Protection for Galvanized Sheets.* Calcutta: Government of India, Central Publication Branch, 1931.

——— *Evidence Recorded During Enquiry Regarding the Grant of Supplementary Protection to the Steel Industry.* Calcutta: Government of India, Central Publication Branch, 1925.

——— *Report of the Indian Tariff Board on Additional Protection for Galvanized Sheets.* Calcutta: Government of India, Central Publication Branch, 1930.

——— *Report of the Indian Tariff Board on Steel Rails.* Calcutta: Government of India, Central Publication Branch, 1931.

——— *Report of the Indian Tariff Board on the Continuance of Protection to the Iron and Steel Industry.* Bombay: Government of India Publication, 1947.

——— *Report of the Indian Tariff Board on the Iron and Steel Industry.* Delhi: Manager of Publications, Government of India, 1934.

——— *Report of the Indian Tariff Board on the Removal of the Revenue Duty on Pig Iron Including Evidence Recorded During the Inquiry.* Calcutta: Government of India, Central Publication Branch, 1930.

——— *Report of the Indian Tariff Board Regarding Certain Railway Materials Made of Steel.* Calcutta: Government of India, Central Publications Branch, 1930.

——— *Report of the Indian Tariff Board Regarding the Grant of Protection to the Steel Industry.* Calcutta: Superintendent, Government Printing, 1924.

——— *Report of the Indian Tariff Board Regarding the Grant of Supplementary Protection to the Steel Industry.* Calcutta: Government of India, Central Publication Branch, 1925.

——— *Report of the Indian Tariff Board Regarding the Increase of the Duties on Steel.* Bombay: Manager, Government Central Press, 1924.

——— *Statutory Enquiry, 1926, Steel Industry.* Calcutta: Government of India, Central Publication Branch, 1927, Vols. 1, 2, and 3.

——— *Statutory Enquiry—1933—Steel Industry.* Delhi: Manager of Publications, Government of India, 1934, Vols. 1, 2, 3, and 4.

Keenan, John L. *A Steel Man in India.* New York: Duell, Sloan and Pearce, 1943. Keenan was associated with TISCO almost from it beginning and during the early 1930's was TISCO's General Manager. His book offers a wealth of information about problems encountered in establishing TISCO's plant.

Majumdar, D. N. *The Affairs of a Tribe.* Lucknow: Universal Publishers, Ltd., 1950. This is a study of the Ho tribe, which is indigenous to the region in which TISCO's and IISCO's ore mines are situated. It is a useful description of the influence of these mines on the tribe.

Morris, Morris David. *The Emergence of an Industrial Labor Force in India: A Study of the Bombay Cotton Mills, 1854–1947.* Berkeley, Calif.: University of California Press, 1965.

Phillips, George B. "The Antiquity of the Use of Iron," *American Anthropologist,* June 1924.

——— "The Claims of India to the First Production of Steel," *American Anthropologist,* September 1924.

Ranade, Mahadev Govind. "Iron Industry—Pioneer Attempts," Essay VI, *Essays on Indian Economics.* Madras City: G. A. Natesan & Co., 1906.

Spate, O. H. K. *India and Pakistan, A General and Regional Geography.* New York: E. P. Dutton & Co., Inc., 1954.

Spiegelman, Robert. *Protection in India During the Interwar Period with Special Reference to the Steel Industry.* Unpub. diss., Columbia University, 1960.

India's Industry and Economy after Independence

American Steel Industry Delegation. "Engineering Data on the Indian Steel Industry." New York, American Iron and Steel Institute, unpub., 1960.

——— *India, Report.* New York: American Iron and Steel Institute, 1960.

Appleby, Paul H. *Re-examination of India's Administrative System with Special Reference to Administration of Government's Industrial and Commercial Enterprises.* New Delhi: Government of India, Cabinet Secretariat, Organization and Methods Division, 1956.

Association of Indian Trade and Industry. *Financial Trends in the Iron and Steel Industry.* Bombay: Examiner Press, 1954.

Boothalingam, S. "Steel in the Third Plan," *Problems in the Third Plan: A Critical Miscellany.* Delhi: The Publications Division, Ministry of Information and Broadcasting, Government of India,

c. 1961. Mr. Boothalingam was formerly Secretary, Department of Iron and Steel, Government of India.
Braibanti, Ralph J. and Joseph J. Spengler, eds. *Administration and Economic Development in India.* Durham, N.C.: Duke University Press, 1963.
Brimmer, Andrew F., "The Setting of Entrepreneurship in India," *The Quarterly Journal of Economics,* November 1955.
Brush, J. E. "The Iron and Steel Industry of India." *Geographical Review,* January 1952.
Carlin, Alan Philip. "An Evaluation of U.S. Government Aid to India." Unpub. diss., Massachusetts Institute of Technology, 1964.
——— *A Possible U.S. Policy Towards Indian Transportation: An Illustration of Improved Sectoral Policies.* Santa Monica, Calif.: The RAND Corporation, RM-4379-AID, June 1965.
Central Fuel Research Institute and the Institute of Fuel. *Proceedings of the Symposium on the Nature of Coal.* Calcutta: Technical Journals of India, Private, Ltd., 1959.
Chatterjea, A. B. and B. R. Nijhawan. "Iron Production in Low-Shaft Furnace Plants with Indian Raw Materials," *Symposium on India's Iron and Steel Industry, Jamshedpur, 1963.* Calcutta: Technical Journals of India, Private, Ltd., 1963.
Chaudhuri, M. R. *The Iron and Steel Industry of India.* Calcutta: Oxford Book Company, 1964.
Coverdale and Colpitts, New York City, and Surveys and Research Corporation, Washington, D.C. "India Coal Transport Study," eight volumes, multilithed, 1964.
Dastur, M. N. *Steel in India—Economic and Technological Possibilities.* Calcutta: *The Statesman,* Commercial Printing Dept., 1961.
——— and R. D. Lalkaka. "Layout of Large Integrated Steelworks," *Symposium on India's Iron and Steel Industry, Jamshedpur, 1963.* Calcutta: Technical Journals of India, Private, Ltd., 1963.
Dastur & Company, Private, Ltd., M. N. (Consulting Engineers, Calcutta). "Preliminary Report to Hindustan Steel Limited on the Establishment of an Integrated Steel Works at Bokaro." Calcutta, mimeographed, 1959. M. N. Dastur & Company has also prepared three subsequent studies about the Bokaro, Salem, and south Indian steel mills.
Dowding, M. F. and A. N. Whiting. "The Case for 100,000 Tonnes/Year Integrated Iron and Steel Plants for Emergent Countries," *Symposium on India's Iron and Steel Industry, Jamshedpur, February 1963.* Calcutta: Technical Journals of India, Private, Ltd., 1963.
Dutt, R. N. *History of the Expansion of the Steel Industry in India.* Calcutta: *Iron and Steel Review,* n.d.

Earle, L. G. and W. S. Walker. "Fundamentals of Small Steelworks," *Symposium on India's Iron and Steel Industry, Jamshedpur, 1963.* Calcutta: Technical Journals of India, Private, Ltd., 1963.

Energy Survey. *Report of the Energy Survey of India Committee.* Delhi: no publisher indicated, 1964.

Ghandy, Sir Jehangir. "Steel in the Third Plan," speech presented to the Indian Rotary Club, October 15, 1959, published in pamphlet form by TISCO. Mr Ghandy was formerly Director-in-Charge, TISCO.

——— "Steel, Some Problems of Development," speech presented to the Engineering Institute of India, Calcutta, December 24, 1959, published in pamphlet form by TISCO.

——— "Technology and Economic Change in the Third Five Year Plan," *Science and Culture,* January 1960.

Ghosh, Moni. *Our Struggle.* Calcutta: Das Gupta & Co. (Private Ltd.), c. 1958. This work is an account of the growth of the Tata Workers Union, written by a person associated with the union for many years.

Gill, K. S. "Suggestions Regarding Major Products of Iron and Steel Development in the Fourth Plan." New Delhi, mimeographed, Indian Planning Commission, 1962.

Guha, A. K. *Location of the New Steel Plant and its Economic Aspects.* Alipore, West Bengal: West Bengal Government Press, 1954.

Hindustan Steel Limited. *Annual Report,* 1957–58 until present.

——— *List of Products* (Printed brochure for each HSL mill). Calcutta: Director (Commercial), HSL, various dates.

——— "Manpower Situation in Bhilai, Durgapur and Rourkela." Ranchi, Bihar, mimeograph, 1964.

Hopper, W. David. "Allocation Efficiency in a Traditional Indian Agriculture," *Journal of Farm Economics,* 47 (August 1965).

India, Government of, Ministry of Commerce and Industry. *Report.* New Delhi: Government of India Publication, 1952–53 through 1956–57. These reports cover the period during which the iron and steel industry was under the direction of the Ministry of Commerce and Industry.

——— Ministry of Finance, Department of Expenditure (Projects Coordination Division). *Annual Report on the Working of Industrial and Commercial Undertakings of the Central Government.* New Delhi: Government of India Publication, various years.

——— Ministry of Industries, *Final Report of the Industries Development Procedures Committee* (Swaminathan Committee). New Delhi: Government of India Publication, 1964.

——— Ministry of Industry and Supply. *Report.* New Delhi: Government of India Publication, 1947–48 through 1949. These reports cover the period during which the iron and steel industry was under the direction of the Ministry of Industry and Supply.

——— Ministry of Labour, Labour Bureau. *Labour-Management Consultation and Cooperation in the Tata Iron and Steel Company.* New Delhi: Government of India Publication, 1957.

——— Ministry of Production. *Report.* New Delhi: Government of India Publication, 1953–54 through 1954–55. These reports cover the period during which the iron and steel industry was under the direction of the Ministry of Production.

——— Ministry of Steel and Heavy Industries, Department of Iron and Steel. *Report.* New Delhi: Government of India Publication, 1961–62 through 1962–63. These reports cover the period during which the iron and steel industry was under the direction of the Ministry of Steel and Heavy Industries.

——— Ministry of Steel and Heavy Industries, Iron and Steel Control. "Price Circular" (for steel, scrap, etc.). Calcutta, mimeographed, various dates.

——— Ministry of Steel and Mines, Department of Iron and Steel. "Notification of Price Changes," *The Gazette of India.* New Delhi: Government of India Publication, various dates. Notifications have also been published by the Department of Iron and Steel when under previous ministries.

——— Ministry of Steel and Mines, Department of Iron and Steel. *Report.* New Delhi: Government of India Publication, 1964–65. This report covers the period during which the iron and steel industry was under the direction of the Ministry of Steel and Mines.

——— Ministry of Steel, Mines and Fuel, Department of Iron and Steel. *Report.* New Delhi: Government of India Publication, 1958–59 through 1960–61. These reports cover the period during which the iron and steel industry was under the direction of the Ministry of Steel, Mines and Fuel.

——— Ministry of Steel, Mines and Heavy Engineering, Department of Iron and Steel. *Report.* New Delhi: Government of India Publication, 1963–64. This report covers the period during which the iron and steel industry was under the direction of the Ministry of Steel, Mines and Heavy Engineering.

——— Planning Commission. *Economic Development in Different Regions of India.* New Delhi: Government of India Publication, 1962.

——— Planning Commission. *First Five Year Plan.* New Delhi: Government of India Publication, 1951.

——— Planning Commission. *Papers Relating to the Formulation of the Second Five Year Plan.* New Delhi: Government of India Publication, 1955.

——— Planning Commission. *Plan Resources and Outlay, a Review.* New Delhi: Government of India Publication, 1959.

——— Planning Commission. *Programmes of Industrial Development,* 1951–56. New Delhi: Government of India Publication, 1952.

——— Planning Commission. *Programmes of Industrial Development,* 1956–61. New Delhi: Government of India Publication, 1956.

——— Planning Commission. *Programmes of Industrial Development,* 1961–66. New Delhi: Government of India Publication, 1962.

——— Planning Commission. *Reappraisal of the Second Five Year Plan, a Resume.* New Delhi: Government of India Publication, 1958.

——— Planning Commission. *A Report on Progress of Selected Projects During the Second Five Year Plan.* New Delhi: Government of India Publication, 1961.

——— Planning Commission. *Review of the First Five Year Plan.* New Delhi: Government of India Publication, 1957.

——— Planning Commission. *Second Five Year Plan.* New Delhi: Government of India Publication, 1956.

———Planning Commission. *Second Five Year Plan, a Draft Outline.* New Delhi: Government of India Publication, 1956.

——— Planning Commission. "Steel in the Third Five Year Plan: Requirements, Availability and Allocation." New Delhi, mimeographed, 1962.

——— Planning Commission. *Third Five Year Plan.* New Delhi: Government of India Publication, 1961.

——— Planning Commission. *The Third Five Year Plan, A Draft Outline.* New Delhi: Government of India Publication, 1960.

——— Planning Commission. *The Third Plan Mid-Term Appraisal.* New Delhi: Government of India Publication, 1963.

——— Planning Commission, Committee on Transport Policy and Coordination, (Neogy Committee). *Preliminary Report.* New Delhi: Planning Commission, 1961.

——— Planning Commission, Perspective Planning Division. "Iron and Steel—Advance Action for the Fourth Plan." New Delhi, mimeographed, 1962.

——— Planning Commission, Perspective Planning Division. "Ten Year Plan for Steel, 1961–1971." New Delhi, mimeographed, 1961. This document contains, "Demand for Steel, Special Steel and Pig Iron in India: 1960–70," one of the Planning Commission's studies of future Indian demand for steel. There has been at least one subsequent study.

Indian Construction News, Bhilai Number, October 1959. Calcutta: Technical Journals of India, Private, Ltd., 1959.

——— *Durgapur Number,* July 1959. Calcutta: Technical Journals of India, Private, Ltd., 1959.

——— *Rourkela Number,* December 1958. Calcutta: Technical Journals of India, Private, Ltd., 1958.

Indian Iron and Steel Company Limited. *Annual Report,* 1919 to present. Accompanying each *Annual Report* is the annual speech to shareholders by IISCO's chairmen. Those of Sir Biren Mookerjee during the past decade are useful expressions of the opinions of IISCO's management on many issues.

Indian Steel Training and Education Program in the United States. *Steelmen for India.* New York: American Iron and Steel Institute, 1960.

Indian Tariff Board. *Report of the Indian Tariff Board on the Fair Retention Prices of Steel Produced by the Mysore Iron and Steel Works, Bhadravati, Bombay, 1949.* New Delhi: Government of India Publication, 1949.

——— *Report of the Indian Tariff Board on the Fair Retention Prices of Steel Produced by the Tata Iron and Steel Company and the Steel Corporation of Bengal.* New Delhi: Government of India Publication, 1949.

——— *Report of the Indian Tariff Board on the Fair Retention Prices of Steel Produced by the Tata Iron and Steel Company and the Steel Corporation of Bengal.* New Delhi: Government of India Publication, 1951.

——— *Report of the Indian Tariff Board on the Works Costs of Hot Metal (Iron for Steel-Making) and Fair Ex-Works Prices of Pig Iron (Basic and Foundry Grades), Bombay, 1949.* New Delhi: Government of India Publication, 1949.

Indian Tariff Commission. *Annual Report.* New Delhi: Government of India Publication, 1952–53 to 1962–63. This source contains summaries of price inquiries made by the Indian Tariff Commission and decisions made by the Government of India.

——— *Report on the Fair Ex-Works Retention Price of Pig Iron for the Period 1st April 1960 to 31st March 1962, Bombay, 1962.* New Delhi: Government of India Publication, 1962.

——— *Report on the Fair Ex-Works Retention Prices of Steel for the Period 1st April 1960 to 31st March 1962, Bombay, 1962.* New Delhi: Government of India Publication, 1962.

——— *Report on the Fair Relationship Between the Ordinary*

Shares of the Steel Corporation of Bengal, Ltd. and the Indian Iron and Steel Company, Ltd., 1952. New Delhi: Government of India Publication, 1952.

——— *Report on the Fair Retention Prices (Ex-Works) of Pig Iron & Steel Produced by the Mysore Iron and Steel Works, Bhadravati, Bombay, 1956.* New Delhi: Government of India Publication, 1956.

——— *Report on the Fair Retention Prices of Steel Produced by the Indian Iron and Steel Company, Ltd., Bombay, 1954.* New Delhi: Government of India Publication, 1954.

——— *Report on the Fair Retention Prices of Steel Produced by the Mysore Iron and Steel Works, 1952, Bhadravati.* New Delhi: Government of India Publication, n.d.

——— *Report on the Fair Retention Prices of Steel Produced by the Steel Corporation of Bengal, Bombay, 1952.* New Delhi: Government of India Publication, 1952.

——— *Report on the Fair Retention Prices of Steel Produced by the Tata Iron and Steel Company, Ltd., Bombay, 1953.* New Delhi: Government of India Publication, 1953.

——— *Report on the Levy of Interest on Special Advances to the Tata Iron and Steel Company Limited and the Indian Iron and Steel Company Limited, Bombay, 1959.* New Delhi: Government of India Publication, 1960.

——— *Report on the Revision of Fair Retention Prices, Ex-Works, of Pig Iron Produced by the Indian Iron and Steel Company, Ltd., Bombay, 1958.* New Delhi: Government of India Publication, 1960.

——— *Report on the Retention Prices of Steel Produced by the Tata Iron and Steel Company, Ltd., and the Indian Iron and Steel Company, Ltd., Bombay, 1956.* New Delhi: Government of India Publication, 1956.

——— *Report on the Revision of the Retention Prices of Steel Produced by the Tata Iron and Steel Company, Ltd., and the Indian Iron and Steel Company, Ltd., Bombay, 1957.* New Delhi: Government of India Publication, 1957.

——— *Report on the Revision of the Retention Prices of Steel Produced by the Tata Iron and Steel Company, Ltd., and the Indian Iron and Steel Company, Ltd., Bombay, 1958.* New Delhi: Government of India Publication, 1958.

Indien-Gemeinschaft, Krupp-Demag. "Preliminary Report for Hindustan Steel, Ltd., May 1954." Unpub., 1954.

International Bank for Reconstruction and Development. "Appraisal of the Tata Iron and Steel Company, Ltd., Expansion and Modernization Project." Washington, D.C., unpub., 1956.

——— "Report and Recommendations of the President to the Executive Directors Concerning a Proposed Loan to the Tata Iron and Steel Company Ltd. in India." Washington, D.C., unpub., 1956.

International Construction Company, Ltd., *Report on the Establishment of an Iron and Steel Works in India.* London: Waterlow & Sons, Ltd., 1949.

Iron and Steel Delegation to China. *Iron and Steel Industry in China, Summary of a Report of the Indian Steel Delegation.* New Delhi: Government of India Publication, 1959.

Iron and Steel (Major) Panel. *First Report of the Iron and Steel (Major) Panel.* New Delhi: Government of India Publication, 1949.

——— *Second Report of the Iron and Steel (Major) Panel on Rerolling Mills, Engineering Industries and Alloy, Tool and Special Steel, 1946.* New Delhi: Government of India Publication, 1949.

Johnson, William A. "India's Iron and Steel Industry: A Study of Planned Industrial Growth." Unpub. diss., Harvard University, May 1964.

Joint Plant Committee. *Indenting Procedure and General Conditions for Sale of Iron and Steel.* Calcutta: Joint Plant Committee, 1964.

——— "Schedule of Prices." Calcutta, mimeographed announcements, various dates.

Kannappan, Subbiah. "The Tata Steel Strike," *Journal of Political Economy,* October 1959.

Koppers Company, Inc., Pittsburgh, Pa. *Indian Steel Report.* Pittsburgh: Koppers Company, 1948.

——— *Indian Steel Report, Supplement, Bhilai Steel Works.* Pittsburgh: Koppers Company, 1948.

Krishnan, M. S. *Iron Ore, Iron and Steel,* second ed. Bulletins of the Geological Survey of India, Series A—Economic Geology. Calcutta: Government of India Publication, 1961.

Kutar, Phiroz. *Choice of Technology in Steel.* Calcutta: Tata Iron and Steel Company, Public Relations Department, 1960. Mr. Kutar was formerly General Manager, TISCO, and Director in Charge of Production, HSL.

——— *India's Steel Industry: A Survey.* Calcutta: Tata Iron and Steel Company, Public Relations Department, c. 1958.

Kutar, P. H. and B. R. Nijhawan. "Some Problems of Iron and Steelmaking in the Hindustan Steel Plants," *Symposium on India's Iron and Steel Industry, Jamshedpur, 1963.* Calcutta: Technical Journals of India, Private, Ltd., 1963. Dr. Nijhawan is Director of the National Metallurgical Laboratory, Jamshedpur.

Lewis, John P. *Quiet Crisis in India.* Washington, D.C.: The Brookings Institution, 1962.

Lindblom, Charles E. "Has India an Economic Future?," *Foreign Affairs*, January 1966.

Lok Sabha (House of the People, Indian Parliament), Estimates Committee. *Ministry of Steel, Mines and Fuel, 33rd Report, Second Lok Sabha, 1958–59.* New Delhi: Lok Sabha Secretariat, 1959.

——— *Second Report (Third Lok Sabha), Ministry of Steel and Heavy Industries, Hindustan Steel, Ltd., Ranchi.* New Delhi: Lok Sabha Secretariat, 1962.

Madan, M. D. "The Tata Steel Works at Jamshedpur," *H. R. H. Duke of Edinburgh's Study Conference 1956.* London: Oxford University Press, 1957, Vol. II.

Madhya Pradesh, Government of. *New Iron and Steel Plant, Supplementary Memorandum.* Nagpur, M. P.: Government Printing, Madhya Pradesh, 1953.

Madras, Government of, Department of Industries, Labour and Cooperation. *Consulting Engineers' Report on Neyveli-Salem Steel Project—A Summary.* Madras: Government of Madras Publication, 1964. This document is a reproduction of the summary report on the Salem project by M. N. Dastur & Company of Calcutta.

Major Industries of India, Annual. M. P. Gandhi, ed., various years. Each annual volume contains an article by a prominent official of India's steel industry.

Malenbaum, Wilfred. *Prospects for Indian Development.* New York: The Free Press of Glencoe, Inc., 1962.

McKee & Company, Arthur G., Engineers and Contractors, Cleveland, Ohio. "General Plans for Increasing the Production of Iron and Steel in India, Report Prepared for the Ministry of Industry and Supply, Government of India." Cleveland, unpub., 1949.

Mohanty, H. B. *Location of a Steel Plant in Orissa.* Industries Department, Orissa Government Press, c. 1954.

Myers, Charles A. *Labor Problems in the Industrialization of India.* Cambridge, Mass.: Harvard University Press, 1958.

Nahai, Lotfollah. *India's Iron and Steel Industry.* U.S. Department of the Interior, Bureau of Mines. Washington, D.C.: U.S. Government Printing Office, 1961.

National Council of Applied Economic Research. *Appraisal of Steel Demand.* New Delhi: NCAER, 1960.

——— *Reappraisal of Steel Demand.* New Delhi: NCAER, 1963, 2 volumes.

——— *Techno-Economic Survey of Madras, Economic Report.* Madras: Department of Industries, Labour and Cooperation, 1960. The NCAER has also prepared techno-economic surveys for other Indian states.

——— *Transport Requirements of the Iron and Steel Belt.* New Delhi: National Council of Applied Economic Research, 1964.

National Metallurgical Laboratory, Council of Scientific and Industrial Research. *Annual Report.* Jamshedpur: NML, various years.

National Metallurgical Laboratory, Jamshedpur. *Proceedings of the Symposium on Recent Developments in Foundry Technology.* Calcutta: Technical Journals of India, Private, Ltd., 1958.

——— *Symposium on the Production, Properties and Application of Alloys and Special Steels, February 1956.* Calcutta: Technical Journals of India, Private, Ltd., 1958.

——— *Symposium on Pilot Plants in Metallurgical Research and Development, February 1960.* Calcutta: Technical Journals of India, Private, Ltd., 1960.

——— *Symposium on the Iron and Steel Industry in India.* Calcutta: Technical Journals of India, Private, Ltd., 1959. Another symposium on problems relating to India's iron and steel industry was held in 1963. Several papers presented at this symposium are indicated separately in this bibliography.

Nijhawan, B. R. "Growth Patterns of Iron and Steel Industry in India's Economic Development," paper presented to the Interregional Symposium on the Application of Modern Technical Practices in the Iron and Steel Industry to Developing Countries. New York, United Nations, mimeographed, 1963.

Orans, Martin. "A Tribal People in an Industrial Setting," *Traditional India: Structure and Change,* Milton Singer, ed., *Journal of American Folklore,* July–September, 1958.

Place, Siddons & Gough (Private), Ltd. *Investor's India Year-Book.* Calcutta: Orient Longmans, Ltd., various years.

Prakash, Om. *The Theory and Working of State Corporations with Special Reference to India.* London: George Allen & Unwin, Ltd., 1962.

Raj Committee. "A Preliminary Report on Steel Control." New Delhi, mimeographed, Ministry of Steel and Heavy Industries, 1963.

——— *Report on Steel Control.* New Delhi: Government of India, Ministry of Steel and Heavy Industries, 1963.

Ramanathan, G. "A Note on the Indian Steel Industry: Its Growth and Its Pricing Structure." New Delhi, unpub., c. 1962.

Rao, B. S. *Surveys of Indian Industries.* London: Oxford University Press, 1957, Vol. 1.

Reddaway, W. B. *The Development of the Indian Economy.* Homewood, Ill.: Richard D. Irwin, Inc., 1962.

Robinson, Harry. *Industrial Development Policy in India.* Menlo Park, Calif.: Stanford Research Institute, 1956.

Rosen, George. *Democracy and Economic Change in India.* Berkeley, Calif.: University of California Press, 1966.

——— *Industrial Change in India: Industrial Growth, Capital Requirements, and Technological Change, 1937–55.* Glencoe, Ill.: The Free Press, 1958.

——— *Some Aspects of Industrial Finance in India.* Bombay: Asia Publishing House, 1962.

Rosentein-Rodan, P. N., ed. *Capital Formation and Economic Development, Studies in the Economic Development of India.* London: George Allen and Unwin, Ltd., 1964.

——— *Pricing and Fiscal Policies, Studies in the Economic Development of India.* London: George Allen and Unwin, Ltd., 1964.

Sandee, Jan. *A Demonstration Planning Model for India.* Calcutta: Asia Publishing House, 1960.

Sankarasubramanyam, K. A. *The Public Sector, A Hindustan Times Survey.* New Delhi: *The Hindustan Times,* n.d. This booklet is a collection of articles written for the *Hindustan Times* in 1961.

Sen, S. R. "Planning Machinery in India," reprinted from *Indian Journal of Public Administration,* Vol. VII, No. 3, pp. 215–235. New Delhi, n.d. Dr. Sen is the Joint Secretary, Indian Planning Commission.

Solveen Committee, Government of the German Federal Republic. "Report of Experts on the Rourkela Iron and Steel Works." New Delhi, mimeographed, Ministry of Steel and Heavy Industries, Government of India, 1962.

Steel Corporation of Bengal. *Annual Report,* 1937 through 1953.

Subcommittee of the Congress Party in Parliament, November 1959, (Krishna Menon Committee). *Parliamentary Supervision Over State Undertakings.* New Delhi: Government of India Publication, 1959.

Tata Iron and Steel Company Limited. *Annual Report,* 1908 until present. The *Annual Report* of TISCO contains addresses to shareholders by the chairman of the company. In recent years these addresses have been useful expressions of the opinion of TISCO's management on many issues.

——— *Tata Steel—A Profile.* Calcutta: Public Relations Department, TISCO, n.d.

——— *The Story of a Strike.* Jamshedpur: TISCO, 1958.

Tata Iron and Steel Company Limited and Indian Iron and Steel Company Limited. *Tata–IISCO, Abridged List of Products (Steel).* Calcutta: TISCO and IISCO, 1961.

——— *Iron and Steel Distribution and Prices of Controlled and Free Categories.* Calcutta: TISCO and IISCO, 1964.

United Kingdom Steel Mission. *Report of the United Kingdom Steel Mission to the Government of India.* New Delhi: Government of India Publication, 1955.

United Nations, Department of Economic Affairs. *World Iron Ore Resources and Their Utilization.* Lake Success, N.Y.: United Nations Publication, 1950.

——— Department of Economic and Social Affairs. *Lignite Resources of Asia and the Far East, Their Exploration, Exploitation and Utilization.* New York: United Nations Publication, Mineral Resources Development Series, No. 7, 1956.

——— *Survey of World Iron Ore Resources—Occurrence, Appraisal and Use.* New York: United Nations Publications, 1955.

——— Economic Commission for Asia and the Far East, *Coal and Iron Ore Resources of Asia and the Far East.* New York: United Nations Publication, 1962.

——— "Review of the Foundry Industry in the ECAFE Region." Bangkok, mimeographed, 1960.

——— "Review of the Iron and Steel Industry in the ECAFE Region." Bangkok, mimeographed, 1960.

——— ECAFE, Subcommittee on Iron and Steel, Eighth Session, October 21–28, 1958. "Asian Steel Consumption, Trends and Future Demand." Bangkok, mimeographed, 1958.

——— Subcommittee on Iron and Steel, Fourth Session. "Development of Intra-regional Trade and Inter-regional Trade in Iron and Steel." Rangoon, mimeographed, ECAFE, 1952.

——— Subcommittee on Iron and Steel. "Intra- and Interregional Trade Development in Iron and Steel." Bangkok, mimeographed, ECAFE, 1951.

——— United Nations Educational, Scientific, and Cultural Organization (UNESCO), Research Center on Social Implications of Industrialization in Southern Asia. *Report on a Preliminary Enquiry on the Growth of Steel Towns in India, a Study in Problems of Urbanization.* Calcutta: United Nations Publication, 1959.

United States, Government of, Agency for International Development. "Background and Summary of a Techno-Economic Survey of a Proposed Integrated Steel Plant at Bokaro, Bihar State, India." Washington, D.C.: Government Press Release, March 1963.

United States Congress, House Committee on Appropriations, Foreign Operations Appropriations for 1964. *Hearings Before Subcommittee,* Part 4, 88th Congress, 1st Session. Washington, D.C.: U.S. Government Printing Office, 1963. This source contains testimony concerning United States participation in the Bokaro project. Of particular interest is the testimony by Mr. William Gaud, former Ambassador John Kenneth Galbraith, and Mr. Norman B. Obbard, Executive Vice President, United States Steel Corporation.

United States Steel Corporation. "A Techno-Economic Survey of a Proposed Integrated Steel Mill at Bokaro, Bihar State, India."

Unpub. report prepared for the U.S. Government, Agency for International Development, March 1963, 4 primary and 3 supplementary volumes.

Warren, E. T. "The Steel Industry—Yesterday, Today and Tomorrow," *Iron and Steel Engineer,* November 1957. Mr. Warren was formerly President of Tata Inc., New York City, New York.

Newspapers, Business Periodicals and Trade Journals

Capital, Calcutta. Of special interest are the annual numbers which sometimes contain articles specifically about the steel industry.

Commerce, Bombay. Of special interest are the annual numbers which sometimes contain articles specifically about the steel industry.

Eastern Economist, New Delhi.

Economic Review, (published by the All-India Congress Committee of the Congress Party).

Economic Weekly, Bombay.

Hindu, The, Madras City (overseas version, *Hindu Weekly Review*).

Hindustan Times, New Delhi.

Iron and Steel Review, Calcutta.

Statesman, The, Calcutta and New Delhi.

Times of India, The, Bombay.

Statistical Sources

India, Government of, Bureau of Census. *Census of India.* 1961.

——— Central Statistical Organization. *Monthly Abstract of Statistics.* New Delhi: Government of India Publication, various months.

——— Central Statistical Organization. *Monthly Statistics of Production of Selected Industries of India.* Calcutta: Government of India Publication, various months.

——— Central Statistical Organization. *Statistical Abstract of the Indian Union.* New Delhi: Government of India Publication, various years.

——— Department of Commercial Intelligence and Statistics. *Annual Statement of the Foreign Trade of India.* Calcutta: Government of India Publication, various years prior to December 1956.

——— Department of Commercial Intelligence and Statistics. *Monthly Statistics of the Foreign Trade of India.* Calcutta: Government of India Publication, various months. Volumes for March contain total imports and exports for the preceding fiscal year.

——— Directorate of Industrial Statistics. *Census of Manufactures.* New Delhi: Government of India Publication, annual publication, 1946 until present.

——— Ministry of Labour and Employment. *Indian Coal Statistics.* New Delhi: Government of India Publication, various years.

——— Ministry of Railways. *Report of the Railway Board on Indian Railways,* Vol. II. New Delhi: Government of India Publication, various years.

——— Ministry of Steel and Mines, Department of Iron and Steel, Office of Iron and Steel Controller. *Monthly Bulletin.* Calcutta: monthly publication, April 1961 until present.

——— Ministry of Steel, Mines and Fuel, Indian Bureau of Mines. *Mineral Production in India.* New Delhi: Government of India Publication, various years.

Reserve Bank of India. *Bulletin.* Bombay: Reserve Bank of India, monthly publication.

——— *Report on Currency and Finance.* Bombay: Reserve Bank of India, annual publication.

Index

Selected RAND Books

Baum, Warren C., *The French Economy and the State,* Princeton, N.J., Princeton University Press, 1958.

Bergson, A., *The Real National Income of Soviet Russia Since 1928,* Cambridge, Harvard University Press, 1961.

Brodie, Bernard, *Strategy in the Missile Age,* Princeton, N.J., Princeton University Press, 1959.

Chapman, Janet G., *Real Wages in Soviet Russia Since 1928,* Cambridge, Harvard University Press, 1963.

Dinerstein, Herbert S., *War and the Soviet Union: Nuclear Weapons and the Revolution in Soviet Military and Political Thinking,* New York, Praeger, 1959.

Dole, Stephen, and Isaac Asimov, *Planets for Man,* New York, Random House, 1964.

Dorfman, Robert, Paul A. Samuelson, Robert M. Solow, *Linear Programming and Economic Analysis,* New York, McGraw-Hill Book Company, Inc., 1958.

Halpern, Manfred, *The Politics of Social Change in the Middle East and North Africa,* Princeton, N.J., Princeton University Press, 1963.

Hirshleifer, Jack, James C. DeHaven, and Jerome W. Milliman, *Water Supply: Economics, Technology, and Policy,* Chicago, The University of Chicago Press, 1960.

Hitch, Charles J., and Roland McKean, *The Economics of Defense in the Nuclear Age,* Cambridge, Harvard University Press, 1960.

Hsieh, Alice L., *Communist China's Strategy in the Nuclear Era,* Englewood Cliffs, N.J., Prentice-Hall, Inc., 1962.

Johnson, John J. (ed.), *The Role of the Military in Underdeveloped Countries,* Princeton, N.J., Princeton University Press, 1962.

Johnstone, William C., *Burma's Foreign Policy: A Study in Neutralism,* Cambridge, Harvard University Press, 1963.

Liu, Ta-Chung, and Kung-Chia Yeh, *The Economy of the Chinese Mainland: National Income and Economic Development, 1933–1959,* Princeton, N.J., Princeton University Press, 1965.

Lubell, Harold, *Middle East Oil Crises and Western Europe's Energy Supplies,* Baltimore, The Johns Hopkins Press, 1963.

McKean, Roland N., *Efficiency in Government through Systems Analysis: With Emphasis on Water Resource Development,* New York, John Wiley & Sons, Inc. 1958.

Meyer, J. R., J. F. Kain, and M. Wohl, *The Urban Transportation Problem,* Cambridge, Harvard University Press, 1965.

Moorsteen, Richard, *Prices and Production of Machinery in the Soviet Union, 1928–1958,* Cambridge, Harvard University Press, 1962.

Novick, David (ed.), *Program Budgeting: Program Analysis and the Federal Budget,* Cambridge, Harvard University Press, 1965.

Pincus, John A., *Economic Aid and International Cost Sharing,* Baltimore, The Johns Hopkins Press, 1965.

Quade, E. S. (ed.), *Analysis for Military Decisions,* Chicago, Rand McNally & Company; Amsterdam, North-Holland Publishing Company, 1964.

Rosen, George, *Democracy and Economic Change in India,* Berkeley and Los Angeles, University of California Press, 1966.

Rush, Myron, *Political Succession in the USSR,* New York, Columbia University Press, 1965.

Speier, Hans, *Divided Berlin: The Anatomy of Soviet Political Blackmail,* New York, Praeger, 1961.

Trager, Frank N. (ed.), *Marxism in Southeast Asia: A Study of Four Countries,* Stanford, Calif., Stanford University Press, 1959.

Whiting, Allen S., *China Crosses the Yalu: The Decision to Enter the Korean War,* New York, The Macmillan Company, 1960.

Williams, J. D., *The Compleat Strategyst: Being a Primer on the Theory of Games of Strategy,* New York, McGraw-Hill Book Company, Inc., 1954.

Wolf, Charles, Jr., *Foreign Aid: Theory and Practice in Southern Asia,* Princeton, N.J., Princeton University Press, 1960.

Wolfe, Thomas, *Soviet Strategy at the Crossroads,* Cambridge, Harvard University Press, 1964.